JT FROM
YAKUTAT TO
SEA OTTER BAY
About 1813

Chil'khat •

Lynn Canal

L'tua Bay

• Akku

Koknau •

Cross Sound

St. Stephen

Iakobi I.

KING GEORGE

Chichagov I.

Passage

Chatham Str.

• Khutsnov

Bay of Islands

ARCHIPELAGO

Kruzov I.

Novo-Arkhangel'sk (Sitka)

C. Edgecumbe

Norfolk or Sitka Sound

Baranov I.

P. Frederick Str.

• Kekau

**South
Point**

**Cape Chirikov or
C de St. Bartolome**

Sea Otter Bay

ALASKA HISTORY NO. 32
and
ALASKA STATE LIBRARY HISTORICAL
MONOGRAPH NO. 9

The Round the World Voyage of Hieromonk Gideon 1803 – 1809

Translated
with an Introduction and notes,
by Lydia T. Black

Edited by Richard A. Pierce

THE LIMESTONE PRESS
Kingston, Ontario : Fairbanks, Alaska

©1989 by The Limestone Press
P.O. Box 1604, Kingston, Ontario, Canada K7L 5C8
and c/o History Department,
University of Alaska, Fairbanks
Fairbanks, AK 99775-0860. All rights reserved.

International Standard Book Number: 0-919642-20-9

Publication was funded in part by the Alaska Humanities Forum, Anchorage, and the National Endowment for the Humanities.

Typesetting by: Gail Knutson

Printed and bound in Canada by:
Brown & Martin Limited, Kingston, Ontario.

CONTENTS

List of Illustrations

Preface

On October 1794 the Russian transport vessel *Tri sviatiteli* (Three Hierarchs, today commonly mistranslated as Three Saints) arrived at Pavlovskaia gavan (Paul's Harbor, or modern Kodiak) bearing promyshlenniki, colonists, and members of an Orthodox Spiritual Mission. Comprising some eight monks and two servitors, under the leadership of the Archimandrite Ioasaf. This small group of ecclesiastics would have a momentous and lasting effect on Russian America, today's Alaska. In spite of many obstacles the priests quickly converted most of the aboriginal population of the Aleutian Chain and some of the mainland people to Christianity, and modified the behavior of company personnel.

In 1894, the Valaam Monastery, whence most of the mission personnel had come, marked the centennial of the arrival of the Orthodox Spiritual Mission in Kodiak by publishing a volume of source materials. These included an account of the mission and its work, papers dealing with Father German (now St. Herman) and Hieromonk Gedeon (Gideon)'s journal of his round-the-world voyage, along with his correspondence and reports concerning his stay on Kodiak and Kamchatka, 1805-1807. A translation of the 1894 volume by Colin Bearne, edited by R.A. Pierce, was published under the title *The Russian Orthodox Religious Mission in America, 1794-1837* by the Limestone Press, Kingston, Ontario in 1978. Since then additional materials have come to light, and are now presented with the part of the centennial volume dealing with Father Gideon, in a new translation. Another volume, on Saint Herman, will follow.

Acknowledgements

I wish to acknowledge gratefully the assistance of several persons. Mrs. Phyllis DeMuth, Alaska State Historical Library, made the project possible. Mr. Jeff Leer, Alaska Native Language Center, University of Alaska, Fairbanks, provided the current Alutiiq spellings and glosses, especially for the songs rendered by Gideon and for the Lord's Prayer in Alutiiq. Mr. H. Theodore Ryberg, Director Emeritus, Rasmuson Library, University of Alaska, Fairbanks, gave invaluable help in rendering 18th century sailing vocabulary, derived from the Dutch, into English equivalents. Richard A. Pierce, Professor Emeritus, Queen's University, Kingston, Canada read the drafts, and Jean S. Aigner, Department of Anthropology, University of Alaska, Fairbanks, edited the introduction. Charles J. Utermohle, Adjunct Faculty, Department of Anthropology, University of Alaska, Fairbanks, offered much needed technical advice. Dr. Richard Dauenhauer of the Sealaska Heritage Foundation, Juneau, aided production. The contributions of the foregoing individuals have made this book truly a joint effort.

Lydia Black
University of Alaska, Fairbanks
May, 1988

Introduction

The papers of Hieromonk Gideon are important to any student of Alaska history and particularly to those interested in the Baranov era. This is the period roughly from 1790 to 1818 which laid the foundation for the Russian Imperial presence on the American continent. They are particularly important for understanding the role of the Orthodox Spiritual Mission in Alaska during the period in question and the role of Gideon himself.

Most important, Gideon's work contains the first in-depth ethnography of the Alutiiq-speaking people of Kodiak Island. Without question, this is the best source of information about the culture of Kodiak Islanders, and it recounts the brutal impact on the population of Baranov's policy of impressment, when the islanders became part of his labor force as well as his army – with their help he established and held outposts in Tlingit territory and later in distant California.

Gideon also provides additional insights on the Russian Imperial Navy's first circumnavigation of the world, supplementing such well known accounts as those of Kruzenshtern, Lisianskii, and Langsdorff.

Other information contained in the Gideon papers sheds light on the complex relationship between the fledgling Russian-American Company and the early Orthodox Mission in Alaska. Specifically, Gideon's papers in the Synodal file in the Central State Historical Archive (TsGIA), clearly indicate that, presumably following the reports to the Synod 1795-1797 by the Head of Mission, Archimandrite Ioasaf, and Hieromonk Makarii about company abuses of the native population, when the decision was made to elevate Ioasaf to the status of Bishop, the newly created Alaska Bishopric (Diocese) was to be financed not solely by the company but by the Synod and a substantial sum was allocated for this purpose. Secondly, the papers show that in 1803 a sum of moneys for the Mission was issued by the Synod to be administered through N.P. Rezanov, who was sailing to Alaska. Apparently, those funds allocated to the Mission were never delivered in full and the impression was created that the Mission's subsistence came from company funds.

Incidental information contained in Gideon's papers provides invaluable historical details: for example, it shows that the first chapel built in the Eastern Aleutians was the chapel of St. Nicholas on Umnak Island, built by the Aleut chief Ivan Stepanovich Glotov, who was the first Eastern Aleut baptized

through lay baptism in 1758 by Stepan Glotov and taken to
Siberia, at the age of 12, by his godfather. His Aleut name in
Russian records is given as *Mushkal'*. He is known to have
returned to Alaska on Glotov's next voyage reaching Umnak
about 1766. He served to the end of his days as the lay reader
conducting regular services. Gideon's records also provide
hitherto unknown biographical data on several persons associated with the early Russian period, including Ivan Banner
and the English Captain Barber, known for his unsavory role
in the Tlingit/Russian conflict over Sitka, and members of the
Netsvetov family.

The available documents suggest that Hieromonk Gideon
played a key role in furthering the cause of Orthodoxy in
Russian America. His report reached the highest levels of the
government and, it is possible, contributed to the decision to
remove Baranov. He may also have contributed to the termi-
nation of the naval careers of Lisianskii and Berkh, whose
anticlerical attitude Gideon reported to Metropolitan Amvrosii.

At the time of his appointment to the first circumnavigating
expedition under Captains Kruzenshtern (the ship *Nadezhda*)
and the ship *Neva*), Gideon was a Cathedral Hieromonk of the
Monastery of St. Alexander Nevskii (Aleksandro-Nevskaia
Lavra).   Amvrosii, Metropolitan of Novgorod and St.
Petersburg, a ranking member of the Holy Ruling Synod of the
Russian Orthodox Church, with the knowledge and support of
the Emperor Alexander I, assigned Gideon to the expedition.
In fact, the Emperor provided Gideon with a monetary gift out
of his own funds. These moneys were to enable Gideon to ac-
quire the necessary kit for the long voyage. The Emperor also
entrusted the church plate and utensils, and the vestry, to
Gideon which were Alexander's gift to the newly established
Church of the Holy Resurrection at Pavlovskaia (or St. Paul's)
harbor (modern Kodiak).

Gideon's commission was to inspect and report on the
conditions of the American colonies (Alaska) and the churches
in Kamchatka. While aboard ship, with the expedition which
sailed from Kronshtat (Kronshtadt) in 1803, he was to act as
ship's chaplain. As a representative of the Synod and of the
Emperor himself, Gideon had to be in close contact with N.P.
Rezanov. At that time Rezanov was the moving power for the
Russian-American Company in St. Petersburg and he was
sailing   aboard   the   *Nadezhda*   as   an   Ambassador
Plenipotentiary to Japan.

The Soviet scholar Roza G. Liapunova recently published
biographical information on Gideon. This followed my publication of excerpts from Gideon's ethnographic account about

Kodiak Islanders in the journal *Arctic Anthropology* (1977 – 14:3:79-108). Liapunova's data are based to a large extent on Gideon's dossier in the former Synodal archive, with additional information from other sources.

Gideon was born Gavriil Fedotov, son of a priest from the Orel region (Liapunova 1970:218), about 1770: his age is given as 33 in 1803. Gideon received his early education at the Sevskaia Seminary where he studied, beginning in 1789, Latin, grammar and poetics, then in 1790, at the Belogradskaia Seminary, reading French, logic, rhetoric, geography, philosophy, and theology. On December 23, 1979 (Julian calendar) he became a monk. Consecration as hierodeacon took place on the 24th and as a hieromonk on the 25th. He had already served for over two years as instructor in the French language at the Belogradskaia Seminary. From 1799 he taught rhetoric and philosophy there, replacing an ailing colleague. In 1801 he taught rhetoric for the upper division. In the following years he continued to teach French and also mathematics, proving himself to be an excellent teacher. His linguistic skills would serve him well later in Alaska.[1] There he organized the collection of vocabularies for a dictionary of native languages. He also initiated the first attempt to provide a written grammar of the Alutiiq language by a team of native students headed by a Kodiak Islander from Karluk region, the "student of rhetoric", Paramon Chumovitskii.

Gideon's assignment as Cathedral Hieromonk to the Monastery of St. Alexander Nevskii came in 1803 and soon thereafter Metropolitan Amvrosii chose him for travel to Alaska and Kamchatka as the "Metropolitan's eye". He would spend over six years in the field.

Gideon returned to St. Petersburg in 1809. According to Liapunova, Metropolitan Amvrosii first assigned him as Superior of the Monastery of St. Alexander Nevskii[2] and of the Zelenetskii Trinity Monastery. Later on he became Superior of the Skovorodskii and Iverskii monasteries. He retired first to the Konev Monastery (which provided at least one member of the first Orthodox Mission to Alaska in 1794), and then to the Andrusov Retreat (*pustynia*) of St. Nicholas in the Olonetsk diocese. He died there in 1843 (Liapunova 1979: 219).

Throughout his travels Gideon, on Metropolitan Amvrosii's instruction, kept a journal and copies of correspondence with various officials and private individuals. The location of the original journals is unknown. The surviving correspondence is but a fraction of what Gideon and his respondents (Rezanov, Baranov, Banner and others in Alaska and Metropolitan Amvrosii in St. Petersburg) wrote.

Three accounts of Gideon's journey around the world exist. Two are in Gideon's hand and one is a scribe's copy. All three versions are synoptic accounts indubitably based on a journal and notes which no longer exist (or remain unlocated).

One version, in Gideon's hand, is an official report submitted to the Holy Ruling Synod of the Russian Orthodox Church through Metropolitan Amvrosii. The original is kept in the Central State Historical Archive (TsGIA) in the Soviet Union. The translation is from a microfilm copy. It will be referred to hereafter as the Synod Version, or SV.

A second version, also in Gideon's hand, is presently located in the Helsinki University Library, Finland. I assume that this version originally was in the archives of the Valaam Monastery, the institution which provided the majority of the clerics who came to Alaska in 1794. It is not known when, why, and how this manuscript became part of the archival holdings of the Valaam Monastery. That manuscript, considered the definitive text, will be referred to hereafter as the Valaam Version or VV.

A third version is a scribe's copy and originated in the Valaam Monastery. Its present whereabouts is unknown, but in the 1930's it was sent to M.Z. Vinokouroff in the United States. He photocopied the manuscript and returned the original to Valaam. This copy, now in the Vinokouroff Collection in the Alaska State Historical Library, Juneau, Alaska, will be called hereafter the Vinokouroff Copy, or VC.

The three versions are not identical. The Valaam Version in the Helsinki University Library and the scribe's copy in the Vinokouroff Collection are largely similar. The minor differences in wording do not as a rule affect the content. Apparently, the 1894 publication by the Valaam Monastery of part of Gideon's account pertaining to his sojourn on Kodiak is based either on the Valaam Version or the scribe's copy (VC), but this publication omits accounts of Gideon's departure from St. Petersburg and visits to Denmark, England, the Canary Islands, Brazil, Easter Island, the Marquesas, and Hawaii. It also omits (as do VV and VC) his departure from Kodiak in 1807, visit to Unalaska, and inspection tour of Kamchatka, as well as the account of his return journey to St. Petersburg by ship from Kamchatka to Okhotsk, on horseback to Iakutsk, by coach to Irkutsk, and from there home. His account of the return journey is found, interestingly, only in the Synod Version.

A microfilm copy (which may be incomplete) of the Synod Version is among the holdings of the Shur Collection in the Rasmuson Library, University of Alaska, Fairbanks. Assuming Liapunova's analysis of the original of the Synod Version to be

correct (1979:216), the microfilm copy lacks the last 20 pages
(ten folios and versos, ending with F 71 and not with 83 verso
as reported by Liapunova).   As a consequence, a definitive
comparison of the three versions is not possible at this time.

As I have indicated, the Valaam Version and Vinokouroff
Copy differ in minor ways only from each other but the Synod
Version diverges to a significant degree from both in wording,
spelling, and different ordering of paragraphs.   A major
substantive difference lies in the inclusion in the Valaam Version and Vinokouroff Copy, but not in the Synod Version, of a
section dealing with labor conditions on Kodiak and the
exploitation of the native population by the Russian-American
Company (Liapunova 1979:216-217 also noted this fact). Some
of the information, however, is present in the Synod files in the
form of letters from Gideon.   Additional material could be in
other correspondence, constituting a separate item or items in
the Synod files, yet to be searched for.

I note that the microfilm copy on hand, which ends with F
71, stops as if in the middle of a sentence. Liapunova's account
is not clear on this point, that is, on the content of the concluding pages of the original, and it is difficult to judge what if
anything is missing from the available copy. She does mention,
however, that the account ends with the description of Gideon's
travel to Irkutsk (a topic already covered on F 70 and verso and
not on F 83 verso).

Several important questions regarding the available manuscript versions remain. One pertains, as already indicated, to
the length of the SV in the Soviet archive and the content of the
last pages from 71 verso through 83 verso. The second involves
the provenance of the manuscript in Gideon's hand now in
Helsinki.   Having examined a xerox copy provided by the
Helsinki University Library, rather than the original, I agree
with Liapunova that this probably is the draft document for the
report prepared for Metropolitan Amvrosii (SV?).   Further
work on the provenance of this manuscript is needed, and it
seems likely that additional correspondence may turn up.

I would also note that in general, the SV is briefer and more
terse, as well as more compressed, than the VV. All personal
observations are carefully edited out – appropriate in a formal
report to an ecclesiastical superior. It seems that the omitted
passages in SV were marked in VV by parentheses,possibly
by Gideon himself. On the other hand, the marks may have
been made by someone who might have edited Gideon's original submission, or by a researcher to note divergences between the VV and SV manuscripts.

In the following presentation, passages present in VV and VC but omitted in SV are set off from the left margin of the page. Words and phrases present in the VV and VC but absent in SV are *italicized*. The very few passages and words and phrases present in the SV but absent in VV and VC are included in brackets [ ]. Passages which differ significantly from the text in other versions are included either in brackets or set off from the left margin; they are preceded with the indication of the text in which they appear: SV, VV, or VC, respectively. When differences between the three versions are minor the Valaam Version (Helsinki University Library text) is used as the definitive one. As the pagination of the VV and VC does not coincide the page numbers of the original text are omitted.

The comparison of the related correspondence presents additional problems. In VV and VC all letters follow the main text. In the SV, the letter received by Gideon from Rezanov in Brazil, for example, is given in the body of the report, in chronological order, following the account of the squadron's stay at St. Catherine's Island. Furthermore, there are discrepancies between the texts of several important letters. The SV letters are usually briefer and less subservient in matters such as form of address, compliments meted out to various officials, and so on. One letter to Rezanov, published by Valaam in 1894 (see Bearne and Pierce 1979:155-156), is not present in SV; nor are the two letters sent by Gideon in secret to Metropolitan Amvrosii (with Lieutenants Arbuzov and Povalishin), but some of the information contained therein is incorporated into the body of the report. Therefore, in this presentation the letters, when warranted, are presented in sets taken from both the SV and VV, or with divergent passages incorporated and sources given in brackets.[3]

Several other letters are included. From copies in the files of A. Dolgopolov, undoubtedly they were part of the original Gideon file kept at Kodiak. It is not known how Dolgopolov obtained the copies. Some were published in the journal *Russian American Orthodox Messenger* in the early 1900's submitted for publication by Tikhon Shalamov, then priest on Kodiak. The originals evidently were lost in 1943 when the church at Kodiak burned. I also include Gideon's report on chrizmations, marriages, and confessions he administered while stopping at Unalaska on his return journey in 1807. The original document is part of the Alaska Russian Orthodox Church Collection, Manuscript Division, Library of Congress, Washington, D.C. Metropolitan Amvrosii's letters of appointment and instructions to Gideon precede the main text.

Gideon's sworn testimony pertaining to questions about the Mission's funding is presented in an appendix.

In the text which follows, I have added section headings such as "weapons and warfare" to the part containing ethnographic description, for convenience. The presentation concludes with translation of the material dealing with Gideon's return journey, following the microfilm copy of the SV available to me. Editorial comments on specialized terms and alternate readings appear in diagonals //.

All dates, unless otherwise indicated, follow the Julian calendar, as given in Gideon's papers. Russian terms are transliterated according to the Library of Congress system, modified. Geographic names are given as they appear in the original, with modern designations, when determined, appearing in brackets. The term "Kad'iak" is used in the text, but modern "Kodiak" in editorial comments.

The name of St. Herman of Alaska is spelled "Herman" throughout, instead of the transliteration of the Russian "German, just as 'Gideon' is used instead of the Russian spelling 'Gedeon'."

Chapter 1 – Departure and Voyage, 1803–1804

Your Holiness,

In the year 1803, the 14th day of July, having had the honor to receive the blessing of Your Holiness for my voyage, I left the Monastery of St. Alexander Nevskii for Kronshtadt at 9 o'clock after midday, aboard a *kater* [cutter]. Toward 5 o'clock in the morning I boarded the ship *Neva* where I left my gear. I remained in Kronshtadt up to the 22nd because both ships were overcrowded, and therefore, because of this unavoidable circumstance I was not yet assigned a cabin.

On the 21st, Mr. Minister of Commerce [Rumiantsev] and Mr. Assistant Minister [*tovarishch ministra*] of Naval Forces [Admiral Chichagov] inspected our ships in person. Some of the staff and senior officers who were not needed for the voyage were taken off. There was plenty of altercation...Finally my lot was decided and I received the cabin of the painter, Collegiate Assessor Prichetnikov. [We] were supposed to weigh anchor on the 23rd. Toward the 6th hour after midday I went aboard the ship *Nadezhda* where, after the blessing of the water, a Te Deum [*moleben*] was sung. The ship was sprinkled with Holy Water. Going on to the eighth hour, the Naval Generals [sic] present in Kronshtadt as well as those who have arrived from Petersburg, Count Kochubei, Count Stroganov, and Messrs. Ambassadors of England and Portugal honored us with their presence.

Our wish [to sail] that day, however, was not fulfilled. Because of adverse winds, we remained for two more days.

[SV: A week after my arrival in Kronshtadt, I was placed on the ship *Neva* because of overcrowding aboard the *Nadezhda* which carried our Ambassador, the Actual Chamberlain and Cavalier Nikolai Petrovich Rezanov and his entourage].

Already on the 26th, *at 8 o'clock after midnight*, having poured out our fervent prayer to the All High Lord who is the hope of all the ends of the earth and those who are on the far seas, we weighed anchors and our ships commenced their trek under fresh [*svezhii*] but favorable wind. The speed at this time was 12 versts per hour.

As I glanced with heartfelt emotion at the waves playing around the ship, their momentary elevation and immediate descent, and imagined the uncertainties, and even the mystery, of human fate, I recalled the words of the

Most Wise Israelite: "The third is impossible to grasp,
and the fourth is not known – the trace of the eagle
gliding in the air, the path of the serpent crawling along
a rock, the track of a ship sailing the sea, and the path
of a man in his youth [VV: the way of a man with a
maid]"[4] .

At nightfall, the weather changed; the wind became strong
and adverse. For this reason, we were forced to continue on
our way by tracking (on) the 27th, 28th, and 29th, in sight of the
[small] (rocky) island *Gogland which is 140 versts from Kronshtadt.*
>   SV: I am not setting down that which usually happens
>   upon the inconstant and inclement sea; I remain silent
>   also about the ship's heaving, the noise of the sails, the
>   squeaking of the blocks [*shkoty*], the coarse shouting of
>   the sailors, and the incessant chafing of the lines. (All
>   these) cause not a little sadness [discomfort] to the in-
>   experienced voyager. But without hesitation I do not fail
>   to record that on the 3rd of August, as we were passing
>   the Swedish island of Gotland, a sailor [Usov] fell over-
>   board and became the unhappy victim of the ferocious
>   Neptune.
>   Finally, on the 5th, under variable wind, we sighted Copen-
>   hagen, and on the 7th dropped anchor, at a distance of one and
>   a half verst from the city. Our entire voyage from Kronshtadt
>   to this Danish capital lasted 12 days.
>   On the 12th [sic, VV: on the 9th], after the celebration of the
>   Divine Liturgy, our Ambassador [Rezanov] and his entire en-
>   tourage visited the castle built two and a half centuries before
>   the Nativity of Christ, in which are kept all the treasures and
>   remarkable possessions of the Danish kingdom and where also
>   the meeting of the State Council takes place once a year, during
>   the Passion Week. In the hall where the Council meeting takes
>   place, in front of the royal throne, stand four large silver lions.
>   The impression is majestic and fearsome. In another [hall] we
>   were shown candlesticks, thongs, and small candelabras [*lius-
>   try*], all made from pure gold, as well as other [paraphernalia]
>   which serve to embellish this house. Our connoisseurs liked
>   most of all the collection of medals of this kingdom, commem-
>   orating various events. There were medals there which date to
>   five hundred years before the Nativity of Christ. In a hall of
>   mirrors, a ratak [VC: row upon row] is so remarkably arranged
>   on the floor, that the spectators see themselves and their sur-
>   roundings in infinite distance.

On the 11th we dined with our minister Mr. Lizakevich at his suburban residence, and on the 13th visited the museum [*kunstkamera*]. The collection of paintings is not worthy of envy. We saw there also icons of Suzdal workmanship in small simple frames [*oklady*]. The Danes consider them to be most ancient, but the [condition of] paint does not support this.

On the 16th we visited the Royal palace in the country, about four versts from the city. The road to it passes, without interruption, along alleys thickly planted [on both sides] with old linden trees. The palace appears very pleasantly situated, because of its elevation, and the park across from it. All Copenhagen assembles here every Sunday for recreation. From 6 to 8 o'clock, the Royal orchestra plays. Occasionally, I visited their various churches. As they lack splendor on the outside, so also does the interior lack any adornment; they are also not very clean. Especially upon entering one is forced to hold one's nose. The pastors deliver their sermons with such fire that foaming spittle from their mouths descends upon the listeners who stand close. On Fridays, theology students explain the Catechism.

We stood in the Copenhagen roads up to three weeks. During this time 54 barrels were fired and once again filled with water; the water in unfired barrels has spoiled during the very short time of our sailing. We unloaded 73 barrels of rye flour, [and] because of spoilage, 70 pud and 24 pounds thereof, three barrels of sauerkraut and five pud of salted meat also were thrown into the sea.

The brine from the meat was poured into 22 barrels and 20 barrels were salted anew. From shore, 58 casks of French vodka were brought, containing 1,556 buckets, also eight casks of salted pork, weighing 16 pud, and freshly salted meat, 14 pud. Other items needed for the ship were purchased: clamps [*zaklepy*], nails, hammers, caulking tools, etc.

On the 27th, at 6 o'clock after midday, we left the Copenhagen roads and close to 12 o'clock dropped anchor in Helsingor roads, where we remained six days, waiting for a favorable wind. Here were also about 40 merchant vessels under the protection of a single English naval frigate.

Helsingor is not a fashionable town; the streets are quiet; its fortress, the Kronburg, is considerable, and, in the opinion of some, the best of the European fortresses. In this town, the customs duty is collected from all ships passing through the Sound [Zund], one Danish thaler per foot of ship's displacement; this constitutes the most im-

portant income of Denmark. Helsingor's location is
pleasant, the land fertile. The distance between Helsingor and the Swedish city of Helsingbjorg is not more than
six verst.

On September 3rd, 7 o'clock after midnight, under a *bramsel'* (steady) [west] wind, we weighed anchors and set out for the
English port of Falmouth, located on the British [English]
channel, where we were to have a rest.

A seven gun salute was fired twice from the ship *Nadezhda*, to which the sentry vessel [*brandvakhta*], as well
as the Helsingor fortress Kronburg replied by the same
number of salvos. About half past five in the afternoon,
we passed Amnout, about 2½ miles to the west, where we
saw a three-masted American merchant vessel stranded
on a shoal. Within the hour, she chopped down her main.
mast [*grotmachta*]. Then our hearts also beat fast, im-
agining our own future fates in this slippery element.

On the 6th [SV: in the German Sea – Nemetskoe More, modern North Sea] we suffered a severe storm which separated us
from the ship *Nadezhda* [SV: which we did not meet again]
until Falmouth. We stopped in the roads of the above mentioned port on the 14th, at 11 o'clock, about one verst distance
from the fortress. On the third day, we were joined by the *Nadezhda*. Our sail from Helsingor to Falmouth lasted 12 days.

Near us stood up to 25 merchantmen, one navy ship,[5] one
frigate, and one tender. On the 17th, going onto 5 o'clock,
the Falmouth battery conducted training in the shooting
of cannon with balls. On the 19th, 8 o'clock after midnight, about 50 merchantmen put out to sea under protection of one English navy ship and two frigates. While
remaining in the Falmouth roads for eight days we filled
all the empty water barrels, caulked the upper deck,
tightened the entire standing rigging, and put up 150 pud
of Irish salt meat for the use of the serving men.

On the 23rd, at 4:30 after noon, we [hoisted anchors and] left
Falmouth with a bramsel' [steady light] wind from the northeast, and entered the Atlantic Ocean [keeping course] toward
the island of Madeira.

On the 24th, at 7 o'clock after midnight, we noticed in the
wardroom [*kaiut kampaniia*] that yellow spots were spreading
on the paint there, caused by long-standing water in the bilge
[*intrium*]. We all suffered headaches. To clear the air, we began to fill the bilge with fresh water every 24, and after a certain time emptied it again. From the 25th to the 30th our sail
was most propitious, and in that time we covered a distance of
1,562 verst. However, from the 1st of October to the 4th, we

were forced to tack toward Madeira. That same date we turned
[SV: Beginning with the 4th we set our course for] toward Teneriffe, the first and most important of the Canary Islands where
on the 7th, at half past ten, we dropped anchors near the island
of Santa Cruz (the Holy Cross)[!].

On the 7th, not too far off this island, about 5 o'clock after
noon, we sighted to the north an approaching frigate
which, having fired a cannon ball under the stern of our
ship, hoisted the French flag and coming near, inquired
from whence and whither we were sailing. She was a
French privateer preying on English merchantmen. The
name of her commander was Gilblaz Snap [sic] and the
ship's name was *Ezhes'ien'* [Egecienne?].

Because of the darkness, we hove to the entire night
and at 6 o'clock in the morning went toward the city of
Santa Cruz on the island of Teneriffe. There, in the Santa
Cruz roads, we dropped anchors at 10:30.

From Falmouth to the above named island we sailed 15 days.
Besides ours, the following ships were in the Santa Cruz
roads: one Spanish naval *kater*, eight merchant vessels,
two Frenchmen, one of these the frigate which queried us,
the other a *kater*, and three English merchantmen taken
by the French. On the 9th, the French privateers brought
here two additional English merchant vessels. On the
11th, at 11 o'clock after midnight, the Spanish *kater* put
out to sea. This vessel brought to the Governor of the
Canary Islands a few days before our arrival here an order from the [Spanish] Court to render us every assistance possible, should we put in at these islands. The city
of Santa Cruz lies under the 28th degree north latitude,
and 16½ longitude by Greenwich, in a small valley on the
southeast coast of the island of Teneriffe. It is protected
by batteries. The construction of the houses, mostly two
and three-storied ones, is beautiful in appearance on the
outside, but within there is little decor. The upper story
has no ceiling. All doors are large, to permit freshening
the air within the rooms. There are three churches, of
Catholic confession, one monastery of a French order and
the Inquisition. The streets are relatively wide, but little
effort is expended to maintain cleanliness. For this reason, during the strong heat spells there is an unbearable
stench, to dispel which many fires are lit in the streets.
Men and women dress in European manner. The main
item of trade is wine.

The inhabitants are employed in cultivation and har-
vesting of various fruits and, in part, in agriculture. The

failure of grain crops occurs due to overplanting [VV: occurs rather often due to frequent droughts] and the cattle
keeping is of small extent because of lack of good pas-
tures and good grasses. Mules, donkeys, cows, steers,
and camels are more noticeable than sheep and pigs, all
of which are fed with barley and millet [VV: by the rich],
and whose numbers are few. The inhabitants for the most
part subsist on fish and produce, such as potatoes,
pumpkins, watermelons, bananas, chestnuts and coconuts. About ten Italian miles from Santa Cruz,
there is in a rather pleasant valley, the city of Laguna, and on
the northwestern shore, at the foot of the mountain Pika, the
city Lorontava [?]. We stood in the Santa Cruz roads seven
days. During this time we put up for the use of the serving men
four *pipas* of Teneriffe wine, each containing 60 bottles, three
casks of vinegar, one cask of salt, 50 [sic] peaches, 400 lemons,
ten bunches of bananas, three barrels of onions, three barrels
of potatoes, and one cask of quicklime to purify the air in the
bilge.

On the 15th it was planned to weigh anchors, and therefore,
at 9 o'clock the Governor of the Canary Islands, Marquis Dela
Casa Kagetal [sic] paid a visit first to the *Nadezhda* and then
to our *Neva* [SV: on the 15th, prior to our leaving the Santa
Cruz Roads, we were honored by a visit to both our vessels by
the Governor of all Canary Islands, Marquis Dela Casa Kage-
tal]

with other officials, up to seven persons. When he was
leaving the *Nadezhda*, he was thanked by an eight gun
salute, which in turn was answered from the Fortress
Cristobal, where the flag is run up, by an equal number
of salvos. When he was boarding our *Neva*, the sailors
were drawn up in the shrouds [*vanty*] and shouted hurrah!
At the very time as the Governor was leaving us, a Spanish three masted ship arrived from the northeast. She
was not permitted to drop anchor because of contagious
disease on board this vessel.

In the first hour after midday, we weighed anchors, leaving
the Santa Cruz roads, and commenced on our way toward the
Brazilian shores of South America.

On the 16th, at 8 o'clock after midnight, in order to avoid
foul air in the ship, some lime was poured into the *ialo*
[head?]. At noon, course southwest, latitude 27°48'. From
this day to the 19th we covered 469 versts, and during the
night from the 19th to the 20th entered the tropics. Our
compass course for the day [*sutochnyi rumb*] was southwest, latitude 23°10', longitude 19°57'.

[SV: In the first hour after midday weighed anchors
and headed toward the Brazilian coast. From the 19th to
the 20th we entered the tropics].

That same day we saw the flying fish, these poor creatures
of the water, *which in fleeing the large predator fish see succor
in the open air but even there find no refuge. As soon as they
emerge from the water,* they are snapped up by sea birds [SV:
while in the water large fishes get them.]

Next day we saw also three sea fish which are called dol-
phins, which followed the ship for a rather long time and
entranced our eyes by their glistening golden scales and
emerald jewel-like fins. On the 22nd, the proud swift kil-
ler whales, marked by their sharply pointed long black
fins, without fear played around our ship for over two
hours.

On the 25th, toward the sixth hour after midnight, we
sighted to the south the Island of St. Anthony, one of the Cape
Verde Islands

about 24 Italian miles distant. At this time calm weather
with very light winds [*malovetrie*] continued, the latitude
was 17°58', longitude 25°47'. The course for the 24 hours
[*kurs sutochnyi*] was southwest. At noon, the level of the
mercury in the Reaumur thermometer was 22½ degrees.
This day, Ambassador Rezanov, gentlemen of the embassy, Court Councellor Foss [VV: a gentleman (*dvoria-
nin*) of the embassy, Court Councellor Fusse], Captain
Kruzenshtern, and Lieutenant Romberg came aboard to
dine with us.

On the 28th, the heat was, by Reaumur thermometer, 23½
degrees in the latitude 14° [SV: we did not experience greater
heat even on the equator itself. Since the 3rd of November, in
the latitude of 7° and longitude 20°40' we encountered light
wind, calm, squalls [strong gusts of wind], rains, torrential
downpours, lightning and thunder, which continued almost every day up to the 10th, to the latitude 4°42' *and longitude
20°47' [VV: 21°47'].*

At 12 o'clock of the same day we sighted a vessel on the
horizon and sailed toward her on the wind [*kontr-gals*].
By 3:30 she could be seen clearer; by 5 o'clock, the ship
Nadezhda together with our *Neva* approached her. The
vessel hove to. A yawl [*ial*] was dispatched from the *Nadezhda* [VV: and from us, under an officer] to inquire
whose vessel it was, whence and heading where? They
were also to deliver to this vessel mail for dispatch to
Russia. The answer was as follows: an American vessel,
sailing from America to Bastiliia [?], putting in at Cape

of Good Hope. She has been becalmed at the latitude of
5° by now for the tenth day.

*From this time on we had finally a bramsel' [steady light]
wind under which, at 10 o'clock after midnight, on the 14th
we crossed the equator at longitude 24°49' west from Greenwich.*

At this time our vessel was about three Italian miles
ahead of the *Nadezhda*, already in the Southern Hemisphere. Consequently, we crossed the line [equator]
sooner.

At 11.30, when by observation we learned that we were in
the Southern Hemisphere, we jibed to the right [*over-stag na
pravyi gals*, to port], and started out for the *Nadezhda*. Approaching the latter, we ran up the flag and the ensign, disposed the sailors in the shrouds, and congratulated her on the
[VV: safe] arrival in the Southern Hemisphere, shouting thrice
hurrah. From the *Nadezhda*, too, came the reply: hurrah!
hurrah! hurrah!

On this occasion a Neptune was dressed aboard the *Nadezhda*, who stood at the rail holding his trident and,
shaking his long thick beard, shouted with all his might:
"What ships?" When he received the answer that we were
Russians, he blanched from amazement and fear, his legs
trembled, his disordered bushy hair stood on end, he
dropped his trident and fled. Only distant grumbling was
heard in his wake: "Russians even here!" At 3 o'clock in
the afternoon, the *Nadezhda* fired her guns twice, the
first time 11 guns, the second time nine.

On the 15th, at 11 o'clock, after the prayer and a thanksgiving Te Deum, the crew was assembled on the quarterdeck
[*shkantsy*], in the presence of the Captain and all Messrs. Officers, and all drank a glass of [SV: Teneriffe] wine to the
health of the Lord Emperor. Then we shouted hurrah thrice.
At 4 o'clock, after the officers' table [SV: dinner] in the mess,
we drank his Majesty's health [SV: and shouted hurrah thrice].

At this time, an 11-gun salute was fired. The day we
crossed the equator occurred during the time of preparation for St. Philip's fast, [*Filipovskii* post]. A serious
time! [VV: Peculiar celebration!] We expected that at the
equator there would be unbearable heat, judging by our
stay at Santa Cruz on the Island of Teneriffe, when the
temperature, with the sun already in southern hemisphere, was 24 degrees by the thermometer of Reaumur
and even higher, but on the equatorial line the temperature was only 22 degrees throughout our entire voyage
within the Northern hemisphere.

From the 14th to the 26th, to the latitude 20°51' and longitude 34°26' the days were clear and the wind favorable. In the course of these twelve 24-hour periods we traversed 2,502 versts, *which means that in each 24-hour period we covered about 208½ and each hour eight and ½ versts.* On this latter date at 6 o'clock in the afternoon, the *Nadezhda* signalled us to heave to; at the commencement of the following hour we secured the topgallants [*bramsel'*] took in a single reef in the gallants [*marsel'*] and mizzen topsails [*kriuisel'*]; at 8 o'clock, the main sail [*grot*] on the mainmast and the large lower sail on the foremast [*fok*] were tightened and main topsails secured to the topmast [*sten'ga*].

In this manner we remained hove to through the entire night, as we thought that Ascension Island, sought by many seafarers, was nearby, but we did not find it.

At 5 o'clock in the morning of the next day, that is on the 27th, we filled our sails and set out west by north ½ west. In this 24-hour period we covered 154 versts, and were in the latitude 20°44' and longitude, by the chronometer 55°50' [sic, VV: 35°50'], the calculated [longitude] was 32°52'.

[SV: Next day, the 27th] not finding Ascension Island, we set our course for SWW and sailed toward the Brazilian coast, aiming for Cape Frio, which we sighted on the 30th at 5 o'clock after midnight in the distance of 7½ miles [SV: at latitude 21°8' and longitude 40°20'].

At that time the depth was counted [VV: by lead] at 40 sazhen'; the bottom was silt and small-size shell. At midday on this date we were at latitude 21°8' and longitude 40°20'. From the 1st to the 5th of December, keeping to the same course, we covered more than 630 versts and were in latitude 26°19' and longitude 46°59'. On the last date, from 9 o'clock and up to the second hour after midnight we were hove to and then sailed by the wind [*beidewind*] because of the nearness of the shore. In the second hour, changed the course to southwest; soon after 5 o'clock sighted an island to the south-southwest. At 7 o'clock, saw a multitude of islands. For this reason, not knowing the route [sealane] to St. Catherine Island, [we] headed northwest, seeking an appropriate passage. By noon, the island nearest to us was about 3 and ¼ to south by west and Catherine [Island] 23 miles distant. Soon after 1 o'clock an overcast developed and all the islands disappeared from our view.

On the 6th of December [we were] tacking toward the Island of St. Catherine.

About half past twelve we sighted a vessel passing near
one of the islands. We put up more sail and followed her.
By 2 o'clock we saw that she was sailing between islands,
and left off our pursuit.

Going on 4 o'clock, it became calm and we heard thunder.
[Soon] we suffered a strong squall, with rain [VV: then a
strong squall with rain hit].

The wind changed first to reef-topsail [strong], then to under-
sail [storm].

[SV: For this reason, having secured certain sails, we removed ourselves from the coast into the open sea].

We secured the rest of the sails, keeping only the foresail [*fok*], mizzen stay-sail [*apsel'*], main topsail [*grotmarsel'*] and the mizzen [*bizan'*], all completely reefed,
setting the course east by south, speed two knots, drift of
[5° *rumbov*].

Approaching 11 o'clock, we came together with the ship
Nadezhda, without sighting her, and were one from the other
not more than five sazhen' distant from each other.

For this reason we brailed [hauled in, *vziali na gitovy*] the
fore and mizzen sails, the main topsail [*grotmarsel'*] was
secured to the topmast, and we went farther north.

This was the first misfortune to happen during our entire
long voyage. The danger was imminent and threatened [VV:
inevitable] destruction of both ships. We owe our salvation to
the resolution, experience, and fearlessness of the commanders
as well as to the efficiency of the sailors.

On the 8th, toward the end of the fifth hour [going onto 6
o'clock] in the afternoon, we were approached by a boat,
which came from the shore, with five Portuguese aboard.
One of them remained with us to show is the way to St.
Catherine, the rest made for the *Nadezhda*. On the 9th,
at midday, the observed latitude was 27°5', the island Al-
varedo lay to the southeast one and a half miles away.
At 1 o'clock, under a topsail (light) wind from northeast
by north, we followed course south, at depth from 20 to
22 sazhen', toward the strait between the islands Alvar-
edo and St. Catherine. At half past two, we passed Al-
varedo Island on the east-southeast about three quarters
of a mile away. Going onto 4 o'clock, an English brig approached and fired a cannon ball under our stern. For
this temerity she received a tongue lashing from our
Captain. Soon after 4 o'clock, we passed the northern
cape of St. Catherine, passing southeast by east about
two Italian miles distant; then, having sailed past two
forts

at 6 o'clock [in the afternoon], lowered our sails and dropped anchors [in the roads of St. Catherine] at a depth of six sazhen'. In the roads were the following vessels: one English privateer and two French merchantmen which she had taken. On the 13th [VV: at nine past midnight] a 13-gun salute was fired by the ship *Nadezhda*, and the Portuguese fortress Santa Cruz responded with an equal number of guns.

The shores covered with pleasant verdure and full of aromatic shrubs and fruit bearing trees offered sweet enjoyment to our eyes and hearts, especially after our long sojourn at sea: our sail from the island of Teneriffe in the Canary Islands to the island of St. Catherine lasted 55 days.

This island lies under 27° latitude south and 48° longitude west. It extends from north to south for about 12 miles, and has a width, from east to west, of not more than two French miles. It is separated from the American [VV: continental] shore of Brazil by a strait which is at its narrowest point 200 toaz [see glossary]. Off this narrow spot, on the western side of the island, is built the city Nostra Senora del Destero. Formerly it was a refuge for vagabonds and escapees from various parts of Brazil, but since 1740 it has been made the provincial capital of the Island of St. Catherine and the lands which lie adjacent to it on the mainland shore. This province extends on [the mainland] Brazil from north to south for 60 miles, from the St. Francis River to the great river Rio Grande [Rio Grande del Sur].

The inhabitants of the entire province of St. Catherine [number] 28,000 to 12,000 on the island and 16,000 on the mainland.

[In SV the following two paragraphs are in reverse order]

Almost the entire island is covered by trees which are green all the time. Among these there is a lot of red wood [*krasnoe derevo*, mahogany] known under the name Brazilian beech, bakautu, and in the orchards the fruit bearing plants: coffee, cotton, lemon, orange, peach, chestnuts, and a few coconut trees.

In the city of Nostra Senora del Destero there are about 500 houses. Their construction is, for the most part, of stone, of very pleasant appearance on the outside as well as on the inside. There are three churches, of which one belongs to the Negroes. It has been built recently, in honor of their Black [VV: Negro] Saint, Benedict. In it there is a carved, almost black, full-size image of him.

The earth is exceedingly fertile and produces almost by itself a variety of fruit and vegetables. The cotton, sugar, and
manioc plantations reward the labor of their owners with great
abundance. The Saracen wheat (rice), wheat, barley, and corn
or the Turkish wheat [VV: Turkish little wheat – maize] bear
very abundantly. Lemons, chestnuts, peaches, pineapples, bananas, pumpkins, watermelons, potatoes, onions, carrots, and
cucumbers are found in great quantities, and there are so many
oranges that even pigs do not eat them.

Their trade consists in rum, granulated sugar, cotton, coffee,
and Negroes, brought from the Spanish [SV and VV: Guinea]
coast of Africa. They are bought for the purposes of labor for
100 to 200 piasters. Their subsistence is most meager, and
their sole food are the pineapples and manioc, a tree root from
which an edible meal is prepared. This meal is so bitter, that
any animal may be poisoned by its pulp. For this reason, it is
soaked in water for a very considerable time, then dried, and
only then used for food.

They go about practically naked, are exhausted by un-
ceasing heavy labor, and are beaten inhumanly. The native Portuguese, however, spend their lives in lazy and
carefree condition.

The Portuguese government forbids trade there by
foreign vessels, but many English engage in smuggling.
For this reason, two of their vessels were arrested during
our stay there and sent on to Rio [de] Janeiro. The Lisbon
Company derives great [VV: all sorts of] profits from
whaling. It [the company] has here three establishments
and sends to Lisbon, via Rio [de] Janeiro, a lot of whale
oil and spermaceti, used for candles which burn better
than the wax ones.

There is sufficient cattle raising, many fat bulls, cows, sheep
[ovtsy i barany],[6] swine and poultry, such as turkeys, chickens,
geese, and ducks; fish are also rather abundant along the
shores of the island.

[Late] in the evening and at night, it is pleasant to observe
luminiferous insects which fill the streets and gardens as if
they were so many tiny lanterns placed there on purpose.

In a word, this country is beautiful, pleasant, rich, and opu-
lent, with everything necessary to satisfy each need of life or
of pleasure in abundance, it flows with milk and honey. There
is only one drawback, and that is that the forests are [thick and]
impenetrable and are always entwined with brambles and lia-
nas [ezhevika i povilitsa, in parenthesis: lian] which during the
torrential rains and great heat causes the air therein to spoil.
The latter can [SV and VV: does] have bad effect on the in-

habitants. Moreover, everywhere there is an incredible number of the most repulsive snakes. Their bite is lethal. There are also many harmful insects. The people are gentle, polite and kindly [SV and VV: hospitable].

Others say that they are mistrustful, suspicious, and jealous. I did not notice this at all, and it was not my business to notice. I shall say frankly that in many homes we were given receptions which might be expected only from the closest relatives or most sincere friends. Their honored superior [SV: most honored Governor], the virtuous Joachim Curado (Kurado), colonel of infantry and cavalier,

VC and VV: the Governor of the entire island and the adjacent lands on the continent exceeds his subordinates in his dignity, politeness, kindness, diligence [effort] and rare hospitality. [SV: excels everyone in his kindness.] [During our sojourn], we dined at his house daily. Our ambassador [Rezanov] took up residence there, while [the governor's] country house was put at [our] disposal as residence of staff and senior officers [oberofizery] from both of our vessels. And I, unworthy one, was offered nowhere greater respect, politeness, and services than in the city of Nuestra Senora del Destero by all its inhabitants in general. When I took a walk in the city, and, as it happened occasionally, it began to rain even slightly, the heads of households would leave their porches, enter the street, and courteously ask me to visit their houses and, at the same time, to take shelter from the weather. They kissed my hands, brought their children to me, and believed that they might receive through me heavenly blessing [VV: for themselves and their children]. When I entered a church on the Feast of the Nativity of Christ, on the feast of the Negroes, that is on the last day of the year, and on New Year's, the clergy met me and escorted me to the Altar, where a large easy chair was placed to enable me to be a witness to their spiritual ceremonies and a spectator of the performance of the services. Everyone in the church knelt, some even through the entire Liturgy, while our Russians and the Ambassador stood full length. It was believed hereabouts that I was being taken to baptize the Japanese Emperor. Pious merchants, when I entered a store, took up their rosaries and recited prayers.

The Year 1804

[In the year 1804, on the 6th of January, I received from Mr. Ambassador a paper of the following content:)[7] .

Most Worthy Father Gideon,
My Dear Sir!

Leaving the Island of St. Catherine, I do hope to have the pleasure of meeting you again on the Sandwich Islands where, as
you know, the last rendezvous of our ships is planned. However, as it may easily happen that the stormy weather around
[VV: at] Cape Horn will separate us, so that our ships will have
to sail even to the very coasts of Northwest America along
routes determined by the circumstances then encountered, I
consider it my duty, in order to better advance the task put
upon us by the Lord Emperor, to express my thoughts in writing, in addition to my earlier communication with you in person.

I have a special regard for the Apostolic calling which you
have so eagerly embraced, and I am convinced that upon your
arrival in America you will in the best possible manner carry
out the August will of the Most Merciful Sovereign who seeks
to encourage the spread of the Orthodox Christian faith for the
benefit of the American inhabitants themselves; that, having
cleansed their minds of prejudice, you shall instill in their
hearts the true ways of rendering homage to God and that re-
moving, by the gentlest of means, all superstition which is not
to be tolerated by true Religion, you shall prepare them for life
in commonality, show them their duty toward the Sovereign
and fellow men, and that you shall make them true sons of
Russia. Success in this important transformation holds promise of eternal fame, good will of the Sovereign, and gratitude
of posterity.

On your arrival in America, try through kindness to gain the
affection of the local authorities and all residents, and do aid
the authorities, by all means at your disposal, to cement the
good accord between the Russians and the Americans. [Make
it clear to them] that they are a single people now, that both are
[sons] of a single Sovereign and that there is no better way to
attract the attention and good will of the Sovereign than by
working everywhere and at all times for the common good,
through respect for humanity and obedience to their superiors.

You may warn them of my impending arrival, and you may
assure them that the Sovereign Emperor, as an expression of
his Most Gracious concern for these remote regions, has
deigned to endow me with the power to reward those sons of
the Fatherland who have served [their country] well; that my
considerations in this matter will be based on substantative
evidence of industry and good deed of each, that it is my duty
to report about each and everyone to the Emperor for whom all

his subjects are equal. If there are those who, due to common human frailty, strayed from the true path, then they still will have time before my arrival not only to mend their ways but even to perform deserving service.

Your Worthiness is aware that in these fortunate times enlightenment in Russia is the main concern of her philanthropic ruler. In accordance with these great plans I entrust to your special care the school on Kad'iak – do transform it into a regular educational institution. To this end, in accordance with instruction issued by me to the Kad'iak authorities, you should receive from them every cooperation that is in their power to give. If the youth there has been taught literacy [*gramota*, reading and writing], introduce to them the true concept of God's Law and of Natural Law, undertake to teach them rules of orthography [*pravopisanie*], arithmetic, and establish the first bases of other sciences [*nauki*].

Agriculture, cattle breeding, and other economic activities do not fall directly into Your Honor's purview, but I beseech you as an educated man, that should you possess any expertise in any aspect thereof, do not deprive the local authorities of the benefit of your counsel, but assist them [in this respect] for the common good and prosperity of the region.

Finally, as I conclude this [letter], I must convey my proposal concerning yourself. In the firm hope that you shall be my foremost co-worker in implementation of these important plans, I do not find it necessary for you to return to Russia aboard Mr. Lisianskii's vessel. Therefore, be so good as to await my arrival in America and to conclude your journey then, together with me. I have already, as befits a humble subject, informed His Imperial Majesty about my provisional disposition in this matter. Now it only remains for us to await the beneficence of the Almighty [*Vsevyshnii*] that he will bless our good intentions with successful outcome.

Brazil, St. Catherine Island
December 25th, 1803

[VC and VV: January 6th, 1804] No.176
We remained in the roads off St. Catherine Island for 44 days. In that time, the masts on our *Neva* were replaced, because of rot; new ones were installed, made of red Brazil wood; the ship was caulked, the rigging repaired, and wood, water, and food supplies taken on.

On the 21st of January, when our Ambassador was leaving the city, he was escorted by the entire regiment, and offered such honors as are offered only to a Portuguese fieldmarshal. The Governor himself, accompanied by se-

veral officials, escorted him to the ship *Nadezhda*.
Throughout the entire time of their passage there was
cannon fire from all forts. When the Governor left the
Nadezhda, he was thanked for his visit by an 11-gun salute. From there he went to the fort, then aboard the
Portugese brig, and finally deigned to visit our *Neva*. As
he was leaving, the sailors were lined up in the shrouds
and shouted four times hurrah! At 2 o'clock in the afternoon, the Portuguese brig weighed anchor and sailed to
the northeast.

On the 23rd, at 5 o'clock after midnight, the ship *Nadezhda*
shook out the lower sails [*marsel'*], while firing a cannon shot;
at 6 o'clock, we followed suit. Because of calm, only at half past
three in the afternoon did we weigh anchors and set out on our
prescribed route. We parted from the Island of St. Catherine
at a season when the pineapples were ripening. For this reason we had the pleasure of tasting this subtly fragrant fruit and
also took some along on the voyage, together with other fruit,
such as bananas, watermelons, oranges, lemons, peaches, and
chestnuts.

From our departure from the roads and to the 7th February,
that is for two weeks, our voyage was accompanied by clear
weather and favorable wind. In this time we covered 2,806
verst [sic, VV, 2,866 verst] and were in latitude 47°34', longitude 62°59'. On the last mentioned date, in the first hour after
midday, thick fog befell us; in order to avoid collision with the
Nadezhda drums were beaten and firearms discharged. At 7
o'clock, as the fog lifted, we sighted the *Nadezhda* a short distance away. Going onto 8 o'clock, sounded bottom by line at the
depth of 55 sazhen'; the bottom was large-grained sand with
small shell. Afterwards, we were visited by Navigator Ka-
menshchikov from the *Nadezhda* who, having discussed fog
signals, returned [to his ship]. On the 9th, we were at latitude
49°49' and longitude, by the map, 66°27', by chronometer
64°50'. Going onto 6 o'clock after midday, while erecting the
yards [*rei*], the lower beam [yard] of the central mast
[*grotmarsel'-reia*] was broken. We let the *Nadezhda* know [VV:
we signalled the ship *Nadezhda*] that we had suffered damage.
It [the yard] was replaced within the hour.

In these latitudes [SV: at the latitude 52° and beyond] we
were often surrounded by whales which were not at all afraid
of our ships, majestically swam in close distance from us, and
by their frequent somersaults and discharge of water on the
top, drew our gaze toward them very often. On the 13th, we
sighted Cape Juan of States Island [States Land?].

Beginning with the 8th of February, and to the 15th we had a calm and good sail. In this time we covered 1,272 versts and reached latitude 56°13', longitude 62°57'.

On the 15th there was hail, snow and rain. At 2 o'clock in the afternoon we were hit from the west with such a severe squall [SV: strong gust of wind], with hail, that our vessel was completely turned around.

Therefore, while we were lowering the sails [VV: in order to lower the sails], we turned to southeast. This day Cape Horn was to the northwest about 36 miles distant.

On the 16th there was a heavy snowfall and a [VV: strong] squall, with hail, hit us also.

About 8 o'clock in the afternoon the wind strengthened, and later turned into under-sail, or a storm, which abated next day in the afternoon.

In the course of this storm the waves broke the false gunwales [falshbort, in VV: naddelanyi bort, also bulwark] on the forecastle [na bake] and carried overboard a barrel of fresh water; afterwards, the waves broke more of the false gunwales, three sections, from the forecastle to quarterdeck, and broke the third yard [beam, bramrei] which was stoved next to them. During this time I barely kept my footing on deck [SV: I swam around the deck] barely escaping being washed into the sea; navigator Kalinin was thrown against the steering wheel [shturval], and midshipman Kavediaev against the hatch to the wardroom.

Afterwards, light winds [malovetrie] prevailed up to the 20th. On that date we were in latitude 59°9' and longitude 67°55'. Beginning with the 20th and up to the 27th we had, once again, light winds, except for the 22nd and 23rd.

Then [SV: on the 27th] we were at latitude 59°30' and longitude 73°48'. We did not proceed beyond this point toward the South Pole.

In the course of the 28th and the 29th we traversed 385 verst, the latitude was 57°48' and longitude, by chronometer, 78°43', by calculation 79°48'.

During this time we passed Cape Horn – a matter of honor among seafarers. Even though we suffered greatly as we rounded this fearsome, stormy, and cold cape, experiencing strong winds, severe cold, hail, snow, fog, slush and rain, we enjoyed hot Russian pancakes with Provence [olive] oil and Holland cheese and tender Brazilian pineapples because the last day of the current leap year fell on the first day of our Russian Cheesefare week [maslenitsa].

On the 1st of March, at 8 o'clock after midnight, upon a signal from the Nadezhda, we approached the latter for a parley, following which Mr. Captain Kruzenshtern, Lieutenant Romberkh [sic], and Doctor Espenberg came on board, and left again an hour and a half later.

From this date [SV: From the 1st of March] to the 12th our sail was quiet.

We traversed 1,612 verst to latitude 48°10', longitude 95°52'.

On the 12th day [SV: on the last mentioned date] we were separated from the *Nadezhda* by thick fog, and were not to meet until the Marquesas Islands.

From the 12th of March to the 5th of April we had clear weather and favorable wind, and traversed 3,197 versts to latitude 27°12' and longitude 110°31'.

On the 4th of April, approaching 11 o'clock, we sighted Easter Island about 30 Italian miles distant.

Easter Island

We cleaned [all] the carronades [*karonady*], loaded five with cannon balls and five with case shot [*kartech'*], in alternate order; two [VV: remaining ones] were loaded with blank shots [VV: and hove to for the night at about 35 verst from the island. Then for four days we sailed around it waiting for the *Nadezhda* – SV: Because of the nearness of the shore we spent the night hove to].

The shores are covered with pleasant verdure, near the settlements are well situated plantations of bananas and sugar cane. Ancient monuments, and a multitude of people frolicking on the soft grass and other objects excited our feelings of extreme admiration, especially after our 70 day long sojourn at sea. However, it was dangerous to drop andchor here because of lack of a [good] harbor. Therefore, we, like so many Tantaluses were forced only to wish for and devour with our eyes only what we could not obtain.

Not a single islander came out to the ship, due, of course, to lack of boats.

On the 9th, under grotmarsel' secured to the beam, we approached the island [VV: we approached the southern end of the island] to about three versts distance from shore [VV: secured the main topsails to the topmast], and dispatched the yawl with, Mr. Lieutenant and Cavalier Povalishin, accompanied by five armed men. He delivered to the inhabitants various gifts and a sealed bottle which contained a note for the ship *Nadezhda* should she come to this island.

About an hour later, we signalled [VV: by means of a cannon shot] Mr. Povalishin to return to the ship, which he did immediately, bringing us presents given as a token of gratitude for our gifts: [some] potatoes, sweet potatoes, yams, bananas and sugar cane. [VV: has a slight change in wording and a sentence appears out of order immediately following the above paragraph, but this does not affect the content of either the preceding or the following paragraphs].

The island on which Mr. Povalishin went ashore is rather high and in the interior there are high mountains. From their foot, the land slopes gradually toward the sea.

The cultivated land appears in the form of well-situated elongated rectangles.

The size and quality of the sugar cane, bananas, yams, and potatoes is evidence of the fertility and richness of the soil. There is no forest on the entire island.

When Mr. Lieutenant Povalishin went ashore, there were present about 700 persons of both sexes. Some of the women wore coverings made of lengths of their own cloth [bark cloth]. These probably were wives of the rich and of notables. The rest, both women and men, were naked, except for a belt of string to which in the front was tied a bunch of grass to cover the genitals and the women wore an additional bunch of grass in the back. Some were tattooed, others had their faces smeared with paint. They consider it fun to jump into the surf, no matter how strong and heavy it is. These Indians [sic] are of full stature, well built, and pleasant in appearance. They are about 5 feet 4 inches tall, and are well proportioned in all parts of the body. In facial features, they differ but little from Europeans. The skin color is dusky or sunburnt; their hair is black. There are no noticeable disfigurements on their bodies, those sure indicators of formerly suffered diseases. One may, therefore, conclude that in general they enjoy good health. They believe it to be a distinction, a mark of beauty, to have their skin painted or tattooed and to pierce their ears. Mr. Povalishin observed that some had their ears extended even to their shoulders. This, of course, is not natural, and one surmises that [the earlobes] are artificially extended also as a sign of greater distinction and beauty.

A short distance away from the shore, there are in many places [VV: island localities] tall [stone] monuments which Mr. LaPerouse and his companion and comrade, De La Langle, consider to be ancient memorials to the dead, as they saw many

human bones surrounding these monuments. These seafarers
landed on this island in [the month of] April 1786.

At 2 o'clock, as soon as Mr. Lieutenant Povalishin returned from shore, we filled the grotmarsel' and sailed to
the eastern side of the island and

at 6 o'clock after midnight set our course for the Marquesas
Islands.

The northern extremity of Easter Island is located st 27°
latitude and 108°31' longitude west. Our speed was 14
verst per hour.

From the 10th to the 25th our sail continued to be a most
happy and pleasant one. The skies were constantly cloudless,
the days clear, the wind steady, with no squalls. Everywhere,
the ship was dry.

To the honor of our Captain, the decks of our *Neva* were
as cleanly maintained as the most conscientious house-
wives maintain their tables and chairs. During those fine
15 days we traversed 3,122 versts. It follows, that we
made 208 verst in each 24-hour period. Our latitude was
11°18', longitude as calculated 136°, by the chronometer
137°28', by the moon 137°.

[The Marquesas Islands]

At 9 o'clock in the afternoon, as we were nearing the
Marquesas Islands, we lowered the sails, put up the
yards, and secured the formarsel' to the stang [*obstengili
formarsel'*] and remained thus through the night. On the
25th, at 6 o'clock in the morning, we sighted in the west,
about 17 versts distant, the Island of Magdalena. All sails
were hoisted and we went to north-northwest. During
this 24-hour period we made 23½ German miles, reaching
the latitude 10°, longitude 136°48'. By 8 o'clock in the
afternoon

we had passed all the Marquesas to the west, namely Magdalena, San Pedro, San Domenique, Christina and Gud [Good?].
On the 26th, we sighted to the north Rios Island, and by 11
o'clock, having passed the latter, saw the Island of Nua-Hiva
[sic, elsewhere Nuka-Hiva] or Kekdri Martins [sic].

Then, having turned toward Rios Island, we tacked near
it until about 7 o'clock; after 8 o'clock, we hove to. On the
27th, going on 5 o'clock, we set sail and went toward the
southern extremity of the Island Nua-Hiva. It was not
possible to note any settlements from aboard ship, because the location is mountainous and the bays cut deep

into the interior: it is on such bays that the islanders have
their homes. Having passed the above mentioned cape,
we then sailed past the northeastern extremity of the island [VV: we sailed past another cape, the northeastern
one].

At that time we were visited by the islanders, who came in
four boats, about 30 men, from the settlement which was located at the last mentioned cape. [VV: On the 27th, we were
visited by the islanders, who came in four boats, about 30 persons, from the northeastern bay].

Their boats were made of the best quality redwood (maho-
gany), in the cleanest possible carpenter's workmanship. A
pleasure to behold! When we saw them [VV: at a distance], we
indicated by various [VV: pantomime] signs that they should
come to the ship without any fear. They, for their part, displayed to us cloth and banana branches, and blew into the
(conch) shell. When they were yet some [VV: about eight sazhen'] distance from the ship, eight of their women [VC: their
women] threw themselves from their boats into the water (VV:
they threw themselves into the water, women are not specified), swam to the ship, and came aboard, with fearless and
smiling countenances. Their first confusion was occasioned by
the sight of our sentries standing on the quarterdeck. They
pointed to their guns, calling them *puga*. They brought with
them a small quantity of cloth, bananas, sugar cane, and coconuts. All were naked,
     except for a few who had a body wrapping [VV: who had
     a belt] of a long narrow piece of cloth. Those were, with-
     out doubt, the most notable among them; the rest did not
     have this covering even, but all
the men had the tip of their genital organs tied with a bark
covering.[8]
     [SV: Some had their entire bodies tattooed or decorated in
     various ways, according to their taste. Some held in their
     hands large fans [*opakhala*]. The heads of all were bare,
     the hair cropped. We offered them some white Teneriffe
     wine, but they did not drink it; neither did they snuff the
     tobacco].
     [VC: They have no hats or caps at all, but many held in
     their hands large fans. In stature they are shapely,
     strongly built. The rich and the notable have their entire
     bodies tattooed in the manner of ancient Roman knightly
     garments. We offered them some Teneriffe wine, but they
     would not drink it; neither would they snuff the tobacco.
     Later, we gave them knives, needles and small pieces of
     iron [*zhelezki*]. In return, they entertained us with their

songs, accompanied by various contortions, and by beat-
ing in time the right palm upon the left shoulder.]

They inspected with great curiosity the chickens, ducks, and
sheep. However, they were most astonished, so that it is even
difficult to depict the same, by the Russian village musical instrument called the *volynka*. As they listened to the song music
being played upon it, they marvelled and grew shy, jumped
around and shouted. After they left the ship, they swam to one
of their boats to inspect a small mirror which Mr. Berkh[9] gave
to one of their notable dignitaries [SV: leaders]. Even from
afar, one could note his expression of pride in having received
such, for him, a rare and unusual item. At 6 o'clock in the afternoon, having left behind the above-mentioned northeastern
cape, we went out to sea and tacked through the night.

On the 28th, under light rain, with little wind, we sighted a
small yawl which was approaching us from the island. In about
half an hour, the yawl came alongside our ship. Aboard the
yawl came Mr. Lieutenant Golovachev from the *Nadezhda*.
With him were four oarsmen and one islander of most imposing
height. We learned from him [Golovachev] that the ship *Nadezhda* arrived safely on the 25th of this month at this island
and lay at anchor in the bay Tai-ogaie or Anna-Maria.

At 10 o'clock, having hoisted sails, we set out for the above
mentioned bay under light breeze. By 6 o'clock in the afternoon, we dropped anchors near the *Nadezhda*. Our sail from
the Island of St. Catherine to Nua-Hiva [Nuka-Hiva, or Kekur
Martins] or Kekodri [VV: Kekdri] in the Marquesas lasted 93
days.

We had barely anchored [SV: we barely reached the anchorage appointed to us] when our *Neva* was surrounded by a
multitude of swimming islanders bearing coconuts, bananas,
and breadfruits. We traded for these the *zhelezki about half a
hand-span long, cut from old [barrel] hoops* which pleased
them greatly.

Even at our first meeting with the islanders, we were able
to note their goodwill [VV: and kindness] toward us and
had, therefore, no doubt that we should be able to put up
here all that we needed. Just the same, we determined to
observe the necessary caution. For this reason, we posted
sentries [VV: with firearms] amidships [*shkantsy*] and on
the quarterdeck [*iut*] and forecastle as well. Beginning
with the 30th, we began to fill the [water] barrels and cut
fire wood. The islanders were obliging and constantly
aided us in these tasks.

Without their help we would have suffered a lot of difficulty,
as the landing was not suitable for oar-propelled vessels. They

[the islanders] carried the barrels through the surf on their backs, and found in this even some kind of sport. As the sailors were hoisting the barrels aboard the ship by means of the capstan [*shpil'*], King Tapega Katenui arrived, in company with all his kinsmen and notables. Our newly arrived guests, seeing the sailors engaged in this work, decided that it was a game and suddenly joined in, singing in their own manner.

Our Tartar, Bek-Murza Iusupov [SV: one of the sailors] began to accompany them on the bag-pipe [*volynka*, see glossary], their most favored and marvelled at instrument. They aided us also in various tasks aboard ship.

They are very strong and agile.

The Island of Nua-Khiva or the Kekedri [VV: Kekdri] Martins belongs to the Washington Islands group and lies under 8°58' south latitude. Its anchorage is to be preferred to all others in the Marquesas Islands. Along its southwest shore are three large bays: first, from the south, Controller [Kontrolerskaia] or Giume; second, Tai-Ogaie or Anna-Maria, where we stood; and the third Zhe Gauskaei [VC: Zhigaiskaia],
near the western cape.

[In the text that follows, SV version is much abridged and paragraphs are in different order. We follow here the VV and VC versions.]

The terrain of this island is mountainous. The islanders have their habitations on [various] bays. [SV: Their number may be estimated to be up to 4,000]. Their subsistence is derived from bread fruits, bananas, coconuts, sugar cane and, in small part, from swine, chickens, and fish.

Their facial features are pleasant and well proportioned. In stature they are large [*rosly*], stocky [portly, *dorodny*], well-built, and so healthy that not on a single person did we notice any blemishes – the usual indications of former diseases – except for [VV: small] battle scars received in the wars. They boast of these just like the old European soldiers do, and displayed their scars for us. Their hair is black, and most have it cut to the roots; the eyes are large, the nose somewhat broad and flattened, ears medium, lips thick, teeth white and so strong that they are able easily and quickly to peel off [VC: with their teeth] coconut skins, while we took these off with hatchets. Tattooing is considered among them a matter of great distinction, and the rich and the notables pay for it dearly.

[SV: but it is used only by the rich and by notables]. It is performed in the following manner: first of all the skin is pierced until the blood shows by means of an instrument with a tiny toothed edge made out of a shell. Then ink is smeared over, and the ink, seeping into the pierced openings in the skin, assumes a dark blue appearance. Masters of this art receive great recompense.

Women with no tattooing, except for a few [VV: small] lines along the lips and on the eyelids which indicate the married state and that of child-bearing.

The wives of the rich clothe themselves into pieces of their own cloth (cloth of their own manufacture), one around the shoulders like shawls which are used in Europe, the other from the waist to the knees. Before they dress, they smear their entire body with a yellow juice of most unpleasant odor, something which is considered among them the height of foppery. They have no head-coverings whatsoever. [SV: Some women, doubtless notables, wind around themselves pieces of their cloth.

Poor women, and all men, go about naked. The latter consider it proper only to tie up the tip of the genitals. Among them, to appear before others without such covering is roughly equivalent to appearance stark naked at a feast among us. Should this covering, unexpectedly, loosen and fall off, they, in great confusion, red in the face, hurry and squat, put their hands between their legs, and turning away, fix it. In their houses, extreme cleanliness is observed.

The walls of their houses are erected upon a stone foundation, elevated about four feet above ground. On it are erected posts, about eight inches thick, which may be in height from two to six [SV: two to four to six] and even up to ten feet. On top of these are tied cross-beams, of the same thickness; against this [frame], three walls are then constructed of thin poles [VV: on the inside] which are covered on the outside by leaves [VV: while on the outside leaves are secured to them]. The fourth wall remains open. The roofs are of cane and coconut tree leaves, single pitched. Over the open wall there is a large awning. Within the houses' interior, on the foundation, there are placed two logs, at right angles to each other. In one part of the house are spread very finely and skillfully worked mats and elongated pillows; one quarter [one fourth part] is separated from the rest by a small barrier and serves for storage. The size of such houses depends on the size [strength] of a family. The houses are surrounded by coconut and breadfruit trees, plantations of bananas, sugar cane, and yams. We did not see any domestic animals with the exception of swine and a small number of chickens.

We traded to the King, for a sow and two piglets, a drake and a duck [VV: of Brazilian breed]. He took them under the stipulation that they produce green-colored offspring. He greatly desired that these be red, and argued at length, with great curiosity asking why they could not produce red colored (ducklings).

The population numbers up to 2,000. We found here two Europeans, an Englishman and a Frenchman,[10] who even here were not able to coexist in amity. Friendship between an Englishman and a Frenchman is in the world [VV: something of the order of] a white crow. The first of these served as an interpreter on our ship, the second left aboard the *Nadezhda* for Kamchatka.

Each bay has its own king, which dignity is hereditary. Following the death [of a king] his office is assumed by the eldest son, in case of minority [SV: of the king's children; VV: of the latter] by the elder among the king's brothers. Each king rules throughout his life in the name of his successor. The latter even is regarded in place of Divinity, and his wife as a Goddess. The kingly power is not great. Without the agreement of the folk, but even more without consent by their Spiritual head, he cannot do anything at all. His income is derived from the practice that every one must send him, as well as to the Spiritual personage [leader], the first and best portion of everything. He [the king] together with the Spiritual Head, tabus houses, localities, trees, and various other objects, which afterwards no one may use.

[SV: The word *tabu* according to their religion, designates either such an object which no one may touch under any circumstances, or a forbidden locality which no one will dare enter.]

Obligation for vengeance for injuries suffered is transmitted from one generation to another. Killing which follows an injury inflicted remains without any kind of investigation and punishment. Wars against the residents of other bays are frequent for reason of the slightest insult, but last only four months per year. Battles take place at sea, by means of boats specially built for military purposes, and also on land, by means of wooden spears, maces, and stones thrown by a sling. Such battles are settled with the death of two or three persons, who (whose bodies) are then eaten in the course of solemn rites.

Only the royal kin have the right to travel by boat; the rest came to our ship by swimming, holding coconuts and various other products in their hands, teeth, or on their backs.

Truly, one could call them seals or sea lions, as they spent most of the day [VV: swimming] in the water. Some swam away from us at 6 o'clock, and by seven women [VV: es-

corted by men] came swimming to offer their services to
the seafarers. Once, *Tapega Katenui* sent, under escort
by the Royal assistant, the Queen and his eldest daught-
er-in law, the wife of his heir, as well as three women
from among his closest kin, to visit our ship and Captain's
cabin, which for this occasion was very well appointed.
Next day, the king himself arrived to ask the Captain for
posy [VV: moka][11] bridewealth, for the visit by the Queen
and his daughter-in-law. This king is very obliging. He,
with his own hands, brought for us from the water coral,
of which there is a quantity to be found in the [VV: local]
bays, and various shells.

We remained in the [VV: this] Bay [Anna-Maria] six days.
When water, firewood, and a small quantity of food stuffs were
put up, on the 5th of May, beginning 4 o'clock in the morning,
we began to weigh anchors.

At half past nine, the ship *Nadezhda*, having hoisted anchors, sailed south. Toward the end of the hour, we, too,
having raised the bram and marsel's [topgallants and
gallants], followed the *Nadezhda*.

About 10 o'clock [VV: at half past ten] the *Nadezhda* was
driven toward the island shore of the bay. She dropped anchor,
firing two cannons, and signaled us to dispatch a *kater*, which
was sent immediately. By the beginning of the twelfth hour
[shortly after 11 o'clock] the current began to press our *Neva*
to the shore also. We dropped anchor at the depth of 15 sazhen', secured the sails, and began to put out storm anchors
[*verpy*]. Beginning with the 3 o'clock after midnight [VV: mid-
day], we began to pull ourselves out of the bay along the haw-
sers [cables, *kabel'tovy*] which were strung out beforehand.
Toward 11 o'clock, we cleared the bay, met an easterly wind,
hoisted sails and sailed away from the island.

The ship *Nadezhda* stood at [VV: dropped] anchor at the
very exit from the bay. At 11 o'clock we hove-to in order
to take up on board the oared craft.

The egress from this bay was difficult and dangerous because of the winds which constantly shifted and drove us this
way and that along the bay. On the 6th
while the wind was strong and easterly, close to 11
o'clock we sighted to the northeast the *Nadezhda*, which
stood hove-to in order to take on board the oared craft
which were separated from her by a sudden squall. [VV:
By 11 o'clock the wind began to abate]. At midday we
were in latitude 9°
toward 9 o'clock in the afternoon, having received a signal
from the *Nadezhda*, we beat against the wind on the right halse

[*pravym gal'som*, to starboard], having beamed [*obstenia*] the grot-marsel'. In this condition we continued through the night, in the hope of finding some unknown island.

On the 7th, under fresh [VV: marsel'] wind from east-southeast, at 5 o'clock, we hoisted the sails and set our course southwest [sic] toward the Sandwich [Hawaiian] Islands.

From this date on, until the 13th, we had a most favorable wind and traversed 1,148 versts. We were then almost at the equator, at latitude 0.5° south and longitude 144°50'.

On the 13th, shortly after 4 o'clock in the afternoon, we crossed the equatorial line from the southern into the northern hemisphere.

The Island Oviga [Oahu] was 321 German miles distant.

From the 13th to the 21st we had very light winds from east and northeast, meeting no calms nor squalls; rains, too, occurred seldom, as did thunder and lightning;

During this time we traversed 855 versts. [We] were at calculated latitude 6°57' and longitude, calculated, 145°39'.

On the 21st we got from the east-northeast fresh wind, and in that 24-hour period covered 140 versts, course north. The latitude was, by observation, 8°17', calculated longitude was 145°39', 149°8' by the chronometer, by distance between sun and moon 149°10'. The Island Oviga (Oahu) was then 181 German miles to the northwest.

The [VV: This] wind held to the 27th, with clear weather. During this time we traversed 1,207 versts and were at latitude 19°10', calculated longitude 149°11', by chronometer 153°57'. The Sandwich Island Oviga [Oahu] was to northwest, five German miles distant. Afterwards, we sailed through the entire night away from the island.

On the 28th, we had a bramsel' [steady] wind from east-northeast, were at latitude 18°54'; the southern end of the Oviga [Oahu] Island was to southeast, about six Italian miles distant. Beginning midday, we were hove-to. About half past one, *Nadezhda* sent to us, for transport to Kad'iak, two [Russian-American] Company promyshlennye and one desiatnik [leader of ten, foreman]. Approaching 9 o'clock, we sailed away from the island.

On the 29th, just after 1 o'clock after midday *when we were off the southern end of this same island [Oahu], about 6½ German miles distant*, Captain Kruzenshtern came to visit us; then, having taken his farewell from us, he left about half past five. Soon afterwards, aboard our vessel and the *Nadezhda*, flags were raised, the sailors were lined up in the shrouds, and on both ships we shouted six times hurrah! Soon after 6 o'clock, the *Nadezhda*, *under full sail* set her course toward Kamchatka, and we toward the Island Oviga [Oahu]. On the 30th, there was, beginning at midnight, a calm, then light wind from 6 o'clock on. Shortly after eight, an Englishman and a young islander came aboard, coming from the island. We kept them with us so that they would conduct us to Karakakoa Bay which is suitable as an anchorage.

At noon, this bay was about ten Italian miles distant, we were in the latitude 19° 17'. After 3 o'clock, because of dead calm, we were forced to use the *kater* and the yawl to tow the ship.

At 6 o'clock [after midnight] we entered the said Karakakoa Bay and dropped two anchors, *dagliks* [larboard] and *plekht* [starboard], at 20 sazhens depth; each line was paid out for 100 sazhen.

From the Marquesas Island Nuka-Hiva or Kekdri Martins to this location we sailed 25 days.

As soon as we stood at anchor, we were visited by five English sailors who live on this island. No islanders were to be seen, even on shore, because this day a tabu was placed on us.

This word, according to their religion, designates objects which they may not touch under any circumstances or a forbidden locality which they may not enter.

This was the reason why no island inhabitants came to visit our ship. This was also the reason why the young islander who was on board [VV: as our guide] hid himself in the hold [VV: as we neared the island]. He was afraid of severe punishment had the English sailors noticed him and then disclosed his whereabouts when they went ashore.

In the evening, our ship was surrounded by women only, about 40 in number, who approached us swimming, and wanted to be permitted aboard; when we chased them away, they shouted, as they were swimming back, that the tabu did not apply to them.

The next day we were visited by a Royal official, *Kamigu*, which means in their language 'tooth'. He was dressed only in sailcloth trousers and satin vest, without a shirt.

King Tomi-omi [Kamehameha] entrusted to him the care for his court and other estate during his own absence. He was, in company with his entire family and other officials, on another island, preparing for war against the king of the Island of Attui [Kauai].

The position of the viceroy is occupied by the Englishman Young, who formerly was an ordinary sailor aboard a merchantman. Nowadays he is very wealthy, possesses much land, laborers, and has a stone house. His son, together with the

King's son, is being educated at the Philadelphia University
[University of Pennsylvania].

The island is divided into numerous districts, each ruled by
an official appointed by the King.

The inhabitants are not as tall, stocky, well-built, attractive
and healthy as the inhabitants of the Marquesas Island Nua-
Khiva [Nuka Hiva] or Kekdri [sic]. Their facial features are
coarse, the eyes are black, the glance quick, cheek bones pro-
truding, nostrils somewhat wide, lips thick, the mouth big, the
teeth wide and white.

We saw plenty of young men who lacked many teeth. This
is because of the custom to knock out, with a stone, a tooth
each to mark the death of a kinsman, a friend, or a superior.
Their hair is black. Some wear it long, others cut it all around;
many, out of vanity, of course, arrange it so on top of their
heads that it resembles a helmet.

The hair which forms the crest of such a 'helmet' is redd-
ish-white, due to frequent application of a white pulverized stone mixed with the juice of some caustic product.

Their entire body is covered with [VV: white] scabby spots,
which are the result of excessive use of a concoction made from
a very caustic root. This concoction also causes them to vomit
[VV: from this concoction they also become intoxicated [crazy
– *dureiut*].

They are subject to many diseases, but especially to
smallpox and venereal disease. Many have on their bodies most repulsive scabs, boils and sores, swellings and
warts [VV: others suffer from *skaznaia* disease][12] .

Tattooing is not much esteemed here nor does it serve as a
mark of distinctions.[13] Many of the notables lack it altogether.
For adornment they wear earrings [SV: pierce their ears for
earrings, VV: pierce their ears and noses and wear rings ther-
ein]. Mostly, they go about naked, wrapping only a narrow
strip of cloth around the waist and the genitals. Others wear
old clothing traded from the Europeans, and the American
English [sic]. Strange to see! One will appear dressed just in
a tunic, without shirt or pants; another only in a *kamzol*, the
third wears only a pair of pants or sailor's trousers.

The women are much shorter than the men, fat, ungainly
and not as beautiful as those in the Marquesas. Their hair is
cut all around, with a small fringe on the forehead [VV: combed
up], which also may be of whitish-red color because of frequent
application of the above mentioned concoction.

They have no tattoo whatsoever, wear a shell on their arm
[shell armband?] and are clothed with their own cloth [tapa or
bark cloth] from two to four lengths combined, or in pieces of

blue and red European cloth. They also go about naked, just
tying a bunch of grass or leaves at the genitals.

Their houses are constructed somewhat like poor fisher-
men's huts, have a small door, and are covered with
grass. There is little cleanliness inside. In the sleeping
rooms grass mats, very skillfully woven, are spread.
Water is kept in *kalabasy* [gourds], which are elongated
and have narrow necks and resemble the *kubyshki* used
in our villages. Long ones, about an arshin in length,
serve them as musical instruments which are beaten,
rhythmically, with both hands to accompany singing.
They shape these to their taste when the gourds are still
on the tree, as green fruit and yet soft; after the insides
are cleaned, they are lacquered and decorated in black
paint in various designs, as one wishes. Their cloth,
worked with indifferent skill from the bark of the silk tree
(mulberry), is also covered with various colors; some of it
resembles our cotton prints [*sitsy*].

The soil is composed of lava and other volcanic matter.
[SV: their subsistence depends on coconuts, bananas,
bread fruit, yams, potatoes or sweet potatoes,[14] watermelons, and sugar cane]. There are plenty of coconut trees,
bananas, bread fruit, yams, potatos or sweet potatoes, and
water melons. Sugar cane grows by itself, without trans-
planting.

During Mr. Vancouver's voyage, bulls and cows were
brought here, and these increased in great numbers among the
mountains where they have become wild. Goats and chickens
are few, but swine are so plentiful that many call these islands
Hog Islands.

Hereabouts one cannot trade anything for the iron from old
barrel hoops. They accept in trade bar iron [*polosovoe
zhelezo*], large axes, broadcloth, ticking, sailcloth, calico
[*vyboika*][15] and old European clothing. The above mentioned
[VV: Royal] official Kanigu gave Mr. Lieutenant Povalishin a
pig for a rather worn uniform coat.

The inhabitants are quiet and kind in character, but they do
have a dreadful custom of offering in sacrifice two persons in
case of the death of a superior and, when a King dies, in addition to knocking out teeth throughout the island, [they kill] four
persons. Moreoover, all sorts of license occurs, injuries are
offered and offenses committed without any kind of penalty.
No woman, no matter how exalted of rank, may at that time
refuse a shameful demand even from the lowest of the low
among the islanders. With this exception, all have only one
wife. [VV: At marriage negotiations] a bride gives the bride-

groom the shell which she usually wears on her arm, while the bridegroom begifts her with a *maru* or *manu* which in their language signifies a length of broadcloth or some jute cloth [*pestred'*]. He begifts also [her] kinsmen. Eating meat is tabu for the entire female sex, both pork and the meat of other animals, while the men are subject to this tabu only until the Spiritual head consecrates it; the King's [portion] is consecrated first of all.

The entire twelfth month is spent in festivity, without engagement in any kind of labor [VV: except for war games]. On the first day of the festival [VV: month], the King must appear before the people [VV: at sunrise] dressed in an excellently well and artfully made festival cape of feathers of a small red bird and in a similar rich and majestic helmet. [VV: For this reason] he first departs in a [VV: small] boat from shore at a point where stands the *morai*, their temple, where his forefathers are buried. Then, he approaches land, and one of the bravest warriors runs to meet him, carrying a war spear. With a great onrush, he casts this spear at the King who [at that moment] discards the cape, fearlessly goes forward to meet the warrior, and, with great and manly demeanor, catches the spear in his own hand. After this, the King is met by the primate among the Spiritual leaders. The latter accepts the spear from the King and places it in the above mentioned *morai* while the entire folk exclaims solemnly. When they emerge from the *morai*, and the ceremony is ended, military games begin.

During the entire festival no one is punished for any kind of crime.

All of the Sandwich Islands are under the rule of a single king, Tomi-omi [Kameameha] who has his main residence in the Bay of Karakakoa on the Island of Ovagi [Oahu], the same on the shore of which famous Captain Cook was killed. Several Europeans are in the service of this king and form his main support. He already has built several small vessels.

Throughout our five-day stay in the Bay of Karakakoa from morning to about 4 o'clock in the afternoon, our ship was surrounded by up to 70 boats and a multitude of the islanders, of both sexes, swimming on top of thin, black, and excellently polished boards. We traded with them, for bar, raw, and sheet iron, axes, sailcloth, ticking, linen, and old clothing, a rather large quantity of swine, chickens, potatoes, bananas, yams, taro, a few coconuts, and two goslings.

Fourth of June, going on 10 o'clock in the afternoon, we weighed anchors, hoisted sails, and under very light wind departed toward the southwest, a short distance away from the shore. On the 5th, the calm continued until about noon, then there was very light wind and gloomy weather hanging over the coast. On the 6th, we traversed, under steady wind, 120 verst. On the 7th, going on 5 o'clock, we sighted the island Attui [Kauai].

About half past ten, the King of this island, Tamori [Kaumualii], came to visit us in a small boat. He was accompanied by a court official who held a small wooden bowl filled with cotton and inlaid with human teeth into which the king deigned to spit. Both were naked, girded only with narrow strips of cloth around the waist and genitals. Tamori is of medium stature, has black uncut hair and a small beard; he himself is spare, and by his face, though dusky, he resembles a European. He speaks English very well. Very convincingly, [up to the point of] evoking pity, he begged us to drop anchor in the Bay of Velie [Waimea?] on his island, promising to supply us with sufficient quantity of food stuffs. He himself had the greatest need for military equipment, as the mighty Tomi-omi [Kameameha] was ready to attack his island.

At noon calm, then very light wind commenced. The latitude was 22°, longitude 159°55'.

Chapter 2 – Kad'iak

[Here begins the portion of the text published by Valaam in 1894.]

On June 8th, 1804, at 1 o'clock past midnight, sailing with a northeasterly topgallant sail [*bramsel'*, steady or moderate] wind, we were by midday in latitude 23°6' and calculated longitude 160°18', longitude by chronometer 160°10'. The east coast of Unalashka Island was 467 German miles distant. Close to 5 o'clock in the afternoon we crossed the Tropic of Cancer.

From the 8th to the 19th, we sailed with fair wind and changeable weather, which was at times clear, then cloudy (overcast), or with a light rain and dampness. On the 17th, going on five o'clock after midday, we ran into a storm which continued only until the next morning. In these ten 24-hour periods we traversed 2,033 versts and were in the observed latitude 42°18', calculated longitude 164½°, by chronometer 163°13'.

From the 19th onward we encountered frequent fogs, rain, cloudiness, wet weather, and dampness, which continued almost to the end of the month. Between this date and the 26th we travelled to the northeast 1,327 versts. On the 26th, just after 2 o'clock in the afternoon we sighted the island of Ukamok or Chirikov. On the 27th, at two o'clock in the afternoon, we also saw the Trinity Islands: Sitkhinok and Tugidok. Going on 12 o'clock, we hove to.

On the 28th, at half past two after midnight, Kad'iak revealed itself before our eyes, with its high mountains which are sometimes covered by snow throughout the summer. As we approached it, we were met, and then escorted, by majestic whales. After 4 o'clock, we ran up the Russian merchant flag and at various times fired the cannon three times. At 2 o'clock in the afternoon, the old baidarshchik Ostrogin arrived from Three Saints harbor, travelling in a three-hatch baidarka. He remained aboard the vessel to guide us into Pavlovskaia gavan' [Kodiak].

On the 29th, we were enveloped by thick fog and throughout the day there was just a very light breeze. On the 30th, after 11 o'clock, the fog lifted somewhat and we saw Chiniatskii Mys [Cape Chiniak], on the English charts Cape Grenville, 10 Italian miles away. Going onto 5 o'clock in the afternoon, having rounded this cape with a bramsel' wind, we fired one cannon shot, using a cannon ball. Upon this signal, a two hatch baidarka came out to us, which we sent back immediately with a

letter to the Manager, Banner, with the request to send baidaras to tow in our ship, as by this time we were becalmed.
From nine to two we fired the cannon and sounded the bell so
that the baidaras dispatched from shore should not miss us in
the thick fog.

On July 1st, soon after 1 o'clock after midnight, having secured all sails, we stood on sea anchor [*verp*] at 5 sazhen' depth,
silt bottom. At that time, Mr. Banner arrived in a yawl, bringing with him two 14-oar baidaras. Toward 11 o'clock the fog
lifted, we raised the sea anchor and proceeded under tow to
Pavlovskaia gavan' [St. Paul or Pavlovskaia harbor, modern
Kodiak].   About 1 o'clock we passed the American vessel
O'Cain which stood in the roads. Going on 2 o'clock, we received an 11-gun salute fired by Pavlovskaia fort. At 2 o'clock,
having sailed past the fort, we dropped anchor. From the Island of Oviga [Oahu] in the Sandwich Islands to Kad'iak our
sail lasted 26 days.

[The information in the next paragraph is presented here
as it appears in SV as continuous text. In VV and VC, it
is contained in separate letters from Gideon to Metropolitan Amvrosii and was published in the latter form in
Valaam 1894].

[SV: On my arrival on the 2nd of July 1804 at the main
establishment of the Russian-American Company I
deemed it my first and most sacred duty to give sincere
thanks in the American-Kad'iak Church to the Giver of
All Benefits for safe arrival after a voyage half-way
around the world. My pen is too weak to convey all the
emotions of my soul when I heard the sweet tidings that
in the New World, in a country so distant that there is no
easy communication with our bountiful Russia, in a
country still untamed, the name of the Triurine [Tri-Hy-
postatic] God is devoutly praised, and that the name of the
Most August of His annointed – the one who Genius of
[our] boundless Russia is worthy of homage – Alexander
the First is pronounced more often than the name of any
other mortal. On the 6th, I moved from the ship to the
quarters of the Spiritual Mission.]

Having completed the inspection of the entire church
inventory, vestry, books, and domestic economy, I set out,
on the 26th accompanied by company interpreters, in two
3-seater baidarkas to visit the entire island of Kad'iak, as
well as the nearby islands of Ugak, Shalidakh [Sitkali-
dak?], Aiakhtalik [Aiaktalik], Sitkhinakh [Sitkinak], and
Tugidok [Tugidak] in order to preach the word of God.

Visiting every one of the Aleut settlements, I attempted
to inculcate among the newly enlightened, in so far as my
abilities permitted, all that is necessary to the faith, civil
virtues, and economic existence. By every possible means, I tried to understand their former prejudices, always
offering friendly counsel in order to expose and demonstrate the obvious vileness and harm caused through the
deep rooting of the same. In this manner I led them to the
bases of true homage to God [*bogopochitanie*]. If one
were to judge by appearances, they willingly listened to
me. It was not a rare occurrence when they sat around,
without rising or moving off, for over eight hours. Everywhere I was received kindly. I was offered, besides fish,
sarana with whale blubber and berries: raspberries,
crowberries, salmonberries, and blueberries. I gave gifts
of tobacco, glass seed beads [*biser*], needles, worsted, and
iamanina, that is, long strands of goat hair.

On the 21st of August, in the strait which separates
Aiakhtalik from Kad'iak, my heart was filled with sorrow:
after calm weather and fog, a strong, most cruel wind
arose accompanied by adverse current. The paddlers
tired, the weather grew worse. The swells constantly
rolled over us. From great exertion, blood spurted from
the noses of the paddlers. We expected imminent destruction, either by being overturned by the savagery of
the waves, or by separation of our baidarkas. Our
strength at the limit of exhaustion, God be praised, we
reached a deserted shore – but just barely. Here we remained for three 24-hour periods. We were grateful to the
Provider thanks to whom we did not suffer from lack of
food: we had yukola and whale meat.

In the course of my tour, that is in the period of two
months and five days, I baptized 503 souls of both sexes,
[mostly] aged from one to ten years of age, but among
them also were 22 souls of mature years [in their forties,
sorokoletnie]. Thirty-eight pairs were married.[16]
[Resumption of VV, VC and Valaam 1894 text]:

In Pavlovskaia Harbor all structures are of spruce. On the
shore, near which the vessels lie at anchor, is located a tackle
[rigging] shop with other [subsidiary] large storage rooms.
Across from it, on the hill, is the new Governor's [Manager's]
house, containing a library. Stretching from it in the form of
an elongated rectangle are eight various family dwellings.

Across from the Manager's house, at the very tip of the pro-
montory, stand the church and the belfry, with dilapidated
roofs. Directly before the entry to the church, on the right side,

is the communal company kitchen [*povarnia*, may also be a
blubbering station] while on the left is located a shed [*sarai*] for
the company baidaras and other gear.   Behind this shed are
food storage warehouses and a balagan – that is, a shed built
on piles, with flooring of poles to allow free air circulation,
where yukola and kachemaz are stored [see glossary].   In the
warehouses are kept whale, sea lion, and seal meat, whale and
sea lion blubber (alternate reading: oil, *zhir*), sarana, and berries: *shiksha* [crowberry], *brusnitsa* [cranberry], and *moroshka* [cloudberry].   All food supplies are brought here from
the artels.

Across from the church, beyond the stream, on an elevation
is the old semi-circular wooden fort.   About a third of it is now
demolished, because of its decrepit condition.   Only the quarters for the office, barracks for the promyshlennye, for store-
houses, shops with cellars, and a bit further away, a
blacksmithy [*kuznitsa*] and metal [*slesarnia*] shops remain.
All these structures are very dilapidated.   Beyond the above,
at the foot of the hill, stands the old Manager's house, which
now houses the Russian-American school, the decrepit quarters for the Spiritual Mission, the communal company bath-
house, a round kazhim[17] wherein live the company kaiury
[indentured laborers, see glossary] and the sick, and the new
cattle yard.   Not far away from the latter are located the house
of the Assistant Manager, Mr. Banner, and quarters for visitors.

Besides this settlement, there are on Kad'iak the following
artels:

1.   The Sapozhnikov artel', near Pavlovskaia Harbor, where
     one wooden barrack has been built for the Russians, a
     cattle yard, a balagan, and Aleut yurtas (dwellings). [VV:
     More cows are kept here than in any other artel']. A small
     quantity of barley and oats is planted with great effort and
     inconvenience.   The plow is pulled by the Aleuts instead
     of oxen (omitted in SV which instead has the phrase: Up
     to 30,000 yukola are put up here].

2.   The Igatskaia artel' [Igak] is located on the south side of
     Kad'iak, in the name of the same bay (modern Ugak Bay).
     Here all the construction is of poplar and alder wood.
     There is a house for the baidarshchik and the Russian
     promyshlennye, a *barabara* [storage structure] for food-
     stuffs, a whale-blubbering house [*povarnia*], a kitchen, a
     steambath, a barn [*ambar*], a new cattle barn, the Aleut

kazhim, a shed, and two *labaz*, that is, slatted platforms on posts on which fish are hung to dry.

About three versts from the artel', at the mouth of the lake, there is a weir, a shed eight sazhen' in the length with three labaz, and an earthern yurta. Here up to 60,000 yukola are prepared. Beginning April 10th, char [or trout, *gol'tsy* – Dolly Vardens and/or steelheads] move from the lake into the sea; about April 23rd or earlier, red fish [red salmon] appear at the weir; about the middle of June *gorbusha* [humpback salmon] and *khaiko* [haiko salmon] come up from the sea. Yukola is prepared from the last three fish species by the women. The latter, using their American knives [ulus] which somewhat resemble our choppers first split the fish in half, then, having chopped off the head, remove the spine in its entirety; these fish strips are then dried on the labaz and then, when dried, removed to the balagan. The kizhuch of the salmon family [silver salmon] arrive at the weir about the middle of September or earlier. It is also used for yukola and for kachemaz, in which the backbone is not removed.

3. The third artel' is in Three Saints Harbor. Here the construction is [also] of poplar and alder wood. There are quarters for the baidarshchik and for visitors, a barrack for ten families, a blacksmith's shop, a blubbering station [*povarnia*], and three barabaras [storage structures] about 15 sazhen' in length. The first of these serves for [whale] blubber [alternate reading: oil] storage and for cutting up the whale meat. Portions of a fresh whale carcass are first cut up into small pieces which are then placed into large vats where they are left to stand without any addition of water for ten days. Then, after water has been added, they are left to stand for additional 20 days. After that, the oil is rendered over medium heat in large kettles, each about 20 buckets capacity, adding to each kettle about eight buckets of water. If, however, the whale has remained in the sea for a long time and begun to spoil from the heat of the sun and the action of the sea air, then, being cut up, it is not placed into the vats but right away into the kettles. A large quantity of water is added and the rendering of oil is done over a very slow fire. Sea lion and seal blubber are rendered without addition of water. If the catch is good, up to 50 barrels of whale oil may be put up. The belly part of a fresh whale is steamed in a special manner separately in kettles, and then, smeared for preservation with fish roe combined with cooked wild sorrel [*kislitsa*], it is stored in

vats. This kind of whale product is called pavlina[18] and here, just for the [consumption by] the Russians, they prepare more than 200 pud of it. The whale product which is cut in strips out of flippers [flukes] of a fresh [killed] whale, and from the belly part of flukes of one which has remained in the sea for a long time, is called *provesna* *[provesnia]*. This whale produce is used for the kaiury.

In the middle (second) barabara yukola is kept, of which over 90,000 are prepared in a good season. In the third there are four vats of crowberries with whale blubber, yielding more than 30 barrels. Between the second and the third barabaras there is a rootcellar [*susek* or *lar'* or *zakram* – all three terms appear in the original], for sarana, which, when the crop is good, is gathered in the quantity of more than 600 buckets. The sarana is dug in June, cooked, crushed, and dried, and then stored in this form in the above mentioned rootcellar. Such [prepared] sarana, mixed with water is called *burduk*.

Not far from this barabara is a cattle barn, a hay storage shed, a shed for [storage of] baidaras and baidarkas, and a dwelling [yurta] for the kaiury.

4.   The 4th, the Alitat artel' is located on the west side of Kad'iak. It is built on a hill, near a small stream, in the following manner: [SV: two plank houses] one plank dwelling (apartment), covered with sod for baidarshchik; a second one, right next to it, with two compartments [*uruny*] for the Russian promyshlennye, a foreroom [*seni*], a cookhouse, a blubbering station [*povarnia*], and a storage room.

Somewhat further away there is the blubbering station and cookhouse for the whale blubber and sarana and two storage barabaras for foodstuffs. In the first are two large vats with sarana, 15 barrels of crowberries mixed with fat, and two vats of whale meat called *pavlina*; in the second are kept whale oil in 25 sea lion bladders [*puzyri*, plural], about 150 buckets. There is a barn for storage of various gear, a cattle yard, a piggery, a hay barn, a balagan with yukola, of which about 70,000 strips are prepared here and, below the hill, a shed for the baidara and baidarkas.

5.   The 5th, the Karluk artel' is on the north side of Kad'iak. On the hill near the river Karluk the fort is surrounded by a low earthen wall, 27 sazhen' long on the sea side, on other three sides about 50. Therein are the following structures: a rather clean and airy barracks, of plank con-

struction, covered with sod, seven sazhen' in length and four in width, with 11 compartments [*uruny*] for Russian promyshlennye, and quarters for the baidarshchik. Above it there are two summer rooms, a foreroom [*seni*], a cookhouse (povarnia), and a balagan eight sazhen' in length and four sazhen' wide. Hereabouts, in a good summer, they put up up to 300,000 yukola. There are two barabaras, one for foodstuffs where are stored 200 native baskets [*ishkaty*] of sarana, 20 barrels, each of 25 buckets capacity, of crowberry, three vats of whale oil and two barrels of cloudberry; the second barabara is for storage of various items. There is also a root cellar for keeping potatoes and turnips, a summer cookhouse, a steam bath, a shed for various gear, and a blockhouse or guardhouse [VV: Behind the fort, not far from the gate, there is a cattle barn, a hay barn, piggery, three sazhen' – square kazhim with a yurta three sazhen' long for the kaiury, of whom at this artel' alone there are 20 men and 18 women on hand. For fish processing, additional 25 women come here from various settlements]. Below the hill is the shed for the baidaras and baidarkas.

Beside these artel's on Kad'iak Island, there are two on the Island of Afognak with similar structures and enterprises; there is one on Lesnoi [Woody] Island, where no yukola is prepared because there is not even a single stream there. On this island bricks are made and salt boiled.

Dwellings

After Mr. Rezanov's arrival here [1805], a few of the Kad'iak tuiuns [sic, normally *toion*, translated as chief] built themselves Russian [style] houses, albeit without stoves, although all of them promised him they would build their houses in the Russian manner. However, they lack the resources as well as manpower to do so. Their usual form of construction is as follows: there is a foreroom or hall, in the Aleut [modern designation *Alutiiq*] language *chikliuiak*, 12 arshin long, eight wide, and two high, lined with planks and having an elongated entryway. Between the support posts which are at all corners, there are placed on a slight incline, on all four sides, three crosspieces [alternative reading: horizontal bars] forming a rectangle [*kletka*]; above these, three more crosspieces are placed but at a steeper pitch, so that on top there remains an opening slightly over an arshin square. On the outside, this

structure is covered with grass and then with earth. Attached
to this central or front room, along the sides, are small square
compartments, of a similar construction [SV: also covered with
earth] which have a tiny window on one side and a small round
entry (just enough for a person to be able to crawl through)
(leading from the front room). Here the people sleep, work, and
sweat themselves bringing in the rocks which were heated in
the front room.   In these sleeping chambers, spears are hung
on the walls as ornaments, and, to commemorate the animals
taken in the hunt, thoracic vertebrae or bladders of seals and
sea otter heads; beneath are stored platters of various sizes,
cups and porringers, spoons and *kaluzhki*, that is, elongated
vessels for water. In the front room, in a special compartment,
are the foodstuffs: yukola, red salmon roe, berries with fat, and
sarana, but all in very small quantities.

A rich toion who has a family has [SV: may have] a square
kazhim [as his chamber), eight to ten arshin long and about two
and one half arshin high, lined with [VV: thick unfinished]
planks, with an entry to the front room. In each corner thereof
there is a firmly placed thick support [post].   Upon these is
constructed a square frame of crosspieces, up to six tiers in
number, spaced just a bit less than one arshin from each other,
and slanting inward in such a manner that a single square
opening [hatch] is left on top.   The latter is covered with sea
lion or seal gut which makes the kazhim very light.   On the
outside, it, too, is covered with grass and then with earth. Inside, along all the walls, there are benches for guests. I saw
only three such kazhims on the whole of Kad'iak. In them festivals [*igrushki*] are held.

Leadership

Until 1784, when Shelikhov arrived on Kad'iak and instituted
toions, each settlement was ruled by an *anayugak*, a husband-
man [an owner, *khoziain*]. He, without fail, had to have his
own kazhim. His office was hereditary, inherited by his children or close kin: a son, a brother, an uncle, a nephew, a son-
in-law.   His successor assumed the predecessor's place
gradually. The anayugak designated his successor well before
his own anticipated death. For such an occasion, he called everyone to the kazhim whither he escorted the designated successor himself, having dressed him in the very best clothing.
In the presence of all he declared the person to be his heir. The
latter had then, without fail, to treat all those assembled to food
and drink. At such times women were not present, except for

girls who had been given male names and brought up as sons. They had the right to attend the assembly. For their right of entry into the kazhim, their fathers had annually to give gifts to the anayugak three times greater than gifts made by others on behalf of males. After the conclusion of the assembly and the [obligatory] food offering, all women joined the subsequent festivity in the evening.

The power of the anayugak consisted in the following: anyone who wanted to absent himself from the settlement had to declare why he needed to do so; the anayugak also made dispositions concerning sending out messengers [alternate reading: on errands, *posylki*]. He had no power to punish others in any way, except when redressing his own personal injuries. He ruled solely over his own family, fosterlings, and *kalgi* [war captives, slaves]. He persuaded his fellows to go to war through counsel and gifts; in the assembly, he took the most important seat and delivered various admonitions. Deep silence was observed in his presence: even a small child was not supposed to move about. This, then, is the distinguishing feature of the honor due him.

Wealth

Among the Aleuts that person was deemed wealthy, who, besides having his family clad, possessed for his own use alone one otter parka, five ground squirrel parkas, five marmot or caribou parkas, five cormorant and five puffin parkas, one baidara of 20 oars [paddles], three baidarkas, many lavtaks, that is sea lion or seal skins which were dehaired after steaming, a sufficiency of whale meat, two sea lion bladders of whale oil, two water containers [*kalugi*], five *kalikakh*, that is, bentwood baskets which resemble our *lukoshko*, full of crowberries with fat, and the same number of sarana, a sea lion bladder of red salmon roe, ten large bundles of yukola, as well as some halibut and cod yukola. Besides the above, and excluding spears and other domestic tools needed by everyone, he should own, for adornment, the following items: first of all, four or more [pieces of] amber which they occasionally find on the Island of Ukamok, formerly, and even now, valuing the light-colored, almost white kind above the yellow amber; secondly, *aiminak* [sukli], that is the very thin small bones which resemble worms, and are about half vershok long, more or less [dentalium shell and/or beads]; thirdly, *kuikak*, that is then plates about one vershok long and one vershok wide cut from

the very center of mother-of-pearl shell; and fourthly, a considerable quantity of various glass beads [*bisery*].

Weapons and Warfare

In warfare they used shields, *kubakhkinakh*, of wooden slats,
not less than half a vershok thick, one vershok broad, and three
and a half handspans [*chetvert'*] long on the back and two
handspans in the front, tightly secured together by sinew
thread. To it they attached a breastplate, *khakaat'*, made of
thin rods which were so skillfully and tightly interwoven with
the same kind of thread that even a spear of a strong warrior
could be easily stopped by it. Sometimes, entire shields were
fashioned like the breastplates. These were used to protect the
torso only.

Over these shields they used to wear a cape, *ulikhtat'*, made
in the same manner of long slats, according to the height [stat-
ure] of the person concerned. A sinew net [this reading after
SV, in VV and VC, it is "uril" or cormorant, an error] served
as a collar. It was tightly twisted and wound around the neck.

Hats were made either of poplar wood or thick animal skin.

They went into battle with painted faces, holding a bone
[tipped] spear in the right, a bow in the left hand. A quiver
filled with arrows was suspended also on the left side. The bow
is usually about two arshins long and made of American cypress [sic, *kiparis*, that is, cedar] which is also called fragrant
[*dushnoe*] wood. The arrow shafts are three handspans or more
long, with the foreshaft or caribou bone about [VC: only], one
handspan long having three 1-handspan long barbs and armed
with a stone or copper blade about a vershok and a half long.

Thus equipped, the brave and enterprising men assembled
during the summer in the settlement of the main originator of
the enterprise, or their general [voevoda], answering a call he
had issued previously. When a sufficient number of such warriors assembled, they entered the kazhim where they took
places on the benches as directed by their leader in his capacity
as owner of the kazhim. He himself sat down on the floor near
the entry [into the kazhim). Then his wife, with self-effacing
mien, brought in a container of water, sat down for a moment
next to her husband, and then left abruptly, as women were not
supposed to be present at such assemblies. Boys, either kinsmen or slaves [prisoners], offered water to drink to each man
in turn, in order of seniority. After that, [the leader's] wife,
assisted by other women from among close kin, brought in

large square or round wooden bowls of *talkushi* [sic, elsewhere *tolkushi*, used here in plural to mean "various"]:

1.   pounded red salmon roe with fat,

2.   sarana pulverized and beaten together with water and fat,

3.   crowberries with fat.

Following that, boiled sea lion and seal meat and raw chopped halibut were served. The latter was eaten to prevent fat-induced belching. Of such feasts, no one dared to speak, except old men. Strictest order was observed in everything. Anyone who moved, as much as stretching a foot, had to pay a fine. After the dinner ended, [the leader's] wife again brought in water, while close kinsmen carried in gifts prepared earlier for this occasion and placed them on the floor in the center of the kazhim.

At this point the war leader, and he alone, their foremost anayugak, rose and took up the rattles, i.e. small hoops to which are attached the red beaks of the sea bird called puffin[19] and began to dance. At this very moment, his kinsmen commenced to beat the drums, that is large hoops, equipped with a handle and over which thin [sea mammal] skin is stretched. They sang about the deeds of their ancestors and fathers, who warred with fame and honor. At the end of such a war song, the host, with his own hands, offered gifts to the guests, in order of rank: sea otter and ground squirrel parkas to the [other] anayugaks [the toions], *lavtaki* [processed sea mammal skins] and cormorant parkas to the old men, amber to some of the young while others received dentalium and glass seed beads, and all the while asking their pardon that he was giving so little and then encouraging them with hopes of the rich booty they would obtain from the enemy.

The next day they prepared to depart without much ceremony. Their wives saw them off, sitting on the sea shore. The men parted from them very casually. Not one would shed a tear or emit a sigh – such would have been considered a sign of cowardice inappropriate in a warrior. As a man climbed into their baidara, he barely deigned to utter as if through clenched teeth a single word: *fayai* [VV: fayeya] – farewell.

They went on such raids in about 30 baidaras, each manned by 20 men, sometimes a few more or less. The inhabitants of the northern and western parts raided the Aliaskans [Alaska-Peninsula inhabitants], while the southerners and easterners went against the Kenaitsy [Denaina, in anthropological liter-

ature Tanaina] or the Chugach. In good weather, they crossed
in two days from Shuyak Island to Kenai Bay [Cook Inlet].

They aimed to attack their adversaries when the latter were
asleep. The old and adult [men] were killed, while young
women, girls, and adolescents were taken prisoners. The minors were left behind together with the old women. All useful
possessions were taken as booty. If the conquered toion took
pity on women and children, he obtained peace through medi-
ation by another village. The victors never refused these neg-
otiations. Both sides exchanged amanats [hostages] from
among the notables and agreed on prisoner exchange. The
hostages were always treated extremely well: they were given
the very best clothing and shown great courtesy. When they
were received, sea otter skins were spread for them and when
the hostages visited, they were given the most valued items as
gifts.

When the Kad'iak people were attacked, they defended
themselves not by the force of arms, but through flight toward
large and high, almost inaccessible, sea rocks where long beforehand they had prepared shelters and left all needed supplies for themselves and their families to withstand a long
siege; sometimes [from such a position] they were able to repel
the attackers with great success.

Inhabitants of settlements that lacked such defensible rocks
in the vicinity, retreated into mountains and took refuge there.

Annual Care of Winter Dwellings

In the fall, after the food supplies have been put up, Aleuts
usually repair their winter dwellings. Grass needed to cover
the same is harvested by bare hands; then the dwelling is [re-
]covered with earth. In the same manner they put up grass
used in winter for pallets in their bedrooms.

All help the owner of the kazhim to finish it. At the end of
the very same day, he [the owner] feasts all those who labored,
in accordance with the ritual [feasting] described above.
Women are excluded from this work.

Feasts

The one who wishes to give a feast calls all his neighbors to the
kazhim. When all have taken their appointed places along the
benches, he brings in the tolkusha, places it in the center, and
takes up his place at the door. All then begin to sing in praise

of his [the host's] kinsmen. At the end of the song, he sits down
on the floor and declares whom he intends to invite, what kind
of present he shall give to each, and when he will send to
summon the particular guest. Then he rises, gives gifts to the
owner of the kazhim and to the old man whose duty it will be
during the feast to entertain with conversation (tales) the
guests, especially in the intervals between songs and dances,
when one song or dance has ended and there is a lull before the
next one. Finally, he himself offered the tolkusha to each man
present, in order of seniority [rank]. They eat politely – in
small quantities – so that there shall be enough for all. Having
thanked their host for the food, all go home. The festivities are
usually held at the end of the fall or beginning of the winter
season, lasting as long as the food stores hold out. They are
held for various reasons and on various occasions. One will
hold a feast to get better acquainted with a person he wishes to
know and establish a closer friendship – friendship is a big
thing among them. Another gives a feast on occasion of a
wedding. A third, to express his gratitude to someone to whom
he is indebted for a loan of something or other. A fourth will
do so simply because it is customary. A fifth will do so out of
vanity to impress the others that he is rich, has a lot of foodstuffs, etc.

The festivities are held in the kazhim, but if a settlement
lacks such, either in the front room or in one of the large
sleeping compartments.

Everyone comes: men, women, and young girls, as well as
the little ones. In the kazhim, the men sit on benches, the
women on the floor beneath the benches, each wife at the place
occupied by her husband.

The old men beat the drums and start to sing songs in honor
of their ancestors and forefathers, remembering and reminisc-
ing about how many baidaras they used to own, how many sea
otters they had, and so on. Following the old men, everyone
sings, while the men, dressed in their festive little hats [sha-
pochki] and embroidered hoods [kolpaki], made especially for
such occasions, dance singly, with rattles in their hands, now
jumping, now crouching down, or swaying their bodies from
side to side, swinging the rattles in time. In these movements
they represent their various hunting activities, for example,
how a whaler spears a whale and then evades the animal, how
a sea otter is being driven[20] and so on. Later, having removed
their festival caps and donning various kinds of strange dis-
guises and all sorts of masks, they dance [again] also to the
accompaniment of songs and carrying rattles, either singly or
by twos, once again representing various actions.

Women and young girls always dance by themselves, without men. They solemnly line up in a row, tightly one behind another, and by slight, almost imperceptible movements, they crouch down, then straighten up in the same manner, now and then swaying to the right and then to the left. At the beginning of their dance they first of all extend slightly forward their left hands, and, with fingers bent, hold them in this position as long as the singers sing without words. As soon as those who beat the drums and sing begin to sing about their dead ancestors, mentioning the name and the death of a particular kinsman, the women, immediately and in unison, turn their palms downward, toward the ground. During the women's dance, old men who are enjoying themselves make every possible effort to make some of them laugh, as according to their custom the father or husband of the woman who succumbs to teasing and laughs must pay a fine for the benefit of the old and the poor: it is enough for a wife or a daughter just to smile ever so slightly while dancing. I myself was given a gift of a lavtak by a father and a sealskin by a husband when their daughter and wife respectively violated this ancient tradition. I donated these items for the benefit of the poor and received from the old men then present much approval and gratitude.

Such festivities last all night – almost until dawn. At the end, the host gives gifts to all whom he has invited: parkas, amber and dentalium beads, and other riches he possessed. He also gives gifts to the owner of the kazhim, the speaker, and others, as he deems necessary. Then they disperse, without any kind of ceremony, but in a restrained manner – without noise, in silence.

Here is a song by Vasilisa Kinuak, a 68 year old woman, sister [cousin][21] of the toion Afanasii, from the Ubaguik settlement on Sitkhinak Island, which she composed on the occasion of her brother's death:

[The songs given below are rendered as follows: 1st line – English translation of Gideon's Russian gloss; 2nd line – Gideon's transcription in Cyrillic rendered in Latin alphabet' 3rd line – modern Alutiiq; 4th line – gloss of Alutiiq text by Mr. J. Leer, Alaska Native Language Center, UAF. Each line is separated by a row of dashes][22] .

Why do I lament this death /it/ is everywhere (ubiquitous)
Amchi   khnvi kennegli; tugu mannia   nuug-naitok
Amci   ggwi qian'irlii tuqu   man'a   nurnaituq
/Yes, truly/ /I/ /let me stop crying/ /death/ /this/ /(it) is
                                                    ubiquitous/

Why do I grieve (sorrow) this death /it/ is everywhere
    (ubiquitous)
Amchi khvi paliunegli; tugu mannia nugg-naitok
Amci ggwi palun'irlii tuqu man'a nurnaituq
/Yes, truly/ /I/ /let me stop grieving/ /death/ /this/ /(it) is
    ubiquitous/

Why do I blacken [VC: besmear] myself this death /it/ is every-
where
    (ubiquitous)
Amchi khvi ikanegli; tugu mannia shuidok
Amci ggwi iqan'irlii tuqu man'a suituq
/Yes, truly/ /I/ /let me stop being dirty/[23]/death/ /this/ /(it)
    has no people.

Even those /proper name of a group/ are not exempt from death
Ikankutliu Kuzhiktigmiut tugum nunytei
Ikankut-llu _____ miu: tuqum nunitai
/And those, over/group name not death abides with them there,
    across/ identified/

Kuzhiktigmiut [VC: Kuzhiktagmiut] in their opinion are those
people beyond whose habitat no more people live. Under this
name they understand the distant Fox Aleuts (Unangan of the
Eastern Aleutian Islands).
    Here is another of their ancient songs communicated to me
by Aleksei Ikuik, toion of Alikhtalik:

Grandfather   diligently   I seek
Apaka   kashkaklia   ivakhpagaka
Apaka   qasqangqertellria;   iwarpagaqa
/my grandfather/   /had riches/   /I am looking
                                            diligently for him/

Grandfather had baidaras Aminak[24] I seek
Apaka angiaklia [VV: antaklia] Aminak ivakhpagaka
/my grandfather/ /had baidaras/ Aminaq /I am looking
    diligently for him

Grandfather diligently I seek, Agnak[25] had sea otters
Apaka kashkaklia ivakhpagaka Agnak
  akhniaklia
Apaka qasqangnqertellria; iwarpagaqa /name/
/My grandfather/ /had riches/ /name/ who has sea otters.

Grandfather Kigiliak was a promyshlennik (hunter, provider)
Apak Kigiliak nakhshchaglia [VC: nakhgaglia]
Apaka _____ /name/ _____ /unidentified but possibly
/My grandfather/ based on the stem nere- to eat/

Grandfather Ukhtaiak used to shout (was shouting repeatedly)
Apaka Ukhtaiak kashliaklia [VV: katliaklia]
Apaka _____ /name/ qalriallria/
/My grandfather/   /was shouting repeatedly

The Kad'iak people like this song very much and during festivities sing it often, with great sadness, because in it is mentioned:

1.   formerly they possessed baidaras while nowadays a rare
      toion owns even a three-hatch baidarka;

2.   formerly, they had sea otters and wore sea otter parkas,
      while nowadays some have great difficulty in obtaining
      even a puffin parka, which in the old days were worn only
      by their slaves; and

3.   their former Anayugak[s] upon their arrival in baidara[s]
      at a settlement, or when meeting guests, shouted loudly,
      and immediately a multitude of people responded, ran to
      the beach and carried the baidara and baidarkas on their
      (backs, shoulders) onto the shore, while to-day many set-
      tlements are almost deserted, even though there had been
      no epidemics.

   On the day following the festivity, about the ninth or tenth
hour after midnight, everybody reassembled in the kazhim and
was treated to tolkusha[s] and berries mixed with fat, which the
women served offering it in the same manner, with the same
modesty and order as described above. The person for whom
such a festivity had been given, was obliged to reciprocate with
the same, without fail, though some time in the next year or
even later.

Birth

When the time approached for a woman to give birth, a midwife was called and the woman was conducted to a specially built small structure somewhat farther off from the front room. There, after the woman gave birth, the midwife washed the infant with cold water, tied the umbilical cord, and then went home. By agreement between husband and wife, if the infant was of the male sex, he was named in honor of the grandfather, father or a close kinsman or friend. A female infant was named in honor or a grandmother, the mother, a kinswoman, or a friend.

At the end of the 5th day after birth, if the mother was an older woman, or the 10th, if a young one, a sweatbath was prepared for cleansing of mother and infant and after that she was brought back to the regular sleeping quarters. When the woman was in the above mentioned [birth] hut [khizhina], no male could enter this structure. In the matter of segregation of women in childbirth from their dwelling, I admonished the toions appropriately, as during the cold season, or in winter, both mother's and child's health could very easily be harmed.

The education of children consists of preventing the child from crying, not just the infants but even seven-year olds. From this one may conclude that mothers and fathers love their children dearly. They never inflict any kind of corporal punishment, either on minors nor adults, resorting only to admonition. If it is noticed that there is no improvement, they scold and shame [the culprit] before the assembly of old men. If this last method does not prove effective, the person, an object of contempt, is deemed to be stupid or savage. Nowadays, fathers and mothers accustom the little ones to bow to others in greeting and to pray to God. Little girls begin to be accustomed to their work at about six years of age: they polish thread, plait cords, and do so with sufficient skill and rather well. The boys, beginning about seven years of age, instead of games are busy making spears, toy baidarkas and toy paddles. They throw spears on the beach and thus become accustomed to future hunting techniques. They help in putting up foodstuffs at the streams.

Beginning with 14 years of age, the boys are trained in handling baidarkas. In calm weather they are taken out to fish and to shoot birds in the bays by means of spears. Beginning with 16 years of age, fathers and kinsmen include them in sea otter hunting parties.

Marriage

They marry when they are able, by their own efforts, to prepare for themselves and their future brides the necessary clothing and wedding gifts. The groom prefers, as a rule, to choose as his bride a girl who knows how to sew baidarka [covers], parkas, and kamleikas even if she is considerably older than he. A son asks his father's permission beforehand, disclosing the girl's name to him. Sometimes, the father approves the son's choice, sometimes he selects someone else. If the son consents to the father's choice, the father dispatches a close kinsman to inform the bride's father. If the desired answer is obtained from the latter, the young man the following night goes to the girl's house, and lies down next to her, fully clothed; in the morning, having risen, he gathers firewood, heats rocks in the front room for a sweatbath, which he then takes together with his bride. As they emerge from the sweatbath, the [groom's] kinsmen bring his gifts which formerly consisted of sea otter, ground squirrel, marmot and cormorant parkas, slaves, amber, and dentalium. These gifts were given to the bride's father and the latter's kin.

On the next day, the newlyweds visited the groom's father who presented to the bride a gift of one parka, one kamleika, and several dentalium shell, glass seed and large trade beads [korol'ki] and offered her tolkusha. When parting, the father admonished his son: love thy wife. After this, the newlyweds returned to the groom's father-in-law where they might live as long as they wanted. The newlyweds had to observe chastity for five days.

In the fall, the groom, if he were rich, organized a feast.

These customs were observed even before conversion to Christianity.

Some used to designate a bride for a boy in infancy, but this happened only among the truest of friends.

Husbands treat their wives with great affection. In the presence of others, they may not speak harshly to each other, nor show a stern countenance; were one of them to do so, the other would consider this behavior an unbearable insult. If the wife notices that her husband does not match her affection, and she becomes angry because of jealousy, she flies at his face and scratches him with her fingernails. The guilty husband sits with head hanging to the left, not daring to lift a hand against this righteous avenger.

Nowadays it happens quite often that husbands chastise their wives if they notice that the latter lead a disorderly life. Formerly, husbands refrained from chastising their wives, because they [the women] used to threaten to run away, go out to the cliffs, to take their lives there or to drown themselves. Indeed, some used to carry out such threats.

It also used to happen quite often that if a man caught his wife in infidelity, and did not observe any inclination on her part to mend her way, he cast her out and, in order that others become aware of her infidelity, cut off the tip of her nose; a really enraged husband bit it off with his teeth. The wives who learned of their husband's infidelity, on the other hand, had the right freely to leave him and join another man.

Some industrious and enterprising women had *polovinsh-chiki* [two husbands] who lived together peacefully, in amity.

Women and girls were, and still are, segregated at the first sign of the monthly infirmity natural to their sex. They are placed in a special small structure, apart from the communal dwelling. Food is handed to them there in separate dishes, and water in a special kaluzhka.

Treatment of Illness

A small sea fish, the *kaiuliuk* [kayuluk, bullhead, *byk*] serves as a remedy against chest congestion and pains [*kolot'e*]. Until the cure is effected, only this fish is eaten, and thereafter they also refrain from eating other fatty foods. The chest congestion and pains are attributed to ripening internal sores which are believed to be caused by uncleanliness of women [menstrual matter]. When such boils are believed to have ripened and ruptured, a different remedy is employed. An infusion is made from the shredded and well-bodied root of the plant *chikinal-iakhpak [cukilanarpak, devil's club], and given the patient to drink in the morning and at night. This infusion is very disgusting and so bitter that some cannot stand its use. At this time, patients eat cod and other non-fatty fish.*

At the first sign of external boils, they lance these with their knives in order to prevent them from coming to a head, [believing that] in the latter stage they become more dangerous.

When the livers [insides] ache, they lance certain places in the groin opposite from the place where the pain occurs; the trunk is lanced also, and after the bad blood has been let, [the incisions] are covered with down.

When a person suffers from puffiness and there appear over the entire body hard swellings [*zhelvaki*], the heels are lanced to the very bone. When a person becomes nauseated, which happens from excessive bloodletting, cold rocks are placed in the groin; otherwise bleeding is stanched by spruce *gnilushka*

[see glossary] [26] pounded into powder. When the heels begin to
mend, they cut out a strip of skin from the top of the head,
about a vershok and a half long and over a vershok wide. When
this is done, there is usually a lot of bleeding, which is stanched
either by means of the above mentioned powder or raw halibut
flesh or with clay.

If a sufferer of stone illness [kidney stones] is reduced to the
state of near unconsciousness from the extreme pain, then,
sometimes, the stones – only small sized ones – are removed by
lancing with their knives the tip of the penis.

In cases of chronic eye disease a veritably fearsome operation is occasionally performed: a thinly worked bear bone, not
thicker than a straw, is used to pierce [the head], from both
sides, beginning just above the end of the eyebrows, and then
pushed through to the nasal bridge in such a way as to pass
behind the eyeballs. In the course of this terrible operation, a
piece of thick spruce branch is placed in the sufferer's mouth,
in order to prevent his biting off his tongue from the unbearable pain. No poultices or bandages are applied after this operation.

Headache is cured by lancing the head to the bone just below
the crown on the side where the pain is experienced as more
severe. After considerably quantity of blood has been let, the
wound is covered with down. Also for relief of headache, blood
is let from the arm on the side the pain is felt; against cough
and sore throat, from under the tongue; against stomach aches,
from legs and arms. The blood vessel is lifted by means of a
needle and then lanced. Bad blood is distinguished by its color
and its flow is stanched with pulverized *gnilushka*.

On the basis of the color of the blood, judgments are also
made as to whether a person will live or die.

Chinkak [*cingkaq*, sing.], the root of the wild parsley, is used,
after steaming, with fat [oil] as food. It is also used to make hot
poultices to relieve swellings.

Atunat [*aatunat*, pl.], wild sorrel [kislitsa][27] , pounded and
cooked, serves as an emetic and sometimes as laxative.

Chavykhat', chistiak or kosichki [Iris sibirica][28] , when an infusion is made from its roots, serves as the very best laxative;
this root is also eaten raw with great success for relief of
constipation, which often is induced by immoderate consump-
tion of raspberries.

Tagnak [Tarnaq?], bitter kutagarnik [also kutogornik][29] , is a root which, when powdered and steamed, over hot rocks, is applied to swellings.

Kyuiukhat' [unidentified]: only small roots of this plant are used, prepared and applied in the same manner as *taganak*, but with far better effect than the latter.

Amagat' [possibly *amara (a)t*]: an infusion prepared from its powdered root is drunk mornings and evenings as a remedy against venereal disease, but most often when one suffers from a sore throat. During the cure, no food is eaten throughout the day. The pulp is used for steaming hot poultices applied to the throat.

The two last mentioned herbs usually grow along the level sandy stretches of beaches.

Shulyalyunak [unidentified]: this blood-purifying herb has leaves similar to our podbel[30] . It grows on the north side of Kad'iak Island, near the Karluk artel'. Its roots are very similar to a decoction sold in the stores. Aleuts cook it in a sealed vessel and use it as a remedy against venereal disease. A small quantity of the infusion is drunk and then [the sufferer] is given the root *mzhulingok* [*mecuilngug*, one that lacks moisture], the chernogolovnik [*Sanguisorba officionalis*], which does not absorb moisture, to chew. The saliva is swallowed, although it gets bitter and caustic.

In general, in the course of any illness, a strict diet is observed. Even small children [VV: little boys and girls] noticing a pimple on their body [VV: small boil], voluntarily abstain from eating, especially fatty foods.

Burial Practices

When an Aleut dies, all kinsmen and friends are called together, with the exception of small children. Having assembled, all sit around the corpse, weeping and lamenting. If the deceased was a man, they lament that he will not hunt animals anymore, give feasts, eat tolkushas, nor whalemeat, go to war, etc. If the deceased was a woman or a young girl, they lament that she won't be wearing parkas, amber, dentalium shell beads nor glass seed beads, will not dance at feasts, sew baidarkas [covers], will not eat whalemeat, sarana, and berries with fat,

such as cloudberries, salmonberries, *kalina* [*Viburnum* spe-
cies] which are their delicacies, etc.

Afterwards, a pit is dug at some distance from the dwelling.
The coffin is made within the grave in the form of a rectangle,
out of wood [VV: when it is on hand]. The body is placed in it,
dressed in the person's favorite clothing and ornaments, then
covered with lavtaki [processed seal skins], surrounded by
rocks, and, finally, covered with earth. On top of the grave
some place long timbers, diagonally [*kos'*], In winter, the dead
are interred in the sleeping chambers [*spal'ni*, VV, in VC and
Valaam 1894 – *spainy*, rock clefts].

Five days later [whether, it is five days after death or burial
is unclear), the kinsmen cut their hair as a sign of grief, and for
a half year or longer visit the grave site daily at sunrise, and
sing mourning songs such as this one: [The text of the song
below follows the SV version]:

Aknak, Akhsinak, Ukhtaiak, Kigiliak, etc.–their ordinary
names–

To each of these names are added the following two verses:

Aknak died as a human being [but] will come back to life
Aknak kaiu   shukhka tugum-agmi, – unuiakhlia
_____ /name/ qayu sugkaa tuqung'armi unguirli or unguillria
_____ /name/ how he /his person/ is to be even though he died
shall
                    shall he come back to life or came back to life.

Enough of lamenting   in this world there is   no immortality
Tvan' kennegli;   tlia una   chakshil'gvidok
Tawang qian'irlii;   lla una   chaksailnguituq
Enough! Let me stop crying; world this has none to whom
                                        nothing happened.

(In the VV and VC, the verses given above are in the reverse
order and are preceded by different sets of names, see below):

Names of Fox Islanders: Aknak, Katiyuksnok [Kashaiuknok?),
Katiliuk [Kashiliuk?], Kinatadak [Kinashadak?];

Names of Kenai inhabitants: Kalchacha, Nishtatu, Kakhtak,
Uninuka.[31]

Social Relations

The Kad'iak people live peaceably and in friendship with their
neighbors, aid each other in case of need, and in times of scarcity willingly lend food supplies to each other; fish is supplied
for visitors, which is left in the center of the foreroom for the
purpose when everyone leaves for work: the women to dig sarana and pick berries, the men to hunt animals [SV: seals and
other species]. In their social intercourse politeness is observed and they censure those who fail to meet an arriving
[guest] or to escort the departing one. If someone turns his
back on another, this is taken as a sign of rudeness [discour-
tesy] and one who commences some task, makes an apology.
If a host offers a guest tolkusha or berries with fat, he must
first partake of the dish himself.

A wife may not stretch her legs toward her husband,[32] even
if she should be sitting with him; if she has turned away, however, she is freed from such prohibition.

Arriving guests must bring food for their host; the host, on
the other hand, must provide food as parting gift for the guest;
besides, the latter also must take with him any remnants of the
food with which he was treated during his stay. Failure to do
so is considered an act of rudeness and of disrespect.

If a visitor engages in unseemly behavior or quarrels with
others, this is deemed an insult. Such a one was driven out not
so much by force as by shaming [*ne tolchkom, a bolee stydom*].

If someone unjustly called another person poor, slow, lazy
or a poor hunter, the injured party called the offender outside
and recounted, before witnesses, the nature of the injury offered him, and finally settled in lieu of vengeance for scolding
the offender in front of others and spitting in his face. They
have no special swear words. In the heat of utmost anger, the
modest Kad'iak person will solemnly say:

"Your father had no baidarka, he was no kind of a hunter – while I never wore a seal skin parka."[33]

There was no corporal punishment for theft. The stolen item
was taken away from the culprit and the latter was shamed
before the entire community and called a thief. It happened,
that if a person did not admit to the theft and refused to return
the stolen item, the latter was forcibly recovered, and to the
culprit's greater shame and as an example to others, he was
stripped of his parka.

The slaves [captives] were punished for theft by beatings
with rods, and in case of great guilt, their legs and arms were
broken.

A diligent hunter goes outside frequently during the night
to observe the clouds, note the weather, and, deciding on the
basis of his observations, leaves very early in the morning to
hunt.

The wife, loving and respecting her husband, abstains from
eating until he returns. When outsiders are present, the husband eats first, then the wife, each from their own dishes; when
by themselves, they very often eat together, and nothing is said
[*nichego ne govoria*]. During mealtimes, children are not expected to move around. Women must wash their hands before
commencing to prepare food of any kind. It is also a wife's duty
to bring water for her husband in his own special vessel [*kaluga*].

Hunting

Sea otters are hunted collectively, on Tugidok Island, from
eight to 15 two-hatch baidarkas departing together, and going
over ten versts out to sea. [VV: Sea otter hunting is done by
various district detachments which muster eight to 15 two-
hatch baidarkas.

The first man who sights a sea otter signals the others by
lifting his paddle. The others try to encircle the place at a distance within range of their spears. Only those who occupy the
forward hatches throw the spears, everyone at will, before each
other, while those in the rear hatches maneuver the baidarkas.
The sea otter belongs to that hunter who was the first to hit it.
Sometimes the sea otter is hit by two spears and in such a case
the carcass belongs to the hunter whose spear struck the animal closer to the head or above the other spear. If the spears
are spaced evenly, then that hunter receives the sea otter who,
before commencing to shoot, uttered the cry: "Ku-ko-ko!". This
is usually done to serve notice to others that the hunter is the
first about to cast his spear. A slow-moving sea otter weakens
with about five wounds, a sprightly one may take as many as
ten.

Seals are hunted by means of a decoy, made out of the same
animal, a *shuak* [sugaq, "doll"]. It is inflated and placed on a
tideflat [*laida*] that is a shallow close to shore, which is covered
by water at high tide, but is dry at the ebb and where these animals usually come ashore. The hunter, sitting behind the decoy and wearing a wooden hat made in the form of a seal head,

shouts, imitating the animal's hoarse call: *"uva!"* As the seal approaches the decoy, the hunter casts a spear on a line which is about ten sazhen' long. The animal is dragged out on shore and finished with a club, the *pikkhudak* [piqrutaq]. Seals are also taken by means of nets made of sinew cords, about 50 sazhen' long and five sazhen' wide, with floats tied to the upper edge and small rocks to the bottom one. The hunter, sailing in his baidarka, attempts to spread this net as quietly as possible almost across the entire bight or cove when the animals are sleeping either on the shore itself or on high off shore rocks. Then he yells with all his might, the frightened animals rush into the water and are caught in the net.

[In SV the next section contains a description of whaling practices, which is VV and VC, as well as in Valaam 1894 appears later on, as a separate topic – see Valaam 1894:234 –. Here, VV and VC order of topics is followed.]

Trade

The northern and western inhabitants of Kad'iak engaged in barter trade mostly with the Americans of Aliaksa [Alaska Peninsula], while the southern and eastern residents traded with those of Kenai and Chugach [areas]. The former obtained from the Alaskans, in exchange for dentalium shell beads and amber, caribou antlers used for spear tips [foreshafts], caribou parkas, and also long caribou hair taken from the animals chest, the latter being used by the Kad'iak women to embroider various designs on their parkas, kamleikas, and on hoods and hats worn by men exclusively when dancing at the festivals. They occasionally hunt caribou themselves, approaching the animal stealthily down wind, as they do when hunting bear or seal, because these animals have a very acute sense of smell.

The southerners and easterners traded ground squirrel parkas with the Kenai people for marmot ones, and with the Chugach for dentalium shell beads and spoons. From the inhabitants of Sitkha they obtained mother-of-pearl plates. They also used to barter [SV: and still do so] among themselves, especially if someone admired someone else's possession.

Nowadays, they exchange the pelts of the animals they hunt, which never remain in their hands except for the lavtaki, for Russian goods – whatever they are given for their wares, as the Russian goods are issued mostly to the Russian hunters, while the Kad'iak men obtain, even prior to the departure of the hunting party, on credit against the future sea otter catch such goods as processed seal skins for their baidarkas' covers, puffin parkas, gut kamleikas, so that it is a rare person who remains not indebted to the company at the end of the party's hunt.

Appearance and Adornments

The Kad'iak Americans are of medium stature, occasionally of good carriage, but the majority are hunched. Their faces are broad and swarthy or ruddy, the nose is average, eyes and hair are black, eyebrows thick, ears broad, lips somewhat thick, and the teeth white.

Both men and women have perforations along the entire circumference of the ear. From these apertures are suspended glass seed beads, dentalium shell beads, and among the rich, two amber pieces. The old people have a slit in the lower lip and in the nasal cartilage.

In former times, every woman had her chin tattooed, and some had their bodies tattooed also, in the form of two wide criss-crossing bands over both shoulders, of various designs. This was a sign of the height of fashion [SV: and distinction]. Some men also sported such bands [SV: the very rich and notable men also sported such bands].

The tattooing was performed by lifting a small piece of skin, with the point of a needle until blood showed. Ink, made of spruce charcoal mixed with blood, was applied, and on the body [against the skin] it assumed a dark-blue color.

Women have five to six perforations at the lower lip, and from each perforation is suspended a string of glass seed beads, about half a handspan long.

Worn under their noses, inserted through the perforated nasal cartilage, is a thin somewhat crooked animal fang. Their ears are bedecked with glass seed beads, dentalium shell beads, and, among the rich, with two amber pieces, an item possessed only by very few [this section differs somewhat in wording and sequence between SV, VV and VC]. On their necks, arms, and legs they wear necklaces, bracelets and anklets made of multicolored glass seed beads each about a vershok wide, while some wear on their arms and legs up to five iron or copper hoops. During festivities, especially when offering tolkusha, and at other joyous times, they paint or rather simply smear, their faces with red or other colored paint, except black; the latter is used only in times of sorrow.

Men, too, paint their faces for the same occasions, but especially when they approach the settlement as they return from
the hunt.

Origins

The Kad'iak folk, according to the legends recounted by the old
people, moved to Kad'iak from Aliaksa [Alaska Peninsula].
Their ancestors formerly lived on the north side of Aliaksa
near a great river, the *Kvignak* [unidentified]. They had an
anayugak [leader, angayuqaq] named Atlivatu. He had an only,
well beloved daughter who disappeared without a trace. He set
out with his command to search for the girl, and also persuaded
another angayuqaq, Iakunak by name, to join him. They wan-
dered over many places for a long time. Nearing the southern
side of Aliaksa, they sighted land and called it Kigikhtak [Qik-
ertaq], which means in their language "an island". This name
was applied to Kad'iak until the arrival of the Russians.

Later on, Atlivatu and Iakunak became curious, inves-
tigated, and all sorts of advantages [on the island] persuaded
the rest with their families to resettle on Qikertaq.

The affinity of the languages of Kad'iak and Aliaksa inhabitants lends support to such [a sequence of] events.

They have the following notions about the creation of the
world: there was once upon a time a Kashshiakhiliuk,[34] a sage,
a trickster. At that time there was neither day nor night. He
began to blow through a straw, causing land to begin to emerge
gradually from the water and imperceptibly to spread. Then,
while he still continued to blow, the sky opened, the sun ap-
peared, and in the evening the stars came out and the moon
rose. Finally they saw animals and people.

They have concluded that the earth is round on the basis of
the following occurrence: their ancestors sent out two baidarkas manned on this journey by young men, who returned as old
men but have failed to reach the end of the earth. It follows,
that as the earth has no end, it is round.

Shamanism

Their shamanistic activities resemble children's games. The
shaman, sometimes naked, sometimes dressed or painted in the
strangest manner, jumps about, goes through gyrations of the
body, howls at the top of his voice, naming the evil spirit, and
runs around the dwelling. In this excessive bodily activity he

brings himself to such a state that his eyes become blood-shot and from exhaustion he falls [SV: almost] unconscious to the ground. [SV: At this time he tells various fantasies]. Some on such occasions employ various tricks. For example, they divined for others what they actually had earlier observed themselves or learned about with the aid of their apprentices. If someone demanded performance of an action beyond the shaman's power, he declined to perform it by a ruse or some outlandish statement such as maintaining that he should bleed to death were he to attempt the deed. For this purpose the shamans prepared beforehand small skin pouches filled with blood and carried them around with them.

Children were designated for this role by their parents at birth. Such [male] children received female names, were trained in skills appropriate solely to the female sex, and then, finally, were apprenticed to a well-known shaman. For this reason, all [shamans] were single and had tattooed chins.[35]

I was not able to obtain detailed knowledge about shamanism, because many of the old shamans had died during the epidemic which raged through all of Kad'iak in [VV: June of] 1804. Others were secretive about it. While I was visiting the Igak [modern Ugak] settlement, one of the shamans pretended that he lost his power of speech from a fright he experienced during a horrible dream.

Miscellaneous Observations

The above mentioned epidemic occurred immediately prior to our arrival on Kad'iak, and started after the arrival from California of the American-Bostonian vessel *O'Cain*, which carried a complement of Kad'iak Americans for sea otter hunting.[36] At first, there was a headache which lasted for about two weeks; as the headache diminished, it was followed by nasal congestion and cough; then ears became blocked and there were chest congestion and pains [*kolot'*]. Finally, the person lost any desire to eat, and weakened. Except for the shamans, very few died.

Formerly, the whale hunters used to secretly disinter recently buried bodies, carry these into the mountains, and render fat from them to smear the points of their whaling spears. For this same purpose they collected worms from the dead bodies, dried them in secret, and then attached them to the whaling spears.

Anyone who was a quiet person, not angry but cheerful, and exhibiting a kindly appearance was considered a good man.

Male cousins preserved the most intimate friendship and shared their innermost secrets.

Their rules for maintenance of health are as follows: those who wish to live in good health and long must, first, never eat to satiety; second, they must never oversleep the dawn; third, they must abstain from intercourse with women; and, lastly, they should be as active as possible.

It is common knowledge that excessive use of the steambath causes them to age prematurely, to lose their eyesight, and to become weak, but it is difficult to leave aside long established habits. The young exhibit a bit more moderation in this respect.

For the most part, the Kad'iak people are taciturn, but in their responses they are quick, clever, and have a good sense of humor. One man, responding to my question as to where he sought remedies against illness, said: "Within myself, my wife, in the water, and on the shore!"

Once I asked another man, when I saw a multitude of sea gulls on the cliffs, if he could count them, "I would," he said, "if they only would stop laying eggs each year."

Kaiurs

[The following section on social conditions on Kodiak does not appear in the copy of SV on hand. As in the available microfilm copy a number of pages seem to be missing [see "Introduction"], it is not possible to say with certainty whether this material was included in Gideon's official report or was submitted by him only to Metropolitan Amvrosii in his private letters.]

The word *kaiur* [see glossary] designates those Aleuts who are taken from various settlements at the will of the company for work in various artel's and at the harbor. At the order of the baidarshchik, they erect about the middle of March weirs on streams for the fish catch, construct labazy [fish drying racks], and begin seining in the localities where there are fish appearing in the bays. When the fish runs begin from the ocean up the streams the seining is stopped, the gates in the weirs are opened, and traps placed therein. As these become filled with fish, the gates are closed to prevent the fish moving upstream. These fish will never return to the sea, but will always try to reach the sweet water at the very source of the stream.

The kaiurs chop wood and transport it by hand from nearby localities, by baidaras from distant ones. They also cut hay. In

the fall, they are dispersed to the *odinochkas* to trap foxes for
the company; in winter, they deliver food supplies to the head-
quarters or to the Harbor [modern Kodiak]. Some are employed
in salt production, brickmaking, and spruce sap collection, and
for other tasks as happen to be required by the company. In
reward for all this, the company issues them clothing, that is,
bird skin parkas, a shirt and breeches and lavtaki to make
boots [*torbasy*] for winter. Some receive in addition a woolen
cloth jacket and trousers.

Their wives and the kaiurki, that is female laborers who are
single, are used to prepare yukola, to dig sarana, ferns roots
which are used to make *kvas* [see glossary], to gather nettles
which they then work into fiber for nets and seines, to pick
various berries, to cut up whale carcasses, to render the whale
blubber into oil, to process bird skins by biting them with their
teeth and sucking out the fat, and to sew those into parkas.
They sew kamleikas out of whale, sea lion, seal, and bear gut
which are customarily used for protection against the rain. As
spring approaches they sew baidara and baidarka covers for
company use. These female workers receive from the company
for an entire year of such labor one bird skin parka, a shirt and
a pair of boots each.

Hunting Parties

1)   On the order of the manager [*pravitel'*] a contingent of the
     best Americans drawn from all settlements is mustered for
     sea otter hunting. In the beginning of April, from the
     southern side of Kad'iak and adjacent islands, the bai-
     darshchiks dispatch the toions of each settlement with the
     assigned number of baidarkas to Pavlovskaia Harbor.
     From there, they go to the American mainland.

     Another section of [this] hunting party is dispatched
     from the north side of Kad'iak and from Aliaksa under the
     command of a special baidarshchik. This party links up
     with the first one at the mouth of the Kenai Bay [Kenaisk-
     aia Guba, Cook Inlet] at the Aleksandrovskaia fort [*kre-
     post'*, modern English Bay, also known as Aleksandrovsk].
     Here the party is augmented by the local inhabitants and,
     while en route, by those sent out by the baidarshchik from
     Voskresenskaia gavan' [modern Resurrection Bay, near
     Seward] and, out of Nuchek (Hinchinbrook Island), by the
     close and distant Chugach. On Nuchek the entire party
     undergoes general inspection. Some baidarkas, because

of their decrepit state, and some Americans, because of their poor health, are left for hunting around Nuchek. From this point, the leader of the hunting party [*partovsh-chik*] spreads the party along the American coast as far as it is needed to achieve their goal. Formerly, the hunting parties mustered up to 800 baidarkas, in the year 1799 – 500, and in 1804 up to 300. During the night and in the foul weather, the baidarshchiks set up tents for themselves, the Americans take shelter under their baidarkas.

Each morning, one of the toions, in rotation, accompanied by his own command, is dispatched to procure food for the hunting party commander and the entire party as well: fish, seals, drift whales, birds – whatever happens to be handy. In times of scarcity, the Americans subsist on molluscs, sea urchins, mussels [*baidarki*, see glossary], and kelp. When the main hunting party leader has located a number of sea otters in a locality, and the weather turned calm, the hunters divide, by settlement, and each detachment so formed conducts the hunt separately.

Sea otters cannot remain long underwater because they need to breathe, thus it is easy to take them during calm weather. At first, a sea otter makes a great dive, but gradually weakening, the dives become shorter and shorter. The direction of its dive is indicated by air bubbles emerging from its mouth. Sea otters are hunted for the most part in the bays beyond the Baranov Island where at present is located the Novo-Arkhangel'sk Port or Sitka [sic, modern Sitka], the most distant establishment of the company along the American coast.

Sea otter pelts, after drying, are taken by the company. Upon their return, beginning in September or somewhat later, to Kad'iak, the hunting party is dismissed for return to their settlements, except for the young hunters, who came along as companions, not having their own baidarkas. These are employed in fox trapping and are so occupied until spring. They are issued by the company a bird parka each if they do not have one of their own, but for this the company deducts from their catch up to five foxes or land otters. Those who obtain a catch greater than the deduction for the parka, are paid in tobacco – for appearances' sake only. Baidarka owners, on company orders, make new baidarkas for use in future hunting parties. For this purpose they hunt seals for lavtaki. Those who are not able to obtain sufficient quantity of seal skins [one baidarka cover requires ten lavtaks], obtain the

lavtaks from the company against the future sea otter
catch.

2) The second sea otter hunting party, consisting of Kad'iak
    inhabitants numbering up to 150 baidarkas, is dispatched
    to the west, toward Unga Island. This party is sent out in
    the beginning of March, under supervision of an old voy-
    ager promyshlennyi to the Island of Tugidok, where they
    hunt until the month of June.

    In the beginning of June, as the weather at this season
    is often dead calm at sea, new baidarkas manned by heal-
    thy hunters are dispatched to Ukamok Island[37] where sea
    otter hunting is conducted also. Later on, they move to the
    Semida [modern Semidi Island] and from there to Sutkhum
    [modern Sutwik] and, finally, to Aliaksa.[38] By the middle
    of July sea otter hunting in this area comes to an end.

    The hunters are then dismissed to hunt for themselves
    birds for their parkas and seals for lavtaks for their bai-
    darkas. They obtain clothing mostly from what they get in
    exchange for sea otter pelts. In the middle of September
    they return to Kad'iak.

3) The third small sea otter hunting party consists of Alas-
    kans [inhabitants of Alaska Peninsula] and residents from
    the north side of Kad'iak Island. To this party are as-
    signed those whose baidarkas are judged to be unsafe for
    travel to Sitka, also the old and the ailing. They hunt sea
    otters along the south coast of Aliaksa, between Kenai Bay
    and Sutkhum.

4) The fourth sea otter hunting party has been in existence
    since 1797. It is composed of about 50 baidarkas of
    Kad'iak residents. They hunt near the islands Evrashechii
    [Marmot Island], Afognak, Shuyak, and the Peregrebnye
    [Barren Islands] and in Kenai Bay. To this party belong
    only those who were among the first to go into the Kolosh
    [Tlingit] party, that is to Sitka and beyond Baranov Island.
    In recognition thereof, they are now assigned to hunt near
    Kad'iak only.

Bird Hunting

5) From the remaining male population of Kad'iak, the com-
    pany drafts old men and boys, up to 100 persons. The

youngsters from 12 to 15 years of age are taken; the oldsters are dismissed only when they are incapable of walk-
ing. Such an enlistment completed, they are dispatched to
the south side of Aliaksa to hunt sea birds called tufted
puffins. Because of the infirmity of the crew, they are
dispatched in groups of two and three to small islets and
off shore rocks off the coast of Aliaksa.

Each is obligated by the company to obtain a number of
birds sufficient for seven parkas. Each parka requires 35
birds. The birds are captured by snares [*silki*] on high cliffs
and rocky outcroppings. If a rock is unclimbable, ladders are
used. Often, people fall, damage whatever health remains to
them, and some even lose their lives.

During the hunt they subsist on the meat of these birds; the
skins, with feathers on, are dried. By the middle of July this
company hunt ends, as the birds, having hatched their young,
leave the nests. It is then that these laborers are permitted to
hunt for themselves up to the middle of September. Upon their
return, the party supervisor collects from them the bird skin
quota and delivers these to Pavlovskaia Harbor, to the company clerk, against a receipt.

Later on, these bird skins are distributed among the female
kaiurs in the artels, as well as among all other Kad'iak women,
for processing and sewing of parkas which then are later sold
to their relatives for sea otters. Thus it is so: a father is sent
to hunt birds, the son to hunt sea otters, or the younger brother
to hunt birds, the elder brother to hunt sea otters; having taken
from everyone all the bird skins, after the men's wives, mothers, or sisters processed the skins and finished the parkas, the
latter are issued to their men – and to others – against the sea
otters they take.

When this hunting party returns, those who are efficient
take up hunting of foxes and land otters. If anyone had not
fulfilled the quote or did not obtain bird skins in excess of that
quota to make his own parka, he is issued a parka from his own
catch, against the future obligation to catch for the company
five foxes or land otters. Those who do not fulfill the company
quota, round out the deficiency either next year, or by borrow-
ing from others. If a person dies, his relatives assume the
obligation to make up the deficit.

Women's Work

The wives of all the inhabitants of Kad'iak, after their husbands leave with various hunting parties, are required to dig sarana according to the following quotas: wives and daughters of those who travel as companions, not possessing their own baidarkas, must collect four ishkats [native grass baskets] each; wives of those men who own their baidarkas must collect two, their daughters four, ishkats each. When the berries ripen, the company compels them to pick berries for winter reserve and each is obliged to provide one ishkat of cranberries, and a second one of crowberries. Other berries, such as raspberries, huckleberries, blueberries, cloudberries, and salmonberries, are collected, depending on the crop, as much as a baidarshchik orders. Those women who cannot fulfill this obligation because of poor health or because they have children at the breast, buy the berries from other women friends and deliver these to the company.

After the end of the berry-picking season, the women face another task: the bird hunters return then, and the company, having collected their catch, distributes it to Aleut wives and daughters in all settlements [as has been mentioned above], to be processed and made into parkas. Following this, they are assigned yet another obligatory labor: to sew kamleikas from whale, sea lion, seal, and bear guts and to make out of sinew cordage for seal nets and to prepare sinew thread.

Thus, almost throughout the entire year, the women are employed in company work.

When the news reached Kad'iak that in 1803 an around-the-world expedition was being planned, they [the company] began to pay these laborers with needles, beads, and other trifles, but only in some settlements, those close to Pavlovskaia Harbor, and for appearances' sake only.

Since 1792 the company has prohibited all inhabitants engaged in its enterprises to make for themselves parkas out of sea otter and fox pelts, and issued the strictest orders that if anyone were to wear such clothing, it would be torn off the person's back and confiscated for the company without any recompense. This has actually happened. This is why nowadays, all inhabitants generally wear bird skin parkas, formerly used only by the poor and the slaves [captives].

Ground Squirrel Trapping

In 1798, the company forbade the Kad'iak people to hunt ground squirrels on Ukamok [Chirikov] Island where they formerly took these animals for their own use in rather considerable quantity. The ground squirrel parkas are valued highly among them. In the same year, the company dispatched thither from various settlements a party of up to 25 men, not counting wives and children, and 15 female laborers, under the command of an old voyager, a Russian promyshlennoi, to hunt ground squirrels there. A quota of ten ground squirrel parkas was assigned to each man. These parkas were then sold to the Aleuts against sea otters.

The wives and female laborers were sent to sew parkas from the pelts of these animals.

In the wintertime the men also hunt seals there, and deliver to the company more than a hundred each season. In inclement weather, they look for sea otter carcasses cast ashore.

The skins of these animals are delivered to the company, the laborers use the meat.

In the spring time, they hunt birds called *urily* [cormorants], and deliver to the company annually up to 200 [cormorant] parkas. In the summer, they join the other hunters for the puffin hunt. Only females remain then on the island to pick berries and dig sarana under the protection of those oldsters who cannot walk unaided [who are practically immobile].

In the wintertime, if no whale carcasses are washed up, they suffer great hunger and subsist solely on roots, mollusks, and kelp, because even though the streams on this island are numerous, fish do not enter them, except one, in the fall in occasional years and even then in small quantity. The fish [taken there] are consumed during the fish run.

Ground squirrels are also hunted on Semida Island.

Whale Hunting

The company assigned about 30 men, the best of the Kad'iak inhabitants, to hunt whales for the company around Kad'iak and Afognak.[39]

They are dispatched to various bays, in groups from two to four persons, depending on the suitability of the locality. The hunters go out singly, in single-hatch baidarkas, choosing yearling whales because their meat and blubber are tastier and more tender.

Once the hunter notices such a whale, he approaches to the distance not more than three sazhen' and tries to aim his spear below the side fin called locally *last*. If the hunter misses the side fin, he aims at the back fin or tail [fluke]. The wounded whale dives for the sea bottom. If the spear hit accurately, the whale will be dead and come to the surface on the third day; if the spear hit to the rear of the side fin, toward the tail, the whale carcass will surface on the fifth or sixth day; if the spear was placed under the back fin, then the carcass will float not earlier than on the eighth or ninth day.

Any hunter who notices a floating whale carcass, immediately notifies the baidarshchik of the nearest artel'. [SV: The latter dispatches men, in a baidara, to tow the carcass ashore, cut it up into small portions, and transport the meat to the artel'.]

The hunter who struck the whale, as it is determined by the spear, is supposed to receive for his labor from the company the lesser half of the carcass, but in practice this is seldom observed. This rule has been established solely for appearances' sake. Fins [*lasty*], that is side fins and the tail, the belly part, and everything else considered choice portions, are taken for the company. Even that portion of the sinews which is given to the hunter is such that it is barely usable. During the summer season some whalers take up to eight, rarely ten whales. The company pays those who kill more than four whales – which is the assigned quota – in goods, worth about five rubles.

Settlers from Elsewhere

Of 70 families brought here in the year 1786 from the Fox Islands [Eastern Aleutians], there remain about 30 men.[40] These are employed in the summer in bird hunting on the Peregrebnye Islands and from the mouth of Kenai Bay to Voskresenskaia Harbor to the Chugach territory as well as on the adjacent islands. They hunt together with the Kenai and Chugach people.

The company quota for them is ten parkas each. Above these, they must hunt for themselves, their wives and children. To anyone not able to obtain what is needed for themselves, the company issues a parka, for which, in accordance with the above mentioned regulation, five foxes or land otters are deducted from the hunter's winter catch, without regard to the fact that each summer he delivers to the company, without any recompense, ten parkas worth, and that for each of these the company obtains a sea otter pelt. If anyone obtains more than above mentioned pelts, the company pays for the catch as much as is the company's will. Their wives are used like the female laborers.

Gideon's Indictment of Company Practices

In 1801 the company drove the Aleuts to join the Sitka [sic] sea otter hunting party in the following manner: they prepared in advance leg stocks and neck yokes, also for the young ones canes, for the adults [in original "thirty-year olds"] lashes, and for the old men sticks, and an armed baidara, carrying cannon and firearms, was dispatched. On the west end [cape] of Kad'iak, the Russian promyshlennye, coming ashore, formed a line with firearms loaded, and announced: "Now, tell us if you are not joining the party, [just] say so!" [the guns were then cocked] – "We'll shoot!"

Under such threats who would dare to express dissatisfaction?

Upon arrival on the Island of Sitkhinak, they fired the cannon, and standing around with loaded arms, spread on the ground the canes, the lashes, the sticks, the stocks and the yokes, saying: "Whoever does not want to join the party, let him choose which of these they want for themselves!" At this time, one man stated his refusal. He was seized, put in irons, and flogged until he was barely able to croak: "I'll go!"

In the same year, in the beginning of May, an old man, one of those assembled for the bird hunting party, was in such condition that he could not crawl to the camp about one hundred sazhen' distant and he and his wife had to spend the night on the shore. In the morning he was summoned – or better said, carried – to the manager's house in order to verify his infirmity. There he was told: "Yes, even though you are unable to walk, you are able to keep watch and see to it that the dogs do not eat up the baidara."

In 1798, about 20 men from the Sitkha hunting party were drowned, and not a few died en route.

In 1799, 140 members of the same party died as a result of eating mussels because of hunger, and an additional 40 died en route.

In 1800, from the party on Tugidok Island, promyshlennyi Lopatin sent out to sea in foul weather, despite their protests, 32 baidarkas, that is 64 men, all of whom drowned.

In 1805, an inhabitant of Ubaguik [settlement] was sent out with the birding party when seriously ill, concerning whom I

interceded by means of the following letter to the assistant
manager Mr. Banner:

Dear Sir,
Ivan Ivanovich!

The inhabitant of the Ubaguik settlement, on the Island of Sitkhinak, Nikolai Chunaginak, is blind in one eye, and is dan-
gerously afflicted with an illness of the throat, which caused a
sore to open at the back of his neck. His lower lip is festering,
he has sores on his legs, and he suffers from such chest congestion that he is unable to speak. Artamonov has dispatched
this unfortunate sufferer to join the bird hunting party. My
dear sir, do judge for yourself what kind of a hunter he will
prove to be, what kind of profit will he bring to the company
while in this pitiful state? Take pity on this enfeebled man and
order, instead, that he be sent to the healing basin, to the kazhim. He is a young person; when cured, he could be of use to
the company, while you, by means of such merciful decision,
will honor all humanity, and will render me a considerable
service in not rejecting my petition.
    Firmly convinced of your magnanimity and with sincere re-
spect, I have the honor to remain etc.

                                                     8 June 1805

In the same year [1805], in the last days of October, about 300
men were drowned while returning from Sitka [sic][41] .
    Due to the onerous tasks imposed by the company, which
have been described above, Aleuts in all settlements in wintertime suffer great hunger; when shellfish and kelp become un-
available as the tideflats are covered with ice, they consume
even seal bladders in which they store oil and fermented roe
of the red salmon, processed seal skins [lavtaki], thongs and
other items made of sinew.
    A compassionate human being can hardly restrain his tears
observing the situation of these unhappy people who resemble
the dead more than the living. After the husbands depart with
a hunting party, their wives, together with the minor children
and old men and women, have neither the means nor the time
to prepare for themselves food needed for the winter, as they
lack baidarkas necessary for this and also because of the labor
required from them by the company throughout the summer,
such as cleaning fish, digging sarana, and picking berries. For
this reason, it often happens that many die of starvation.
    Is not all of this more onerous and destructive than the ia-
sak, collection of which was abolished in 1794?[42] Is this evi-

dence of kindly and friendly treatment? The words "kindly and friendly treatment" are always the first on the lips and papers of the company, but not in reality.

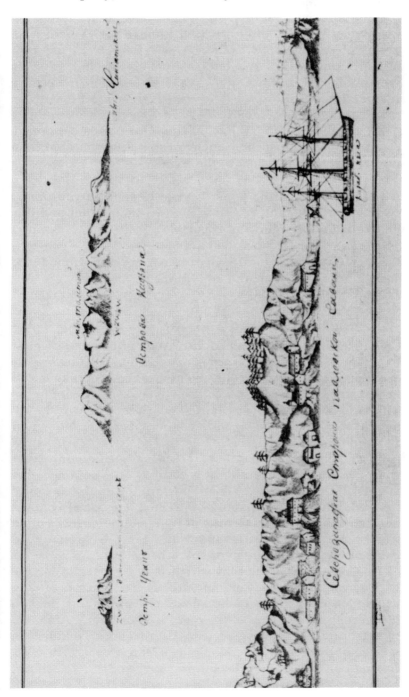

Pavlovsk Harbor, Kad'iak Island, ca. 1805

Chapter 3 – Correspondence

The correspondence is arranged as follows: Gedeon's reports to Metropolitan Amvrosii, and the enclosures, as indicated by Gedeon himself; other letters, which appear in VV and VC, published in Valaam 1894, manuscript letters from the collection of A. Dolgopolov and letters from the Kodiak Church Archives published in the *Amerikanskii Pravoslavnyi Vestnik (American Orthodox Messenger)*. *For readers' convenience, the letters are numbered sequentially, and are in chronological order.* As noted above, in SV part of the information contained in the letters to Amvrosii and enclosures is incorporated into the body of the official report to the Synod.

In the year 1805 I had the good fortune to send to your Eminence via Mr. Lieutenant Arbuzov and Mr. Lieutenant and Cavalier Povalishin the following reports:

1. Hieromonk Gideon to Metropolitan Amvrosii, June 1805, describing the voyage and conditions at Kad'iak.

    Most Holy Archpastor!   Copy

    On my arrival on the 2nd of July 1804 at the main establishment of the Russian-American Company I deemed it my first and most sacred duty to give sincere thanks in the American-Kad'iak Church to the Giver of All Benefits for safe arrival after a voyage half-way around the world. My pen is too weak to convey all the emotions of my soul when I heard the sweet tidings that in the New World, in a country so distant that there is no easy communication with our bountiful Russia, in a country still untamed, the name of the Triurine [Tri-Hypostatic] God is devoutly praised, and that the name of the Most August of His Annointed – the one who Genius of [our] boundless Russia is worthy of homage – Alexander the First is pronounced more often than the name of any other mortal.

    But let us put aside that which it is impossible for me to describe and permit me, Most Holy Archpastor, to take up the following: The Bishop-designate of Kad'iak, Ioasaf, left here four members of the clergy: Hieromonk Afanasii, to celebrate the sacred services; Hierodeacon Nektarii, in charge of the vestry, and Monks Herman [German, now St. Herman of Alaska] and Ioasaf, in charge of the [mission's] economy, all men suited to their appointed tasks. All of them tried to the best of their ability to instruct the local people; by their own labor they have started vegetable gardens from which in some years they harvested up to eighty *chetveriki* of potatoes, as well as a sufficient quantity of turnips and winter radish. The potatoes were used to make flour, the turnips, cut up into small pieces, were pickled. A lack of salt was made up by the use of sea water. [This pickle] was used throughout winter and summer instead of cabbage. The remaining surplus of the [fruit of] their labor was used to aid the destitute inhabitants. In their status as preachers they dealt with the latter kindly and thus instilled a good opinion of themselves in the minds of the Americans. In the past year of 1804, as an experiment, they sowed four pounds of barley in manured soil, and harvested one and a half pud. The soil is fertile only in those locations where there were formerly Aleut settlements. These are quite numerous on Kad'iak and the adjacent islands.

On the 6th of the aforementioned month I moved from the vessel to the Spiritual Mission quarters, and after inspecting the church utensils, vestry, books, and domestic economy, I set out on the 26th accompanied by a company interpreter in two three-hatch baidarkas to spread the word of God around the entire island of Kad'iak and also the adjoining islands of Ugak, Shalidak, Aiakhtalik, Sitkhinak, and Tugidok. Visiting all the Aleut settlements, I tried, to the best of my ability, to impress upon the newly enlightened [people] that which is necessary for faith, civic virtues, and economic life. I tried to the utmost to understand their earlier superstitions, exposing almost imperceptibly, through friendly counsel, their obvious vileness, and the harm stemming from their being so deeply rooted. In this way I led them toward the true homage due God. To judge by externals, they listened eagerly to me. It happened often that they sat over eight hours without arising or moving away. Everywhere, they received me kindly, and treated me, not only to fish, but to sarana with whale fat, and to berries: raspberries, crowberries, salmonberries, and huckleberries, also mixed with whale fat. I gave them gifts of tobacco, glass seed beads, needles, worsted, and iamanina, that is, long goat's hair.

On the 21st of August in the strait separating Aiakhtalik from Kad'iak my heart was filled with sorrow, as, following calm and fog, a strong contrary wind arose, coupled with adverse current. The paddlers were tired, the weather grew worse, we were at our wits end. However, God be praised, we just, absolutely just, managed to reach a barren shore where we remained three days and nights. We thanked Providence that we suffered no shortage of food, that is of yukola and whale meat.

In the course of my entire inspection tour, that is in two months and five days, I baptized 503 souls of both sexes aged from one to ten years, also 22 souls in their forties; I married 38 pairs.

On the 21st of November the Russian-American Company decreed a celebration to be held to mark the successful taking of the Tlingit [Kolosh] fort to Sitkha on Baranov Island and incorporation of these localities under the Scepter of the Russian Empire. After the Liturgy, a thanksgiving prayer service [blagodarstvennyi moleben] was offered to All-Bountiful God for the health of His Imperial Majesty and of the entire August House. The day before, a panikhida [service for the dead] was held for those killed at the storming of the fortress, ten men in all, that is three sailors from the ship Neva, three Russian promyshlennye, and four Kad'iak Aleuts. The wounded were Manager Baranov, Lieutenant Povalishin, the assistant surgeon [podlekar'] assistant navigator [podshturman] quartermaster, a cannoneer, eight sailors, and seven promyshlennye.

The rest of the time, at my leisure, I took up composing and delivering sermons on Lord's Feast Days, solemn holidays, and on some Sundays. I exercised myself translating from French into Russian Bourdaloue and Blaire [Blere?] and also prepared Hierodeacon Nektarii to become a teacher in the Kad'iak school. He is very eager and has good aptitude for sciences, especially for mechanics. Before my arrival, without any guidance from others, he mastered Russian grammar. In the same way he learned how to make wall clocks. I introduced him to the basics of other sciences: arithmetic, history, geography. He is also learning French.

In the year 1805, I opened the Kad'iak school, dividing it into two forms [classes]. In the first, 30 students are taught proper reading, writing, students' rules, and the short catechism. In the second, 20 students are taught Russian grammar, arithmetic, Sacred and civil history, and geography. Besides the sciences, the subjects relating to the economy were not forgotten: instead of [taking time for] recreation, the students are shown how to prepare the ground for vegetable gardens, plant and sow vegetables, weed, collect needed herbs, roots and to fish.[43]

There is also a section for the shoemaker's and cobbler's craft.

This small but growing Russian-American vineyard urgently required the benevolent moisture from above. Thus, the American Kad'iak Church, turning its emotion-filled gaze toward the Russian Zion, calls upon Thee:

Most Holy Archpastor!
Arise in the north, arise in the south – blow through this vineyard – let the aromas emanating from Thee flow – for the greater benefit of this but newly enlightened region.

I myself, in the hope of your unexpressed mercy, dare to utter this: as I shall call upon you in the hour of my need, hear me – and help me – do not abandon me.

Your Eminence's, etc.
Year 1805, 1st June, Kad'iak.

2. Hieromonk Gideon to Metropolitan Amvrosii, June 2, 1805, describing conditions at Kad'iak. Copy. (Secret)

Magnanimous Metropolitan!

Since the receipt of reliable information about the unfortunate wreck of the vessel *Phoenix* on which His Grace Ioasaf, Bishop of Kad'iak, left Okhotsk the following has happened to the clergy remaining here.

Besides spreading among the Aleuts all sorts of harmful nonsense, everything that could be invented by the company to the detriment of the honor of the clergy, out of envy of the great love evidenced by the child-like [*mladenchestvuiushchii*] folk for their enlighteners, the manager Baranov, construing this as an infringement on his authority over the Americans oppressed by various labor for and demands by the company, on July 14th 1800, in a letter sent to the Spiritual Mission's steward, Monk Herman, forbade the clergy to have any contact with the Americans (underlined in VV) and ordered that those who were given kind reception as part of the preachers' duty were to be driven off.

In accordance with the Imperial Manifesto of 1796, the Kad'iak people ought to have been administered the oath of allegiance to the Russian Throne[44] but because the company sends them far away and because of other impediments this was not done. Therefore, on January 1st, 1801 Hieromonk Afanasii sought Baranov's permission to do so. For doing this, the Hieromonk was cursed and driven off with a warning not to come back. Then, some twenty men from various settlements, with their toions, assembled to plead with Baranov to free them from any further distant trips with the Sitkha party, promising to hunt [for the company] near their villages. They were chased away, with most severe threats, and all ordered to get ready for the spring trek. This saddened them immeasurably, and in their desperation they dared to declare to the Spiritual Mission that they did not want to join the hunting party because so many of their kinsmen had died on these that many of the settlements had become depopulated. Should Baranov, because of their refusal, kill them, [they were ready] having brought with them a new parka each, and they were asking the clergy to bury them in the same and bear witness to the murder of the innocents.

To this, having called together Navigator Tallin's officers and the interpreter for the Spiritual Mission, Prianishnikov, the clergy listened in horror, and tried to persuade them to bear all adversity with magnanimity, assuring them of the mercies of His Majesty. Thus, having but barely consoled them, the clergy proposed that they take the oath of allegiance to the Emperor. They eagerly agreed and promised to obey in all things. Having been escorted to the church by the self-same officers, Hieromonk Afanasii administered the oath. When they left the church and were boarding their baidarkas, Manager Baranov's deputy, Kuskov, and his promyshlennye seized one well-born toion and took him to the company barracks. There the toion was put in irons and confined in a dark closet where not only the windows, but every crack had been boarded up. Others, too, where chased by men armed with guns in a baidara, but none were taken.

Following this incident, Baranov wanted also to seize and confine another toion, the Bishop's godson, who came out of friendship to visit the clergy. The latter, surmising as much, decided to send him off in the night, but first, as a precaution, Hieromonk Afanasii ordered his own baidarka to be made ready. He then went to it, intending to travel a short distance. Suddenly, a group of promyshlennye acting on Manager Baranov's orders stopped his baidarka and seized the Hieromonk. Then Baranov himself, in a towering rage, began to curse, calling the Hieromonk a run-away serf and the entire clergy and the two officers mentioned above mutineers.

Faced with such an unpleasant event, Monk Herman asked Baranov to make known in decent language, devoid of obscenities, the reason for his displeasure. The Manager just continued to shout: "Here! You found some kind of an oath of allegiance! You have corrupted all the Americans!"

To this the humble elder responded: "The Imperial Manifesto was published for all; if the Spiritual Mission in any way acted illegally, shouldn't the matter then be submitted to the Government where everything can be examined in accordance with the law?"

Baranov, paying no attention, kept on screeching: "What Manifesto? What Law?" and in the heat of anger threatened the clergy variously, to send them to Unalashka in irons, and to fence in and board up the mission's quarters so that nobody would be able to visit them nor they get out. As a result, the clergy were greatly afraid and expected anytime to be dragged somewhere by the promyshlennye on Baranov's orders, or to be beaten [variant reading: to be killed – *nachnut bit'*]. They hardly dared to return from the shore to their house, around which they could see for some time afterward promyshlennye armed with guns. For the same reason they did not even dare go freely to the church, but conducted all services in the house [VV: for more than a year] not only out of fear but also because doubt was cast about their loyalty through this prohibition [of administration] of the oath of allegiance.

When the time came to assemble the sea otter hunting parties, Kuskov armed the baidara not only with guns but also with cannon and set out for the settlements where lived those who had taken the oath of allegiance. In order to achieve greater effect, the partovshchik [hunting party commander] Kondakov was ordered to travel ahead. Approaching the settlement, the latter shouted with various obscenities and ridicule addressed to the clergy: "Come out and meet us! The popes[45] are coming, and Osip [this was the interpreter's name] is here to help you swear the oath!" When the baidara rudder was carried ashore, all yelled: "Here is your cross! Come and kiss it!"

It is too shameful to even mention what kinds of injuries, violence, and debauch were committed against the islanders.

Baranov covered up this crime under the pretext that the Americans, on behest of the clergy and the above mentioned officers, were allegedly about to rebel and slaughter the Russians, and that Kuskov on his trek, in fear of this anticipated rebellion, was collecting hostages. Afterwards, Baranov began in every conceivable way to oppress the clergy, in respect to preparation of food supplies and in other vital necessities.

In the year 1802, on Holy Easter [*Paskha*], promyshlennyi Chernov, drunk, came on Baranov's orders and with great coarseness ordered, in Baranov's name, Hierodeacon Nektarii to unlock the belfry. The Hierodeacon did not want to surrender the key, as the church and the belfry were locked with the same lock, and besides, the large bell was cracked.[46] The above mentioned promyshlennyi in great agitation threatened either to drag the Hierodeacon there by force or to break out the windows of the belfry.

In the meantime, the interpreter Prianishnikov, who was ill, had sent a note asking the Hieromonk and Hierodeacon to visit his house with the Holy Cross. No sooner did they arrive there, when Baranov and his promyshlennye came running. Baranov was beside himself with rage, shouting obscenities, cursing, and threatening to put the Hieromonk in a baidarka and send him to an unknown destination. He grabbed the Hierodeacon violently by the chest and threatened to hang him from the belltower. Fearing this, the Hierodeacon was forced to yield the church key.

Whenever such brazen acts occurred, the promyshlennye, sure of their Manager, used to say: "God is high, the Tsar is far away – all is fine as long as our boss is alive and well!"

For reasons described above, the Americans no longer dared to visit the clergy openly, and the clergy, on their part, were afraid to have the contact with them that their calling demanded and which would have afforded them the opportunities to instill in them Christian teachings. Thus, the success of the Spiritual Mission did not come up to expectations.

The majority of our compatriots who contracted to serve the company are of a most immoral disposition, and the local manager himself often in conversation attests that they are people "of the Kama or Volga."[47] The Americans are so burdened by the endless labors and so incensed that wherever new settlements are established they evoke hatred.[48] Even among the people in distant regions the name "Russians" has become an object of hatred. The women kill their babies in the womb, and even after birth, rather than let them suffer at the hands of the company.

In this current year, in the settlements on Shalitok Island mothers deliberately stopped feeding children aged between eight and ten years, so that they should not become laborers for the Russians, and five died of starvation.

Growing fearful that officers arriving here aboard the company vessels would report the refusal to administer the oath of allegiance [to the natives] and the oppression of the clergy, the Manager attempted to smooth over his [earlier] actions. For this reason he found himself compelled to [finally] forward to the Spiritual Mission the Manifesto together with all other dispatches belonging to it which he had previously retained, appending a communication in which he asked [the clergy] to administer the oath of allegiance to all [see below, no.4]. Thus the clergy, no longer fearing any suspicion of disloyalty on their part, as of September 15, 1802 resumed the conduct of Divine services in the church, while Baranov began to exhibit signs of his benevolence toward them: first he sent them two pounds of tea and four pounds of sugar, then a barrel of whale oil, a barrel of whale meat, and a barrel of crowberries, a berry known in northern Russia as *voronitsa* but not eaten by the folk there, mixed with fat. Subsequently, a paper was sent to the clergy in which it was stated that the local [company] office had, in recognition of commemorative mention at Services of those who had died at Sitka [sic], assigned to the Mission's credit 500 rubles which they may use to take out goods. Finally, a paper was sent by the above office stating that through the efforts of individual promyshlennye and the Manager, over three thousand rubles were donated [to the Mission] at the annual sharing out of profits, donations having been made by each as much as they saw fit, with the stipulation that the greater part of this sum be expended for the church, the lesser for the bretheren.

Against these sums they [the clergy] charged what they needed at the company store, at the highest possible prices, such as: a pud of tobacco for 75 rubles, a pound of sugar for 3 rubles 60 kopeks, a pound of tea at 8 and 6 rubles, one pud of dried wheat bread at 20 rubles, a measure [*shtof*] of vodka at 25 rubles, and hempen cords of the poorest quality for their household needs, by weight at 1 ruble per pound.

The clergy all live in one house alloted them by the company, situated in a cramped location between the Manager's house and the communal company steam bath. They obtain their subsistence for the most part by their

own labor. Besides working the vegetable gardens, they
collect various berries and mushrooms, and they fish. A
part, however, is supplied by the company.

All these tasks are carried out with the help of Americans whom they have befriended and whom the company
by every means at its disposal attempts to drive away.

The clergy wear clothing and footgear from the stock
remaining since the time of Bishop Ioasaf. They also have
a supply of grain [remaining] from the same source, as
originally there was brought here, from Shelikhov, 250
pud of rye, 20 pud of wheat for communion bread, and 20
pud of various groats, while later, before His late Grace's
departure, 150 pud of rye were shipped to the account of
the Bishop's residence.

Hierodeacon Nektarii, 36, and monk Ioasaf, 32 years of
age, both wish ardently to return to Russia and from the
bottom of their weary hearts they ask and beseech you,
most holy and all-merciful Father, for your Archpastoral
blessing to do so. Let their prayer reach you, oh Christ's
hierarch, like aromatic incense, for their hearts are full of
sorrow. Comfort them, thou blessed Comforter of the
Russian Church!

The Hieromonk [Afanasii] is 50, and Monk Herman 48
years of age. Both are lovers of solitude and wish to remain in America. But because of the fact that the house
allotted to them is right next to the secular ones, making
it impossible for them to escape the idle gossip, boundless
temptations, and various ugly and inhuman acts committed by the Russians in part among themselves, but
more often against the Americans, and also because firewood and other household necessities must be fetched
from far away and the location is inconvenient and
cramped, they are very depressed.

Their intention is to remove themselves from this tur-
bulent situation and to lead a quiet life apart, have a
church nearby [in a locality] where, if support in respect
to food and other necessary supplies will not be forth-
coming from either the governmental or through a private
agency, they will be able at least to support themselves by
their own labor. Consequently, they would want to choose
a location near a wood, to have timber for construction,
and near a stream so that they may fish, and also one that
is suitable for establishing vegetable gardens.

Most Holy Archpastor!
Hear my cry also! Do not turn thy face away, most merciful father from this lesser son separated from thy house, for I suffer. Hear me soon, soon. Lead my soul out of prison to confess in thy name.

Your Holiness', etc.
2nd June 1805, Kad'iak

3.   Hieromonk Gideon to Metropolitan Amvrosii, no date, describing difficulties of voyage on the *Neva*. Copy.

Most Worthy Eminence, Vladyko!

Carrying deep in my heart the impress of Your Eminence's apostolic instructions, I have tried in all things to act in accordance with them, but people's characters are different, as was the case among those with whom it was my misfortune to spend almost an entire year aboard the ship *Neva*. Captain Lisianskii and Midshipman Berkh are people of troublesome character and caused me much offense, against which my only cure was magnanimous patience. Even now I shall pass in silence the many prohibitions against performance of the Divine service on Sundays and Lord's Feast Days, the only solace at sea for those who know God. I am ashamed to mention various scathing remarks ridiculing Religion. The son of Archpriest [protoierei] Lisianskii from the town of Nezhin, one who, one should think, had been born and raised in the very lap of Religion, often took leave at table, drinking the Teneriffe wine, to address me with these words: "Father! The Health of the Mother of God!"

During our stay on the Island of St. Catherine in Brazil, he, under the guise of consideration for myself, tried to estrange me also from His Excellency [Rezanov][49] .

En route from the stormy Cape Horn to Easter Island, on the 25th March 1804, I, the humble elder, suffered another storm, this one emanating from the Captain. He wanted to lock me up, board me up, in my cabin simply because I was sitting on the quarterdeck [*shkantsy*] while he was taking a walk along the deck. I was protected [only] by the love of other officers who interceded for me and protected me.

While in the Marquesas Islands, he ordered the crew not to permit me to go ashore because the evening before, returning from the ship *Nadezhda*, did not go to the Captain's cabin to report my return to him in person, although it was made known to the officer of the watch.

Without patience life is impossible. Therefore, I bore all such unpleasantness with magnanimity. While in Sandwich Islands, I did not go ashore at all. On Kad'iak, the Captain was no longer able to offer me violence of the above mentioned sort, but instead he told the Gubernia Secretary (Banner), the acting manager, that I had been sent there as punishment. He used all means at his disposal to take away the two boys being trained by the Spiritual Mission for the Church, although there were many others in the Kad'iak school [he may have used]. He finally persuaded the office to request me in writing to send those two boys [to him]. I refused, basing myself on the lawful imperative, and I enclose a copy of my refusal.

All the earlier incidents were sufficient proof of his hate for Religion and the entire spiritual realm. He gave additional proof thereof when he carried away with him when leaving the local harbor one of the very best of the boys, one who has already been educated and was able to perform a deacon's office.[50]

There is attached to this a copy of a communication addressed to the Spiritual Mission in which I am entrusted with the care of God's Temple here and and of all spiritual matters and also a copy of a document given me by His Excellency Nikolai Petrovich Rezanov.[51]

Most Holy Archpastor!
Both sweet and bitter waters flow from a single source. Firmly trusting to Thy inexhaustible mercy, again and again I cry: lead my soul out of prison to find confession in Thy name.

[date omitted]
Your Holiness', etc.
Enclosures

4.   Baranov to Kad'iak Spiritual Mission, September 15, 1802.

[The following document which relates to Gideon's discussion of the difficulties the clergy encountered in administering the oath of allegiance to the Kad'iak Islanders and Baranov's subsequent attempt to smooth over the incident is translated from a published version in *Amerikanskii Pravoslavnyi Vestnik* 4:6:125-126, 15/28 March 1900. This document, along with several others, including letters by Gideon, St. Herman of Alaska, and Ioasaf were

copied and submitted for publication by Father Tikhon
Shalamov, then Kodiak parish priest. The originals were
in the Kodiak Church archive, and are presumed to have
perished in the church fire in the year 1943.]

To the Kad'iak Spiritual Mission, to the worthy fathers, the
[Mission's] Superior Father Hieromonk Afanasii; to Hierodeacon Nektarii.

Communication from the Manager of the Kad'iak office
of the American Company which is under the August Protection of His Imperial Majesty, Baranov.

There are being forwarded together with this eleven
envelopes delivered here from Okhotsk which are addressed to His Eminence, the local Kad'iak Bishop Ioasaf,
from the Holy Synod and others, also six particular [pri-
vate?] letters and two printed copies of manifestos: the
first about the end of Lord Emperor Pavel Petrovich, of
blessed memory, and the ascension to the throne of the
Heir, Aleksandr Pavlovich, the second about the oath
which goes with it.

As there is no Bishop here at present, and the former
one was overtaken by unhappy fate en route from Okhotsk
here, let the one of you whose duty it is decide if you
should open the packets delivered to you from the Holy
Synod and others prior to arrival here of a Bishop or [other
ecclesiastical] Superior. [Also] in accordance of the August manifesto, do hold in the God's temple here appropriate Divine services, first of all, a panikhida (memorial
service] for the departed monarch, then a vigil and a Te
Deum for the health and well-being of the Emperor Alexander Pavlovich, who has but newly ascended the throne,
and of His entire August House and Family notifying me
and all the local people [about the time]. After conclusion
of the Te Deum service you are to administer to all of us
an oath of allegiance which we are to sing as per attached
[form].

This oath is later to be administered to all of those who
(for one reason or another) did not take it on the first occasion.

September 15, 1802
Aleksandr Baranov

[Gideon's account of the incident of the "oath of
allegiance" should be compared to the account given by
Rezanov in a letter to the Directors of the Russian-American Company, dated 6 November 1805, from Novo-

Arkhangel'sk (Sitka), published by Tikhmenev, in English translation in 1979, by R.A. Pierce and A.S. Donnelly, *History of the Russian-American Company*, vol. 2, pp. 153-173 no. 42. An excerpt, after Pierce and Donnelly 1979:167, is given below:]

"As for the ecclesiastical mission, they have baptized several thousands here, but only nominally. Seeing that the ways of Kadiak natives become milder I find less explanation for that in the work of the missionaries than to time and their own aptitude. Our monks have never followed the path of the Jesuits in Paraguay by trying to develop the mentality of the savages, and have never known how to enter into extensive plans of the Government or company. They have just been "bathing" the Americans [baptizing by immersion] and when, due to their ability to copy, the latter learn in half an hour how to make the sign of the cross, our missionaries return, proud of their success, thinking that their job is done. Having little to do they try to take part in the civil government of the country, calling themselves government representatives. The restless officers use them as their tools against the Manager. The result is grief and there is danger of our losing the whole country. I will give you an example. At the time of the coronation of the Emperor, the monks, without a word to the manager sent out orders calling all natives to Kad'iak to take the oath of allegiance. There were no provisions at Kad'iak and if the manager had not stopped the people from gathering by sending his men to their villages, several thousand of them gathering at Kadiak would have killed everybody from starvation alone."

5.   Enclosure to #3 (see above).   Copy

From the Kad'iak office [of the Russian-American Company] to the Kad'iak Spiritual Mission

His Excellency, Actual Chamberlain and Cavalier of various orders, Nikolai Petrovich Rezanov, in a dispatch dated 23d December 1803, #175, addressed to His Honor, Collegiate Counsellor and Manager of the Russian-American Regions, Aleksandr Andreevich Baranov, deigned to make the following dispositions.[52]
    No matter how we wish that the sad rumors about the loss of the *Phoenix* would prove false, the lack of any news about her tends to confirm them. Therefore, His Excel-

lency has petitioned for the appointment of a clerical person in order to facilitate the spread hereabouts of Orthodox Christianity. Hieromonk Gideon has been selected for this task. [His Excellency] therefore has recommended this worthy man [to us], and instructed that he is to be entrusted [VV: upon his arrival here] with the care of God's Temple and all Spiritual affairs, since to our heartfelt sorrow we have become deprived of His Eminence, Ioasaf [SV: if it should prove true that we lost His Eminence Ioasaf].

The Spiritual Mission is hereby being informed accordingly and will carry out the will of His Excellency.[53]

23rd January 1805, no. 99
Pavlovskaia Harbor, on the Island of Kad'iak
With absolute respect,
Acting Manager, Gubernia Secretary
Ivan Banner

6. Cathedral Hieromonk Gideon to the Kad'iak office. [This letter also was one of the enclosures to letter 3, above, and documents Gideon's refusal to surrender to Lisianskii two bilingual students trained by the Mission. The available text is in a clerk's hand but not explicitly marked "copy."]

One of the most important concerns of His Imperial Majesty is the faith, the church, and its propagation in this region, a fact of which the company is not ignorant. For this reason, His Eminence Ioasaf, who formerly was in residence here, taking into account the difficulty of bringing clergy over here, considered it amatter of the utmost importance to prepare local minors for the offices of Celebrants and Servitors of the Church, and he left them here [for training] with appropriate written instructions on the subject. [VV: Furthermore, the local church has no staffed positions for deacons and sacristans.]

Therefore, I, in the line of duty wishing to see the church in good and orderly state to the greater Christian pleasure and instruction of the parishioners, find it absolutely necessary to keep at the church not only the two boys, Prianishnikov and Kulikalov, who are being illegally demanded by the office, but all the others at the Spiritual Mission who have already been instructed in performance of church offices and in other matters pertaining to the conduct of Divine services.

Moreover, the office is well aware of the expectations of that exalted personage, who by the will of the August

Sovereign has been delegated to be the Organizer of the local lands, the Actual Chamberlain and Cavalier, Nikolai Petrovich Rezanov. Therefore, all matters pertaining to the Spiritual domain shall be left pending His Excellency's arrival.

Consequently, I dare not to send the above mentioned boys to the Commander of the company vessel *Neva*, Captain-Lieutenant and Cavalier Lisianskii.

Cathedral Hieromonk Gideon
March 11th, 1805

In the year 1805, on July 28th, Kad'iak was pleased by the arrival of His Excellency, Mr. Rezanov.

On the 7th of August I received from His Excellency a document of the following content:

7. Copy.

Most Worthy Father Gideon,
My Dear Sir!

As I am organizing all aspects of [the management of] the American territory, I deem it one of my first duties to understand the present situation of the Spiritual Mission which is in residence here and to undertake firm measures to alleviate the needs of those pious men who, rejecting all secular concerns, seek in the Lord's Name to enlighten and educate ignorant humanity.

As, with all due respect, I do justice to their enthusiastic achievements, and express to you personally, as their leader along their way [*putevodets*], my gratitude, I humbly request Your Worthiness to inform me what is required annually for the upkeep of the clergy and beautification of the Temple of God, thus affording me the pleasure to employ all the means at my disposal [to satisfy the same], as evidence of that unalterable respect in which I hold all the worthy fathers and Your Worthiness personally,

Ready always to be
Your most humble servant,
Nikolai Rezanov
7th August [1805]

I replied to this as follows:

8.   Your Excellency,
     My Dear Sir!

Accepting with warmest gratitude Your Excellency's solicitude for the maintenance of the local Spiritual Mission,
I find the following absolutely necessary:

1)   construction of houses and the necessary appurte-
     nances thereof [tools and materials]: saws, iron for
     axes, shovels, mattocks, spades for gardening, nails,
     hemp, pitch, sail cloth for boats, window glass, woo-
     den and copper dishes, cooking pots, teapots, rope,
     candles, writing paper.
2)   Provisions should be issued in kind, as is done for the
     naval chaplain[s], rationed for each person, with the
     exception of meat and beer, but with addition of tea
     and sugar.
3)   Each person should receive, as is appropriate to cler-
     ical status, two sets of winter and summer clothing
     and footwear, also five shirts and underwear each,
     per year; also crepe [silk cloth] for cowls and cotton
     velveteen [*plis*] for monks' hats [*kamilavki*] and cuffs
     [*mufty*].
4)   In lieu of payments to the Americans who aid in
     household tasks and in other necessities, also for
     greater success in their education and enlightenment
     and so as to show our affection for them, [the follow-
     ing items] are needed: tobacco, woolen worsted
     [*sukno*], cotton cloth [*kitaika*, unbleached muslin], li-
     nen, glass seed beads [*biser*], needles, and crosses.

All of the above was refused with great indignation and I found
myself forced to reply to His Excellency thus:

9.   Your Excellency,
     My Good Sir!

Accepting with the warmest gratitude Your Excellency's
benevolent solicitude for the necessary annual maintenance of the Clergy, the Fathers of the local Spiritual
Mission, Hieromonk Afanasii, and the monks Herman and
Ioasaf, have declared to me that they leave it entirely to
your good will to take measures to alleviate their yearly
need in respect to food, clothing, and all other domestic
necessities.

As far as the beautification of the Temple is concerned,
I have the honor to inform you that it depends upon the
efforts of benefactors and lovers of God.

Absolutely necessary for the church are the following:
flour for communion bread, wine, incense, candles, and
vegetable oil. Above all, it is imperative to fix the leak in
the church [roof].

I have the honor to remain, with sincere respect,

Your Excellency's etc. etc.
9th August 1805

That very same day I received another document from His Excellency as follows:

10. Having observed the excellent work done here by the Fa-
    thers of the Spiritual Mission who engage in agriculture,
    I humbly ask Your Worthiness to provide me with infor-
    mation as to which grains were experimented with and
    when, and which vegetables they do grow and in what
    quantities, and append also brief practical observations by
    these industrious laborers. This will enable me to do jus-
    tice to the efforts of these pious men when I report to His
    Majesty on this very important activity here in America.

    With absolute respect, I remain the most humble serv-
    ant of

Your Worthiness,
My Dear Sir,
Nikolai Rezanov
9th August 1805
Pavlovskaia harbor

My answer:

11. Your Excellency, My Dear Sir!

    The Fathers of the local Mission began agricultural ex-
    periments as early as 1795, when they sowed carrot, onion,
    mustard, poppy, turnip and tobacco, and planted potatoes,
    winter radish, beets, rutabaga, cabbage, cucumbers, wat-
    ermelon, pumpkin, melons, green peas, beans, and maize
    (which in Russia is sometimes called garden wheat), sun-
    flowers, and other cultivated flowers. Of all the vege-
    tables, the laborers were rewarded with a crop by only
    potatoes, winter radish and turnips. The rest, though they
    sprouted, soon disappeared.

In 1796, abandoning the earlier lot as unsuitable to bear crops, experiments were conducted at other locations, taking care to fertilize the soil with manure. Aside from an average crop of potatoes, turnip, and winter radish, they obtained outer cabbage leaves which did not head, and rutabagas.

In 1797, further experiments were carried out on the site of an abandoned Aleut settlement, where even beets bore a crop, though the roots were small in size. Turnips were of considerable size though, the largest up to ten pounds, while potatoes and winter radish gave the best yield ever.

In 1802 they learned by experience that kelp improves fertility of the soil very much. That same year, garlic was planted and it was observed that it can bear a crop.

In the year 1804, four pounds of barley were sown in soil which had been manured, a pud and a half was harvested.

On the 25th April of the current year of 1805, ten pounds of barley and ten pounds of wheat were sown at the same time but in various soils, on soil which had been manured, on unimproved soil, and at the site of an abandoned Aleut settlement. The grain sown on the manured soil and at the abandoned Aleut village had good stalks and heads. Barley began to form heads earlier and there is definite hope that it will ripen soonest, while the wheat began to form heads much later and there is little hope of its ripening. Only time will tell what success is to come from these beginnings. With sincere respect, I have the honor to remain, etc.

10th August 1805
Pavlovskaia harbor

[In the context of the above exchange, and other documents pertaining to the Mission's activities and especially their educational effort, Rezanov's letter to the Directors cited above (6 November 1805 from Sitka) assumes an extraordinary importance, substantiating the charge made by Gideon in one of his letters to Metropolitan Amvrosii that the company was spreading lies detrimental to the Clergy.

The excerpt presented follows the text as given in Pierce and Donnelly 1979:]

"Now that the monks understand their mistakes they do their best to help the company in agriculture and in education of the younger generation" [Pierce and Donnelly 1979:168].

On the 15th of August [1805] the Russian-American School, numbering 50 students, had the pleasure to demonstrate the fruits of its labors at a public examination held in presence of the trustee, the Organizer of the Russian-American Territories, Nikolai Petrovich Rezanov, and of the esteemed guests, such as the senior naval officers, and a certain anonymous cleric [Gideon], as well as the notables from among the newly founded citizenry of Kad'iak. Those [students] who had distinguished themselves by their diligence, success in their studies, and good behavior, received personal awards from the generous hand of His Excellency.

On the 20th of August Mr. Rezanov departed for Baranov Island, to the port of Novo-Arkhangel'sk [Sitka]. From there I received on September 29th the following letter from His Excellency:

12. Most Worthy Father Gideon,
    My Dear Sir!

Having reached by the Grace of God the port of Novo-Arkhangel'sk on the morning of this past 26th of August I found myself here at close quarters with a life still far from peaceful. We are awaiting the hunting party from hour to hour, but as yet it has not returned. We live on the rock [kekur] with some men armed at all times, and the cannon primed. I therefore thought it necessary to warn you in respect to sending anyone here to propagate the Word of God, that such a feat is impossible in this region. Aleksandr Andreevich [Baranov] will let you know when it becomes possible. I ask you to inform the Fathers of the Spiritual Mission that they are to follow their calling to the glory of the Triurine [Tri-hypostatic] God within the borders of the Kad'iak region, where His Holy Name has begun to be heeded. Besides, accommodation is very scarce here, and food even scarcer. Our life here is very tedious, each day there is torrential rain, and however necessary the work, the rain prevents the same. In the meantime, a wharf is being constructed here and slipways have been cleared for two vessels. We are felling timber little by little, and soon, with God's help, we shall have on the stocks a 16 gun naval brig and an eight gun tender, for which the plans and budgets have been drawn up.

I expect you to facilitate the success of the school, a matter close to my heart, and I also request you to impress on all that obedience to authority is to be maintained and that the Americans are to carry out their prescribed duties without protest, until we have improved this region. Otherwise, all may be lost and should there be insufficient number of men for the hunting parties, then the knives under the threat of which we lead our lives here, will again be used to annihilate the Russians. It is amazing how barbaric the local people are. They are at the moment held in check by fear, but malice remains and indescribable inhuman acts, we hear, are being committed against our people who are held prisoners by them. I plan to spend the winter here, but I think that Aleksandr Andreevich [Baranov] will be in your parts.

Thus, entrusting myself to your continued good favor, as always with absolute respect,

the humblest servant of Your Worthiness,
Nikolai Rezanov
11th September 1805
Baranov Island
Port of Novo-Arkhangel'sk

[This letter, as well as the letter Rezanov dispatched to the company directors on 6th November 1805, clearly indicates that the clergy, indeed, strongly opposed Baranov's oppressive labor policies and supports Gideon's contention that the company countered by spreading malicious libel. In particular, the clergy's missionary activity came under attack, focusing on the death of Father Iuvenalii, laying the foundation for erroneous interpretations of that man's fate which persist to this day. The calumny stated by Rezanov was later repeated in print in the account of the voyage to America by Lieutenant Davydov. Clearly, an attempt was made to muzzle the clergy and control their activities and intercourse with the natives. The excerpt from Rezanov's letter follows the text as given by Pierce and Donnelly 1979:167-168:]

"Sometimes, unknown to the manager, they [the clergy] would set off uselessly to make new converts. On the Aliaksa peninsula trade, which promised big profits, was opened with the hill na-

tives, on Lake Iliamna, sometimes called Lake
Shelikhov. The monk Juvenal went there immediately to propagate the faith. He baptized them
forcibly, married them, took girls away from some
and gave them to others. The Americans endured
his rough ways and even beatings for a long time,
but finally held council, decided to get rid of the
reverend and killed him. He does not deserve pity,
but the Iliamna natives in the exasperation killed
the whole crew of Russians and Kadiak people.
Since then this people think of revenge and fearing
that the Russians will settle there again, show no
mercy at the slightest misstep. Last year they
killed Russians again.[54]

I told the holy fathers that if any of them took
another step without first getting the Manager's
approval, or if they meddled in civil affairs, I would
order such criminals deported to Russia, where for
disrupting the peace of the community such people
would be defrocked and severely punished, to make
an example of them. They cried, rolled at my feet
and told me that it was the government employees
who had told them what to do. They promised me
to behave, so that the Manager would have nothing
but praise for them in the future. I admonished
them thus privately in the presence of Father Gideon but in public I have always shown respect for
their dignity."[55]

13. Rezanov to Gideon:
     Secret   Copy

My Worthy Father Gideon,
My Dear Sir!

The wish you have expressed to see the port of Novo-
Arkhangel'sk and your willingness to accept my challenge
to share with me my labors for the good of the Fatherland
[expressed] during my stay on Kad'iak, as well as my sincere respect for your merits, obliges me, should this letter
find your disposition unchanged, to propose that you take
part in a secret expedition I am planning for this very
same year.[56] A three-masted copper-sheathed ship, the
Juno, bought by the company from the Bostonians, has
sailed, under command of Lieutenant Khvostov, to Three

Saints Harbor to fetch provisions.[57] He is to return as soon
as possible. Thus, since he may not delay for even one
hour, I humbly beg you, if my proposition appeals to you,
to hasten to the above mentioned harbor by a baidara,
without even a hint of disclosure of [this matter] to anyone,
but using the pretext that I have need of you in Sitka: thus
I shall soon have the pleasure of meeting you again.

I remain your most humble servant,
My Dear Sir,
No.498
Nikolai Rezanov

P.S. There is no need for a field church. In this raw climate, where all buildings still lack stoves, it will rot to no
purpose. Just bring an icon for the ship, so that prayer
service may be held occasionally. Let me say again, incidentally, that your arrival here depends entirely upon
your willingness to come.

4th October 1805
Baranov Island
Port Novo-Arkhangel'sk

Gideon to Rezanov.

[The text in this letter, as it appears in SV, shows several
substantive differences from the text in VV and VC, and
Valaam 1894. The SV version is polished and slightly
abridged but includes two passages not in the other, fuller
versions. These have been inserted in the text presented
here.]

Your Excellency,
My Dear Sir!

Having the honor to be a witness to the sincerity and en-
thusiasm of Your Excellency's diligent efforts for the good
of the Fatherland, and remembering with pleasure the
train of your thoughts in this respect, I considered it my
most pleasant duty to obey, with gratitude, your most flattering invitation to accompany you aboard the ship *Juno*
on your secret expedition. But, to my great regret, circumstances combined to block the fulfillment [of this
plan].

When, on the 24th of October of the last year [1805] I
received your most flattering epistle, Ivan Ivanovich Banner refused to send me to the Old Harbor [Three Saints

Bay] and said angrily to my messenger, the monk Ioasaf:
"There are neither baidaras nor men to take him there,
while here the vessel *Elizaveta* is ready to sail. Let him
go on her!"

So I was forced to travel to Baranov Island on the aforesaid vessel *Elizaveta*. We left the harbor on the 26th of
that same month [October 1805] but encountered fierce
contrary wind as we rounded Lesnoi [Woody] Island,
where we stopped at anchor. On the 28th in the evening
we finally set out on our true course. Though we grounded
twice on the Gorbunov shallows [Humpback Rock?], this
did not prevent us from continuing our voyage. During the
night of the 9th of November we were driven by the fier-
cest of storms toward land in the vicinity of Icy Strait, near
the entrance to Cross Sound. We barely managed to stand
off, avoiding obvious danger. Several times we sighted the
L'tuia [Lituya] mountains, and their striking appearance
only increased our sadness at our troublesome voyage.
Changeable weather, either freezing cold or slush, or severe contrary winds, or fog, gave us little hope of seeing
the Port of Novo-Arkhangel'sk. Danger followed upon
danger. On the 23rd, at night, we were brought again to
Okoisk – [to the edge of despair?][58] but, having poured out
our contrite hearts in prayer, we were spared by the Almighty. On that same day, toward evening, we sighted
Yakutat Bay but only for a short time although we stood
off it about three days and nights.

On December 1st we sighted Mt. St. Lazarus [Mt. Edge-
combe] and for a whole night we looked upon it with eager
eyes from a short distance, but in the morning to our great
sorrow we had to part from this Novo-Arkhangel'sk colos-
sus because of a severe contrary wind. Nevertheless,
thrice more we ventured to hope to reach Baranov Island,
i.e. on the 3rd, the 6th, and the 7th we again approached
this mountain as close as before, and again the contrary
winds which grew even stronger drove us off. What misfortune! The men were exhausted, and sickness began to
break out. Because of unending drizzle it was impossible
to dry out our clothing. Water was growing scarce. Then,
freezing cold set in, and, what was even sadder, the sails
which were being spread by means of hand levers [gansh-
pug] froze, and neither our hands nor teeth were of any
avail. We were very far from the coast we longed for.
What was there to do? On the 10th of December we were
forced to make for Kad'iak.

On the 18th, at midnight, we sighted Kad'iak. Apparently, we were quite close to it. We started tacking but were driven by the current to the shore of Cape Tonkii, a short distance from the Island of Ugak, where, running violently against a rock at 6 o'clock in the morning we dropped two anchors. On the 19th, about midday; the wind increased, the anchors failed to hold, disaster became inescapable. We began to lighten the masts, and then, with tears in our eyes and groaning hearts, we cut down the mainmast [grot-machta]. Oh, what a terror that was! Even now, my feelings fall into disarray! Finally, with surf running so strongly that the sand upheaved by the surging elements blinded us, the vessel was cast ashore. It was already dark. With limbs quaking from the wet and the cold, and with warm tears of gratitude to the Almighty, all came safely off the vessel. Thus was our fate decided.

Our entire voyage was unfortunate. The lateness of the season, the strong contrary winds, the changeable weather, our skipper lacking a second in command, the obstinacy, or better said ungovernability, of the promyshlennye, and the skipper's poor health – who, on the 23rd of November attempting in his pitiful state to gain the deck, fell and to our misfortune injured his right hand – all of this, combined, was no mean obstacle to the achievement of our intended goal. As far as maintenance of good order, thrift, and the care of the preservation of the cargo and food supplies, I am an eyewitness that they were to the honor and evidence of Mr. Karpinskii's merits. It was unfortunate that the men carried out his orders unwillingly, and, after the ship was wrecked, showed overt signs of disobedience. Had it not been for the presence of the kaiurs [native laborers] on this occasion, the greater part of the cargo would have been lost. In his [Karpinskii's] absence, no work was done due to the obduracy of the promyshlennye and, therefore, he was compelled to be present at all times while the ship was being unloaded, although he was unwell.

On the third day following the wreck, I was forced by the cold to set out, on foot, donning the native foot gear [torbasa], for the Igak artel' [in the vicinity of modern Ugak Bay]. The way there was very uncomfortable and difficult because of the deep snow, many high mountain ridges, and steep cliffs [SV: We ascended the ridges with the aid of thick staffs, which we firmly planted in the snow and stamped out a path for a bit, then moved them again, to the new height; when descending, we aided each other with these staffs].

I remained in this artel' for two weeks, leaving on the 6th of January of the current year [1806] after completing all the requested sacred offices [*treby*]. I travelled by a baidarka and just barely managed to land at the place where the wrecked vessel lay. Fierce storms, cruel cold, and most unusual blizzards commenced, and these detained me further on this barren shore.

On the 14th, I returned to Pavlovskaia harbor where I suffered aggravations no less than before [SV: I returned to Pavlovskaia harbor where I reside at present].

Wishing to increase the effectiveness and success of the school, which is in accordance with Your Excellency's ardent wish, I made the decision to appoint a teacher of arithmetic, geography, and art [drawing – *risoval'noe iskusstvo*], in order to offer these subjects in this school, the more so as Hierodeacon Nektarii is unwilling to teach arithmetic. Besides, he is busy with other matters, and this makes it difficult for him to teach and also is a barrier to success therein. Mr. Borisov with great diligence and willingness has taken this task upon himself, out of love for and the benefit of the local youth. His success in teaching two boys he had previously taken on, and the procedure he followed, served both as the reason for his appointment and a guarantee of his success. I informed the office about my intention, leaving the final decision and confirmation thereof to Your Excellency. The office, however, replied in terms very insulting to me, indecently reminding me of my position [as they see it], rudely prescribing their own rules, and accused me of wilfulness, having read into my choice, so well-intentioned, with a view for the common good, some absurd animosity toward the authorities. Moreover, there is evidence that some members of the office are disturbing [the peace of mind of] the clerics Hieromonk Afanasii and Hierodeacon Nektarii, who had been very rude to me following the wreck of the vessel. Well, the senior officials here themselves egg them on in this. [SV: omits the foregoing paragraph, having instead the following: I am busy with the school and various religious matters. My health is suffering great weakness, but especially from having my side when the vessel was wrecked. My legs swell before a change of weather for the worse, my chest is congested and often I feel dizzy. The bruised area feels numb.]

Thus it is that I am impatient to meet with you again, here on Kad'iak as you had promised me earlier, and hope to see my lot eased.

Until such time I entrust myself to your protection, with sincere and constant respect,

I remain
Your Excellency's, etc.
14th April 1806
Pavlovskaia harbor.

On the 21st of April 1807, The Russian-American School has the pleasant opportunity to hold the second public examination in the presence of the Manager, Collegiate Counsellor Baranov, captains of the foreign vessels, and other visitors. In recognition of the students' success the Manager thanked me with the following letter:

14. Your Worthiness,
My Dear Sir!

As an expression of my recognition of the foundation laid for education of the local youth gathered here in the Kad'iak school which bears the impress of your guidance, and of my innermost feelings called forth by the fact that this goal, so long desired for the common good and the glory of the Fatherland, of enlightenment and building up of these untamed and remote regions, but all under the single All-Russian scepter, is being accomplished during my tenure of office, I have the honor to present Your Worthiness, out of my own surplus, five hundred rubles as well as an additional two hundred rubles for those students in the first form who show greater aptitude in the study of the rules of sciences which you reach and who also are able to teach the same to others, because of the level they have reached in their knowledge.

I leave it to your discretion to determine which items from those that are on hand in the store will be charged against my account in the amount of the above award. The clerk [prikazchik] shall be informed accordingly. Your Worthiness may do the same, if you desire to take [the donation made to you] in goods. If not, you may obtain it in money, either from the Okhotsk or Irkutsk [company] office when you leave here. In this case also you may have access to my account.

In order to reward students who excel in study, the
company shareholder, Mr. Vasilii Ivanovich Malakhov,
will assign store credit in the amount of one hundred rubles, to be used at your discretion.

I remain, with all due respect,
Your Worthiness' humble servant,
Aleksandr Baranov
23 April 1807
Pavlovskaia harbor

On the 12th of May [1807] there arrived from Sitka the vessel
Sitka, newly built from the aromatic wood of the American cypress (cedar), and on the 15th I informed the Manager of my
return to Russia:

15. Your Honor, Dear Sir!

My business requires that I leave for Okhotsk aboard the
vessel *Sitka*. Therefore, I humbly ask you, dear Sir, to
order a berth to be made ready for me, to provide me with
food supplies and other necessities for the voyage and also
to do the same for the two older students who are to accompany me, Prokopii Lavrov and Paramon Chumovitskii,
as well as for the minor Aleksei Kotel'nikov, as per the
attached list.

As far as spiritual matters are concerned, I shall inform
Your Honor forthwith.

remain with complete respect, etc.

On the following day the Manager explained to me many difficulties and the great expense of maintaining the above mentioned students en route and, incidentally, asked me to reveal
what was the will of His Excellency Nikolai Petrovich Rezanov
in this matter, promising in the meantime to give me satis-
faction. I answered his representations as follows:

16. Your Honor,
     My dear Sir!

I had the honor to receive Your Honor's clarification. The
advice you are proferring out of your long experience is
all the more welcome and pleasing to my heart because [I
realize that] your acute and farsighted intelligence will
protect me through exercise of caution, thus giving me
greater peace of mind, on this [forthcoming] journey.

Availing myself of this important parting counsel, I feel myself indebted to you, My Dear Sir.

The will of His Excellency, Nikolai Petrovich Rezanov, the Organizer of these territories, in this matter is as follows: in his correspondence with me he has deigned to state that, in accordance with the Sovereign will of His Majesty the Emperor, there was placed upon him, as well as on me, the flattering duty to improve this region. Thus, in his many communications with me, both verbal and written,paying especial respect to my clerical calling, he acknowledged me to be his eager collaborator in the diligent implementation of measures designed for such improvement. I, for my part, to justify His Excellency's high opinion of me, with all possible effort attempted to foster the general good, for which I think it is necessary to enhance the education of these students in St. Petersburg, thus rendering a service to the fatherland, and at the same time making them of use to this region, to the honor of their patron, the Russian-American Company.

Having revealed to you the will of His Excellency and the trend of my thoughts in this matter, I remain with total respect, etc.

16th May 1807

[The above correspondence shows a hiatus in communication between Gideon and Rezanov in the year 1806. Rezanov left Novo-Arkhangel'sk [Sitka] for Okhotsk in June 1806, aboard the *Juno*, commanded by Lt. Khvostov, reaching the Siberian port in September. If, as it is natural to assume, the ship put in at Kodiak, Gideon must have tried to see Rezanov. Gideon's silence on this is inexplicable, and suggests that the meeting or meetings were not successful from the clergyman's point of view. No documentary evidence which would be useful in clarifying this pointhas come to light, but the opinion that amity was lacking in any encounters between the two men following Gideon's failure to join Rezanov at Sitka is strengthened by Rezanov's letter of November 6, 1805, portions of which have been quoted above. Another excerpt presented below follows Pierce and Donnelly's text, 1979:168-169]:

"In the field of education Father Nektarii shows talent and aptitude so I made him director of the school and have promised to intercede so that a salary will be paid to him, which he deserves for his labors. I gave Father German twenty boys to be trained in agriculture. They will be taken to Spruce Island to experiment with sowing wheat, planting potatoes and vegetables and to learn how to make preserves of mushrooms and berries, how to make nets and cure fish, etc. During the winter they will be returned to school where they will learn to read and write and will receive religious training. In this way I will make ready for you the first twenty families of agricultural settlers and think that after they get used to work these boys will become reliable and literate farmers.

I also explained to the monks of what missionary work consists. I shamed them for not yet knowing the American language, telling them that not only prayers but even sermons must be translated into the American Language. I commissioned them to make a dictionary, so as not to be at the mercy of the interpreters, who often interpret what is told to them incorrectly. Because a job of this kind looked as big and forbidding as a bear, I began to make this dictionary myself. This dictionary took quite a bit of work and enclosing it here, I beg you to publish it for the American schools and to send bound copies here. I hope that owing to its novelty there will be a demand for it in Russia also and that several percent can be deducted from the sales for the benefit of the school pupils. As far as the ecclesiastics are concerned you see that they are now living up to sound and strict rules.

Speaking of school pupils I will point out here some means for boarding them. Mr. Baranov has generously subscribed five shares for the school. I believe that fifteen shares given by the company to the late Father Ioasaf can be transferred to the school, so that the school pupils will have twenty shares. Because a dividend is paid once very two years and money for the pupils is needed each year, the company should try to buy these shares, charging the purchase price to the shareholders and letting them have the dividend when it is due ... [the rest of the text is omitted by Tikhmenev]."

[The above statements are clearly at odds with Gideon's letter to Metropolitan Amvrosii, in which he reports the organization of the school prior to Rezanov's arrival on

Kodiak. Rezanov's remark that he had appointed Nektarii [whom Gideon, a professional teacher and linguist, was training] as the school's director, may explain the difficulty Gideon encountered when he selected a Russian settler, Borisov, to teach.

Another difficulty is presented by Rezanov's reference to linguistic work. It is known that Gideon undertook translations into Alutiiq [the translation of the Lord's prayer survives]. It is also known that under Gideon's guidance a comparative dictionary of the Alaskan languages and a grammar of the Alutiiq languages were being compiled.

None of these works have survived. Or did they? Rezanov, whose dictionary of Alaskan languages has long been known to linguists, and is very much appreciated, arrived at Kodiak 28 July 1805, leaving for Sitka 20th August from where he mailed the completed seven-language dictionary of several hundred entries by November 6th. If he did compile such a dictionary, and did not appropriate the work of the clergy and their students, as seems possible, this was, indeed, an incredible achievement, not to be duplicated by modern trained linguists.]

On the 17th [May 1807], I notified the Manager that I had entrusted the Spiritual Mission to the Worthy Father Herman:

17. Copy

Your Honor,
My Dear Sir!

I think that it will not be unknown to you, Your Honor, that it pained the Trustee and Organizer of the Russian-American Territories [Rezanov] very much to hear that, as he expressed it in his communication to me "depravity and violence have been permitted on Kad'iak" due to administration's laxness, and that he was being forced "to resort to strict measures to uproot such evil for ever." He also informed me with regret, deeming it to be almost improbable, that even among the clergy there arose personal dissatisfaction. Reliable rumors have reached him that Hierodeacon Nektarii did not accept my authority, and neither did Hieromonk Afanasii.

Anarchy is harmful wherever it occurs, and a Republic is in no way acceptable to His Imperial Majesty [VV: in any part of his domains]. As it is clear from the earlier in-

structions by Ioasaf, Bishop of Kadiak, Hieromonk Afanasii, who lacks any aptitude for leadership due to infirmity
of mind, as well as because of his limited literacy, was
made the responsibility of Hierodeacon Nektarii to the extent that he was even forbidden "to leave the Harbor or
even to go to the small islet [in the Harbor], except perhaps
for a walk in the woods, and no distant treks were even to
be contemplated; for disobedience and insolence he was to
be chastised variously, by prostrations, fasting, and so on
as was deemed fit; he was to be prevented from becoming
violent, but should it happen, as it had occurred before
frequently, he was to be chained and kept thus until, re-
penting his transgressions, he asked for pardon."

During my stay here, the justification for the above was
found in Hieromonk Afanasii's behavior, which was stub-
born, self-willed, unjustified, and insolent.

On the other hand, the late Bishop entrusted to Monk
Herman   the   care   of   the   entire   house,   estate
[imushchestvo], and the Mission's economy.   The rest of
the clergy were placed in his care also.   He was charged
to treat them according to his own judgement, decisively
reject any whims, and make dispositions in all matters put
before him according to his will, dictated by circumstances
which might arise.

For these reasons, I, too, departing from St. Petersburg,
and contemplating with especial respect the great merits
and rare qualities of mind and heart of this enlightened,
experienced, industrious, and most honorable elder, in
firm conviction that through his diligence, watchfulness,
and insight nothing will be omitted, entrust to his care,
with eagerness and utmost pleasure, the leadership of the
local Spiritual Mission and ask you, My Dear Sir, to please
address him in all that pertains to religious matters, and
assist him by all means at yours disposal to suppress any
and all indecencies that might occur.

I shall report this, my impartial choice, as is my duty,
to the Senior Member of the Holy Ruling Synod, Metropolitan and Cavalier, Amvrosii. Beyond that, I must sincerely admit to you, I am comforted and encouraged in this
choice by the fact that often I have heard from Your Honor
yourself great praise for this meek and gentle elder, filled
with humble wisdom, whom you named a man of experience, worthy of great honor, a man who has all his life
been praised for his labors for the benefit of the Fatherland. This praise is for him of greater importance than
any other.

With absolute respect,
I have the honor to remain, etc.
17th May 1807

18. SV of the letter from Gideon to Baranov presented above
under no. 18:

Your Honor
My Dear Sir!

You are aware that anarchy, anywhere, is harmful. You
also know that Hieromonk Afanasii, because of his lack
of aptitude for leadership, limited capacity, and limited literacy, has been made the responsibility of hierodeacon
Nektarii.   Father Herman, on the other hand, was entrusted with the care of the house, estate, the economy [of
the Mission], and maintenance of the clergy.

For this reason, I, too, departing from St. Petersburg,
and contemplating with special respect the great merits
and rare qualities of mind and heart of this enlightened,
experienced, industrious, and most honorable elder, in
firm conviction that through his diligence, watchfulness,
and insight nothing will be omitted, entrust, with eagerness and utmost pleasure, to his care the leadership of the
local Spiritual Mission.   And I ask you, My Dear Sir, to
please address him in all that pertains to religious matters, and assist him by all means at your disposal to suppress any and all indecencies that might occur.

I shall report this my impartial choice, as is my duty, to
the Senior Member of the Holy Ruling Synod, Metropolitan
and Cavalier, Amvrosii. Beyond that, I must sincerely admit to you, I am comforted and encouraged in this choice
by the fact that often I have heard from Your Honor yourself great praise for this meek and gentle elder, filled with
humble wisdom, whom you named a man of experience,
worthy of great honor, a man who has all his life been
praised for his labors for the benefit of the Fatherland.

This praise is for him of greater importance than any
other,

With sincere respect,
I remain etc.
17th May 1807

[The above letters, informing the Kodiak office of the
Russian-American Company about Gideon's appointment
of Father Herman as the Head of the Spiritual Mission

must be understood in the context of the fact that Herman
occupied the lowest rung on the monastic hierarchical
ladder. He was never consecrated as a celebrant, not even
as a deacon and, therefore, Hieromonk [a priest-monk]
Afanasii outranked him. Gideon, as did Ioasaf before him,
ordered Afanasii superceded. Hierodeacon Nektarii, an
able man, who also outranked Father Herman, had departed for metropolitan Russia in the fall of 1806, as is
evidenced by letters from Gideon to the Kodiak office
published in *Amerikanskii Pravoslavnyi Vestnik*
4:6:126-127 in 1900. These letters are given below:]

19. Draft

To the Russian-American Company, Kadiak office
In response to the request of the office submitted in
connection with the departure of Hierodeacon Nektarii for
Irkutsk, the Kad'iak Spiritual Mission informs that:

1)　the heavy burden of the school, specified in the said
request, is found to be light by Hieromonk Gideon;
2)　in the matter of the investigation going forward in the
said office about throwing Hierodeacon Nektarii out
of the window, no defense lawyer [*advokat*] is
necessary.[59]

4th day of August 1806, no. 9

[The editor of the *Amerikanskii Pravoslavnyi Vestnik* remarks that the document is in the hand of Hieromonk Gideon.]

20. To His Honor, Fleet Lieutenant Mr. Andreian Vasil'evich Mashin from the Kad'iak Spiritual Mission, communication.

On petition of Hierodeacon Nektarii, who because of
illness is not able to fulfill either churchly nor teaching
duties, the Spiritual Mission dismissed him to Irkutsk,
[placing him] under the authority of the local Bishop. The
Kad'iak office was duly notified about this and the Kad'iak
office responded in writing that it is not within its powers
to make any obstacles in this matter and that it yields
[jurisdiction] to the Mission.

For this reason, the Kad'iak Spiritual Mission requests
that you accept Hierodeacon Nektarii aboard your vessel.

As documentation copies of Hierodeacon Nektarii's petition and of the correspondence between the Spiritual Mission and the Kad'iak office, which you have inspected in originals, are enclosed.

No. 11, 7th August 1806

Cathedral Hieromonk of the Aleksander Nevskii Lavra, Gideon

[According to data published in *Pamiatnik Trudov Pravoslavnykh Blagovestnikov Russkikh s 1793 do 1863 goda*, published in Moscow in 1857, in a footnote to Veniaminov's *Sostoianie Pravoslavnoi Tserkvi v Rossiiskoi Amerike* (originally published in St. Petersburg in 1840) Hierodeacon Nektarii arrived safely in Irkutsk in the year 1806, later on was consecrated as a hieromonk, and died in 1814 in Kirenskii Monastery. However, according to a document in the Synodal archive, submitted by RAC, Nektarii died on the return journey on 11 December 1808 in the town of Mal'myr (Microfilm, Shur Collection).

At Gideon's departure the Mission consisted of Father Herman, Hieromonk Afanasii who remained on Kodiak until 1825, and Monk Ioasaf, who died on Kodiak in 1823 (p.203, note)].

[It seems appropriate at this point to include a letter from Gideon to the Kad'iak office, undated, but presumed to have been written prior to his departure on the basis of the rather authoritative tone of the letter which indicates that 1) the leak in the church was not fixed; and 2) that the plate and utensils in the Kodiak church were the gift of the Emperor Alexander I.   This   communication was published in *Amerikanskii Pravoslavnyi Vestnik* 4:6:127, in 1900 .

21. To the Kad'iak office of the Russian-American Company which is under the patronage of His Imperial Majesty, from the Dean of Clergy of all Russian settlements in America and Kamchatka, Cathederal Hieromonk of the Alexander Nevskii Lavra, Gideon, communication:

As the entire church, including the altar area itself, has enormous leaks, it is impossible to avoid damage to the vestry [and its contents]. It is therefore imperative to cover that part which contains the [vestry] but newly brought over here, the gift of His Imperial Majesty. If at all possible, the entire vestry area should be covered with

oil cloth or any other suitable material to insure its better
preservation.

On the 18th of May [1807] the Manager sent me the
provisions needed for my journey and on the 19th I addressed him about the following:

22. Your Honor,
     My Dear Sir!

In his correspondence with me, His Excellency [Rezanov]
has mentioned that when, in accordance with the August
Will of the Sovereign Emperor, he commenced the organization of the American territory, he needed to know the
number of inhabitants in each locality. But, as he himself
deigned to express it, "in the office on Kad'iak I [Rezanov]
found no reliable population census apart from the information collected in 1800." For this reason he has asked
me that the number of births, deaths, and marriages be
annually reported to the company's Kad'iak office. However, Your Honor is aware that the Spiritual Mission lacks
a clerk. Therefore, My Dear Sir, be so kind as to assist
through your office Hieromonk Afanasii in cases when
baptisms and marriages are to be registered.
     In respect to performance of marriages for those Rus-
sians who should express the wish to remain here permanently and will become local citizens, I shall issue
appropriate instructions to the Head of the American-
Kad'iak Clergy, His Worthiness Father Herman. As far as
deaths are concerned, it is absolutely impossible for the
Spiritual Mission to obtain such information.
With sincere respect, I have the honor to remain, etc.

23. Gideon to Baranov, marked "Copy":

Your Honor,
My Dear Sir!

By the will of His Imperial Majesty, as expressed in the
words of His Excellency [Rezanov], a common task has
been put upon both him and myself, and he had firm faith
in me as his collaborator therein. The [above consid-
erations] move me to remind Your Honor of the trend of
thoughts of the Trustee [and] Organizer of this region di-

rected toward the better implementation of the August Will.

The organization of this region engaged his [Rezanov's] spiritual and physical strength totally, to which I myself am witness, and many aspects of the task disconcerted him sometimes to the degree, that he could not find the means to cope. He deigned to disclose in one of his communications to me that [he felt] "the attitude of the Russians living here has up to now been based on premises incompatible with humanity." "Those of depraved minds," he continued in another communication, "go nowadays to America solely with the aim of growing rich, and then, upon their return, in a few days scatter like dust the riches obtained by many years of others people's tears. Can such desperate people respect their fellow human beings? They, being removed for ever from family life, have no good model to follow. Thus, the poor Americans become a sacrifice to their debauchery, [VV: to Russia's shame]. The promyshlennye are such people, that one may say that up to now their existence, for the most part, served only to harm the Fatherland as well as America."

For these reasons, His Excellency sincerely requested me in his absence to attract the minds of all to the three basic principles he had enunciated and which, in his opinion, will soon benefit this region:

1) agriculture,
2) enlightenment, and
3) increase of the population.

I, though named his collaborator and inspired by the same emotions, am bound to the love of humanity not only by the will of the humanitarian Monarch, but much more so by the law of the King of Kings in whom the powerful find truth, and thus I attempted to the limit of my powers to assist him [Rezanov] in carrying the heavy burden of this task.

His Excellency, however, did not forget, in one of his communications to me, to request all the Clerics who are here to join, in order to strengthen the labors expended for the common benefit, their ardent efforts in the achievement of these lofty aims. He did this again in person, especially at his departure for your [Baranov] Island, when he asked the Worthy Father Herman, in the name of the will of the Sovereign Emperor, to give special care to this region.

I have already had the honor to inform you, My Dear
Sir, that upon my departure, the affairs of the local Spiritual Mission will rest in the hands of this industrious
elder. Presently, I shall issue instructions to him, in accordance with the August will and the zealous care about
these regions on the part of the Trustee [and] Organizer
[Rezanov], relative to the above enumerated three basic
principles, the foundation of which was already established, even before the arrival of His Excellency here under the watchful guidance of Father Herman with the
desired success.

1)   In regard to agriculture, for several years exper-
      iments were conducted with various seeds on a vari-
      ety of soils [SV: and vegetable gardens were
      established with great success].
2)   In regard to enlightenment, His Excellency deemed it
      imperative to settle "at least several families who by
      the example of moral conduct and husbandry would
      soften the savagery of the inhabitants and thus const-
      itute the first step toward enlightenment." But Father
      Herman, as is his duty as a propagator of the faith
      among a folk of savage custom [v dikonravnom nar-
      ode], by means of kind treatment accustomed some of
      the Americans to industry, friendly contact, and hus-
      bandry and these were rewarded for their obedience
      to him [Fr. Herman] by the authorized person [Gi-
      deon].

      The Trustee and Organizer [Rezanov], observing
      all of the above with great and benevolent attention,
      deigned not only to appreciate such an unexpected
      beginning so well made in respect to the basic prin-
      ciples, but he even requested me to provide him with
      information about these experiments, their successes,
      and comments thereon in order to enable him to do
      justice to the outstanding efforts in agriculture on the
      part of the Fathers of the Spiritual Mission, and of
      their main leader in his report to His Imperial Majesty
      on this ever so necessary aspect of economy in Am-
      erica.

      The Russian-American School established by me
      here falls under the second basic principle. Your
      Honor is aware that it was formed upon my arrival on
      Kad'iak, on the 20th of March 1805 from the virtually
      defunct former Kad'iak school. By the 15th of August
      of the same year it grew to 50 students, and with this

complement I had the pleasure to demonstrate the fruits of the school's labors at a public examination held in the ardently appreciated presence of the Trustee-Organizer of the Russian American territories Nikolai Petrovich Rezanov [who arrived on Kodiak 28 July 1805] and other welcome guests: Senior Naval Officers, one anonymous clerical person [Gideon], and notables from among the citizens of Kad'iak.   Outstanding students, who distinguished themselves by their application, success in learning, and model behavior, were rewarded by the generous hand of His Excellency in person.

Soon after the departure of the Trustee-Organizer for the port of Novo-Arkhangel'sk on Your Honor's Island [Baranov Island], the school, including the section of practical agriculture, grew to 80 students from various tribes [*plemena*], and after your arrival on Kad'iak in 1806, due to your benevolent care for the poor orphans, imperceptibly it grew to 100 students, including even the Tlingit hostages, who have willingly embraced our Greco-Russian Orthodox faith on the 23rd of November of the same year 1806. The names of these Tlingit hostages are:

a)   Nikostrat L'kaina, 25 years of age;
b)   Niktopolion Tygike, 19;
c)   Nirs Shukka (Tukka?), 19;
d)   Narkis El'k, 18; and
e)   Kashkinat (Katkinat?), 17[60].

With the above mentioned number of pupils in the Russian-American School, I had the pleasant opportunity on the 21st of April 1807 to hold a second public examination in the presence of Your Honor [VV: in your capacity as) the first Trustee of the charitable institutions in America, and of your co-worker, Father Herman, as well as other clerics, foreign sea captains, and the notables of the newly constituted Civil Community of Kad'iak.

The noble sentiments about the improvement of this region which filled your soul when you observed the fruits that have been born were made evident to me through your generous communication of the 23rd of April and also through the noble reflection of your example in the action by the shareholder Mr. Vasilii Ivanovich Malakhov.

Presently (I am telling you frankly), the receipt of the news that some students of the Russian-American

School have already assumed the posts of teachers, will be sweet balm for the heart of the kind Trustee-Organizer [Rezanov]. [61]

Also, on special instructions of His Excellency, work has commenced under the guidance of the senior student Paramon Chumovitskii to collect a dictionary of the Aleut [Alutiiq] language. Moreover, a basis for a grammar of the same language has been laid. On Your Honor's advice, I am leaving this student [Chumovitskii] here, under special supervision by the Head of the Clergy, Father Herman.

I humbly request that you, My Dear Sir, do not separate him from the Russian-American School. Because of the shortage of food supplies here, he can, in the autumn, for common good, move with an entire detachment of students for the winter to the Alitat artel' [Alitatskaia], to his godfather and benefactor, the honorable baidarshchik Timofei Leont'evich Chumovitskii; in the spring, by 1st of May, he must present his detachment for public examination, and then continue his business at Pavlovskaia Harbor until the [next] fall. That is, he is to engage in correction of the dictionary and in translation at the discretion of the Head of the Spiritual Mission, Father Herman, of whatever the latter deems useful, depending on the circumstances.

The student of grammar, the minor Aleksei Kotel'nikov, remains here also, attached to the teacher Ivan Kad'iakskii [Ivan of Kodiak] and his associate Khristofor Prianishnikov. All of the last named have been commended by me to the direct supervision by the man whose piety is an ornament to him – Father Herman – so that they should be taught the fear of God as the basis of true wisdom.

3)   In respect to the 3rd principle, i.e. population increase, it is the will of the Trustee-Organizer [Rezanov], in accordance with the August will, that the clergy assist in this respect the Kad'iak office of the company by giving counsel how to better preserve the people.

In conclusion, I appeal to you most humbly, as to one who loves this land, to assist the Spiritual Superior, Father Herman, in implementing the enunciated basic principles, the first and the second as much as possible, and in respect to the third, to instruct all, entrusted with civil authority in your absence, in compliance with the will of the above named Reformer, not to reject the counsels of the clergy, with sincere respect,

I remain, etc.
26th May, 1807

24.   Your Honor
      My Dear Sir!

His Excellency, the ardent benefactor of this region, casting his benevolent gaze upon every detail, has deigned to write to me the following:

"Establishing order in all aspects in the [administration of] this region, one of my first obligations is to investigate the true condition of the Spiritual Mission in residence here and take firm measures to safeguard its Fathers from need." Bestowing many flattering [expressions of] praise upon their efforts, and continuing: 'with all due respect, doing full justice to their zealous successes, and stating my most sincere gratitude to their main leader,' he asked me to inform him about the yearly requirements for the maintenance of the clergy and for the beautification of the Temple of God, so as to enable him to institute measures which were at his disposal to satisfy these needs.

Upon receipt of my response, he assured me that the annual requirements for the [clergy's] maintenance will be met, upon their request, by the Manager of the Russian-American territories, and that the Kad'iak office of the company will be instructed accordingly. Therefore, I hereby humbly ask Your Honor to issue food, clothing, and other essentials required for domestic needs in accordance with the promise made by His Excellency to these men whom the Plenipotentiary himself called "those devout persons who, leaving behind them worldly

preoccupations, go forth in the name of the Lord to
enlighten and educate ignorant humanity."

In a certain hope of this, I should report, as is my duty,
to the Senior Member of the Holy Synod, Metropolitan and
Cavalier Amvrosii accordingly. [Omitted in SV: In respect
to beautification of the Temple of God, I responded to His
Excellency that the same depended on the efforts of benefactors and of those who love God. Absolutely necessary
for the church are: flour for communion bread, wine, incense, candles, and vegetable oil. But most important of
all, it is necessary to stop the leak in the church.]

With complete respect,
I have the honor to remain, etc.
27th May 1807

25. Your honor,
     My Dear Sir!

When I, with the help of the Almighty, shall return to St.
Petersburg,it will be my duty to report without fail to the
Senior Member of the Holy Ruling Synod, Metropolitan
and Cavalier Amvrosii, about the disastrous fate of His
Eminence Ioasaf, who formerly was in residence here [SV:
about the disastrous fate of the vessel aboard which was
His Eminence...] and also about the evidence thereof, such
as washed up parts of the vessel or other items: where,
how much, and specifics of what was found.
     Your Honor shall be so good as to provide me with this
information in detail.

For my part, I have the honor to remain,
with sincere respect, etc.
27th May 1807

In response to my last two communications, I received on
the 28th [May 1807] the following clarification from the
Manager, Mr. Baranov [VV: which I append here in original, in which His Honor mentioned the experiences and
wreckage washed ashore from the company vessel *Phoenix*, states that it will be his pleasure to support the clergy
in all their needs until the status of the Kad'iak Spiritual
Mission is officially determined, and, among other matters, asks me to rule if he is to issue the supplies only to
the Head of Mission, Father Herman, or to each person
separately.

26. [This letter is presented here after VV, which appears to be in Baranov's hand, while SV contains a copy in Gideon's hand]. To the Cathedral Hieromonk of the Alexander Nevskii Lavra, Father Gideon, lately attached to the Kad'iak Spiritual Mission from Manager Baranov:

My Benevolent Sir!

In response to your communication of the 27th of May I have the Honor to offer the [following] explanation:

1) Regarding the wreck of the company frigate *Phoenix* and the loss of His Eminence Ioasaf and his entire entourage, who were on board, and the vessel's crew:

The said vessel sailed from Okhotsk in the fall of 1799 directly for Kad'iak. It was sighted on the 28th of October of that year not far from Unalashka, off the Island of Umnak, by local Russians and Aleuts. To the present time no reliable intelligence has been obtained where exactly she was wrecked. As to the cause of this misfortune, it is surmised that the deadly epidemic which raged in Okhotsk at the time of the vessel's departure, manifesting itself in cough, bloody flux, and fever, may have been it. Many people died and it may be that among more than 70 promyshlennye who were sailing with this transport some were already infected and from them the disease spread to others. It is possible that the skipper, Collegiate Assessor Shilts [Shields] died of it. As there was no other [navigator] on board, the leaderless vessel may have been left to the mercy of unbridled action of the elements, of the seas and of the winds. However, when she was sighted off Unalashka, she was under sail in heavy weather and on course for Kad'iak.

The wreckage began to appear on Kad'iak and the adjacent areas toward the end of May (after wintering at Sitka, I returned to Kad'iak in this month) and beginning of June.

The wreckage consisted of the vessel's planks, beams, bowsprit, spars, and a capstan [*bramshpil'*]. On Tugidak there was washed ashore a birchbark *tuntai* [container] with butter. On Shuyak and Ugamak, as well as in other locations, even at Unalashka, were found wax candles, several empty flasks, and others filled with [spirituous] drinks mixed with saltwater. One such was also found near Cape St. Elias by members of the hunting party, while on Suklia [Montague] Island in Chugatskaia Guba [Prince William Sound] were found two large leathern book covers and a number of wax candles, of medium and small size. These, as all others which were found, were given to the local church. In that same year, 1800, in the fall, the rudder from this vessel was found near Sitka, and two masts in a bay on Rumiantsev Island, about 56° north latitude.

No other wreckage has been reported and no reliable information about the actual place where she was wrecked was ever obtained, except that one of the American skippers, Joseph O'Cain, heard from others [foreign skippers] that in Bucarelli Bay, otherwise Bobrovaia Bukhta [Sea Otter Bay], where Chirikov of the former Bering Expedition made a landfall, there was seen among the local savage peoples in the year 1801 clothing, whole and in bits and pieces, lined with fox fur, of a kind which these peoples neither have nor which is supplied by those intruders who trade with them. Therefore, it was surmised that this clothing was Russian. It is impossible to ascertain if this is true.

2) Regarding the maintenance of the clergy who remain with the Mission.

During the past sojourn of the Spiritual Mission here, nothing was refused, either company food supplies or the rest, in so far as there was surplus and circumstances permitted. In the future, I shall deem it my pleasure to support them in [satisfaction of] all their needs, if they have a shortage of something that the company has on hand.

Besides, the company is indebted to the Mission, as His Excellency [Rezanov] took 40 bags of rye flour, and also for various goods valued at a considerable sum received earlier [from the Mission] as a loan.

Though we have not even a pound of the first on hand, there is a sufficient quantity of rice [sarochinskoe psheno] and it is possible to replace the rye, pud for pud. Other goods, whatever is on hand, also will be issued [to the clergy] at their request without any hindrance.

In the meantime, we should await, as promised by His Excellency, final decision, [to be] made known by a new regulation, in respect to the status of the Spiritual Mission, regarding the size of their staff and other matters.

I, however, humbly beg you to decide if goods are to be issued at the request of the Superior, Father Herman only, or to each individually? Moreover, for the audits of the accounts of the clerk and the church elder [*starosta*], the office needs documentation [requisitions and receipts] from the Mission.

I remain with due respect,
a humble servant of
Your Worthiness Aleksandr Baranov.
No. 39
May 28th, 1807, Kad'iak I.

27. Your Honor,
    My Dear Sir!

You wish to know, in order to be able to check accounts of the church elder [*starosta*] and the store clerk [*prikazchik*], if goods for the clergy remaining here are to be issued solely on request of the Superior or to each person individually. I have the honor to state to you, briefly, that of course by all the rules of any hierarchy, all issues are to be made in the name of one person only, the [Mission's] Superior, Father Herman. If such rules of order are violated, the result is that of the proverb "if pulp is the boss, the head is pulp [*lyko za nachalo, a golova za mochalo*]."

With constant lifetime respect,
I have the honor to remain, etc.
29th (month omitted)
Pavlovskaia Harbor

On the 1st of June I entrusted Father Herman with the following:

28. Copy

Most Worthy Father Herman!

In accordance with the kind communication to me from His Honor Aleksandr Andreevich Baranov, dated 23rd of April of this year, I empower you to receive a sum of three hundred rubles designated for rewards of those pupils of the Russian-American School who have at the public examination on the 21st of the same month distinguished themselves by exemplary success in learning and model behavior and demonstrated considerable aptitude for teaching others.

The sum is to be distributed as follows: 90 rubles to Ivan Kad'iakskii [Ivan of Kad'iak], 90 rubles to Paramon Chumovitskii, 80 rubles to Khristofor Prianishnikov, and 40 rubles to Aleksei Kotel'nikov.

I have the honor to remain,
with sincere respect etc.
1st of June 1807

On the 11th [of June 1807] I issued the following instruction to the [Mission's] Superior, Father Herman:

29. [This letter, as published in Valaam differs substantively from SV and VV, as well as VC.]

Most Worthy Father Herman!

Setting out for St. Petersburg, I find it essential, in the course of my duty, to entrust to you the headship of the American-Kad'iak Spiritual Mission, and I have already so notified His Honor, Collegiate Assessor and Chief Manager of the local regions, Aleksandr Andreevich Baranov.

For the sake of better organization, I feel it to be my duty to express my thoughts to you in writing in addition to our verbal exchanges.

1) Rendering all due justice to your merits and expressing my appreciation of your zealous solicitude for the good of this region, I sustain myself with fond hope that you shall not cease by virtue of your wise counsel to instill in the hearts of Russians and Americans the rules for the true cognizance of God, love for the Fatherland [SV: rules for rendering reverence [homage] to God, and of Christian virtues – "love for the Fatherland" omitted] and friendly bond[s] between the two nations [plemena].

You know that it is the first duty of the clergy to exemplify the Christian ideal of sainthood by virtue of their own lives. I have no doubt that you will give them proper guidance in this respect. It is within Your Worthiness' responsibilities especially to see to itthat every one, whatever his appointed office may be, fulfills the same diligently, honestly and beneficially [blagougodno].

2) The entire church building is leaking greatly, of which the Kad'iak office has been notified by me earlier. It is your duty to insist that it be re-roofed.

The care of the vestry, church utensils and vessels and Divine Service books should be made the responsibility of either Hieromonk Afanasii or Monk Ioasaf, as you decide. Have a special care for the preservation of all of these.

3) Upon my arrival here from St. Petersburg I observed with pleasure your rare sense of moderation [frugality] and exemplary husbandry in the conduct of the [Mission's] economy, such as reliable ways to preserve [store] grain, for which even His Excellency expressed his appreciation when he was lent 40 bags [of rye flour) to support his sea voyage. Therefore, it is really superfluous for me to remind you to continue to take the same care as before of the economy, the remaining grain, and the rest of the estate. I am fully convinced that nothing pertaining to these matters which depends on your zeal will ever be omitted.

4) His Excellency [Rezanov] informed me that: "In the future, until the will of His Imperial Majesty is made manifest, no marriages are to be performed except for those [employees] who wish to remain here permanently. In such cases, written declarations are to be obtained from them, witnessed by the Manager, and three persons who have declared themselves permanent local citizens standing bond." Please continue to follow the procedure as already established by the local office.[62]

As far as providing the office with an annual population census, the records of births, marriages, and death [SV: for the Americans] is concerned, this is impossible not only because the company is dispersing people of both sexes, from their settlements, to the most distant countries without providing the Spiritual Mission with any information, but also because the Spiritual Mission has at its disposal only one Hieromonk[63] for whom it is impossible to go far from the church or the harbor. The people who remain at their settlements are under the jurisdiction of their baidarshchiks from whom the Mission also does not receive any information about births and deaths.

As the Spiritual Mission does not have a clerk [scribe, *pis'movoditel'*], you are to request the office's assistance should you need to register baptisms or marriages. I have already informed the local Manager accordingly.

5) Upon my arrival aboard the *Neva* in this untamed and remote region my feelings suffered a shock of terror when I first experienced the severity of the climate and the naked savagery of nature. But when I saw the fruits of your zealous labors, so ardently desired, the kindly treatment of the Americans, their success in agricultural enterprise and in domestic economy, an unexpected pleasure filled my spirit with sweet contentment. Even His Excellency, when he arrived, looking with similar pleasure upon your achievements in this untamed land, rewarded in your presence the Americans who have been attracted by your kindness for their obedience to you and their industry, in order further to motivate them.

Then he defined three basic principles which are to serve as the basis for further development of this region:

a) agriculture,
b) enlightenment [education],
c) population increase.

He asked me to turn the minds of all toward these ends, so as to benefit this land the sooner. Therefore, I, for my part, at my departure, remind you, the one who has already established here the beginnings of [the application of] these principles, to devote even greater attention to them. However, I find it superfluous to explain their details to you, as you have plenty of experience therein. You ought to receive assistance in these matters from the company. His Excellency issued appropriate instructions to the office and I myself have communicated about this with His Honor, Aleksandr Andreevich Baranov.

6) It is with very special pleasure that I entrust to Your Worthiness' care the Russian-American School which I have established.

[SV: In the first form the children should be taught reading, writing, and short catechism, in the second grammar, arithmetic, Sacred and civil history, and geography. Besides the sciences, do not forget the subjects relating to the economic sphere. Instead of recreation, instruct them in preparation of vegetable garden plots, how to sow and plant vegetables, collect needed herbs and roots, and how to fish.]

The order which has been established should be kept in the future also. I left my instructions with the School.   Ivan Kad'iakskii has been appointed the (head) teacher, Khristofor Prianishnikov as his Associate, and Aleksei Kotel'nikov as their assistant. Paramon Chumovitskii has been entrusted with the compilation of a dictionary of the Aleut [Alutiiq] language, with assistance of others and also with producing a short outline of its grammar. He also should serve as your interpreter.

Exercise due care and supervision of the detachment of students of agriculture. It is the duty of the company to provide the means therefore.

Above all, strive to fill the young hearts with the rules of the faith, fear of God, and or morals. Chastise their transgressions. Your love for all that is good leaves no room for doubt that you shall carry out all of the above in the best possible way.

7)   Your [Mission's] maintenance has been entrusted to the care of the local Manager, according to the assurance of His Excellency [of which you are aware]. For my part, I, too have petitioned him about it. For the sake of better maintenance of order, all requisitions should be made in your name only.

8)   [For this concluding admonition, Valaam 1894 has Fr. Gideon state merely: "Maintain peace and harmony among your brethren," but all three versions, SV, VV and VC have an additional passage. There are minor differences in wording between the three versions. VV text is followed here]

[VV: Above all, strive to preserve peace among the brethren.] I hope that monk Ioasaf, your spiritual son, will not despise your admonitions, but Hieromonk Afanasii, due to his infirm mind, obstinacy and wilfulness will prove a burden to you [SV: will, of course, be difficult for you as he was even under the former Bishop...] He was unbearably insolent to the former Bishop Ioasaf, and I found confirmation thereof during my stay here [SV: when he was frequently rude to the local authorities]. Therefore, I direct you, by authority of this instruction, to chastise him as you see fit should he be disobedient or insolent.

From the instruction left here by the [former] Head of Mission at his departure for Yakutat[64] it is evident that he [Afanasii] was then subordinated to Hierodeacon Nektarii and it was ordered that he be punished for violence not only by prostrations, fasting and other means as deemed necessary, but by keeping him on a chain until, mending his ways, he should ask forgiveness for his transgression. Should it come to such an extreme, I leave it up to you, being truly convinced that you, an experienced and skillful spiritual healer, will preserve due moderation in everything.

I, on my part, beseech and pray before the All High Giver of Gifts that he should send you strength and fortitude to do and act in accordance with His Benevolent Will.

Cathederal Hieromonk of the
Alexander Nevskii Lavra Gideon
June 11th, of the year 1807
On Kad'iak, Pavlovskaia Harbor

30. [This brief letter was published in *Amerikanskii Pravoslavnyi Vestnik* for September 1899, 17:469].

Most Worthy Father Herman!

My books which I am leaving here, I entrust to your care, as also all other items. I beg you to keep them safe until my return.

Cathedral Hieromonk of the
Alexander Nevskii Lavra Gideon
June 11th, 1807
Pavlovskaia Harbor

31. [This note, dated 18th [May 1807], was found in the papers of the late A. Dolgopolov (see "Introduction")].

Manager Baranov's order is that I be issued from the store for the journey a cask of two pud weight of groat flour [*krupchataia muka*], two pud of dried bread, also of groat flour, sugar in equivalent of two heads by weight, half a bucket of French vodka [brandy], two eighths measures of vinegar, and three pud of rice. Also a length of finished striped [one word unclear] ticking.

The casks for brandy and rum, and copper [one word unclear] are to be searched for and issued.

Aleksandr Baranov

32. [This brief but important document is also extracted from the A.A. Dolgopolov files. It is dated 20th (May 1807) and is suggestive of the presence of serfs in the early Russian

colony. It also gives us additional data on I. I. Banner, Baranov's deputy on Kodiak):

I was the witness when the landowner [*pomeshchik*], Guberniia Secretary, formerly *berggetvoren* [engineer?] of the Mining Service [*Gornaia sluzhba*], Ivan Ivanovich Banner issued the manumission letter to the widow Praskov'ia Sergeevna Efremov, together with her minor son Ivan and daughter Matrena.

My signature was appended to the same [Gideon, the document was also signed by Banner].

[Report, Gideon to Metropolitan Amvrosii, 1809, on the voyage to Kamchatka and Okhotsk, and the overland journey to Irkutsk.

The material presented in the following section appears as part of Gideon's official report to Metropolitan Amvrosii, submitted in 1809, the SV.   As stated in the "Introduction," this portion of his report has never been published and is not contained in the VV or VC. The account commences with a description of Gideon's departure from Kodiak on 11th (23rd) June 1807, microfilm copy of SV: Folio 70].

That same day [11th June 1807], approaching 5 o'clock in the afternoon we sailed out of Pavlovskaia harbor.

Mr. Chief Manager [Baranov] and the Spiritual Fathers escorted me to Lesnoi [Woody] Island, while his assistant, the Gubernia Secretary Banner, accompanied me aboard the *Sitkha* to Unalashka. Our departure was not a fortunate one. Contrary wind accompanied by fog and rain arose and kept us in the vicinity of Kad'iak until the 17th. On that date, about 5 o'clock in the afternoon, Kad'iak disappeared from sight. On the 23rd and the 24th we suffered a severe [*zhestokii*] storm.

On the 29th, we sighted Unalashka and just after 6 o'clock in the afternoon dropped anchor in Barboskaia Bay [modern Constantine Bay?]. From there the next day we went on foot to the Aleut settlement called Imagnia [at modern Summer's Bay, Morris Cove]. The way was unpleasant because of uneven and pathless terrain.

From Imagnia I went by baidara to the settlement of Soglasie [Accord, also Good Accord, the modern town of Unalaska] where is located the main establishment of the Russian-American Company.

During my one week stay here, besides the appropriate instruction [teachings] which I offered, I annointed with Holy Myrrh [chrizmated] children of both sexes, of whom 91 were males and 50 females, united in marriage five Russian and 35 Aleut couples.[65]

The inhabitants of the Unalashka Island, as well as of the entire Aleutian Chain, are strongly devoted to the faith. They know and reverently observe all major Feasts, lovingly and very willingly listen to the teachings offered, and follow these in real life. They are very intelligent, diligent, gentle, industrious, and honest. Their yurtas are cleaner and better appointed than those on Kad'iak. Some keep their own vegetable gardens in which only potatoes and turnips are grown.

On the Island of Umnak, through the efforts of the literate toion Ivan Glotov, a chapel has been built which is dedicated to the Church Teacher [*Sviatitel'*] Nikolai [St. Nicholas]. He himself conducts there morning prayer services and the Hours on Sundays and Feastdays. This chapel has been supplied by the Unalashka office with the necessary books and other needs in respect to beautification (blagolepie)[66] .

We left Unalashka on the 7th of July [1807]. In the course of the [following] three weeks, sailing under adverse winds, we passed the Fox, Andreianov, and Rat Islands and were approaching the Near Islands so called. On the 14th of August we sighted the Land Kamchatka. On the 21st we had already entered the 1st Kurile Strait (when) toward evening a severe storm from the southeast arose and drove our vessel almost to the very shore. Providence alone saved us. Following this [occurrence], we tacked against the head wind in the vicinity of the 1st Kurile Strait, trying to pass it. However, lateness of the season, shortage of provisions, water, and firewood, as well as the continuing contrary winds forced us to turn toward Kamchatka heading for the Petropavlovskaia Harbor (Petropavlovsk).

On the 4th of September, due to a mistake by a promyshlennoi, we sailed past it [Petropavlovsk]. In the evening it became calm. At that time we were just a short distance from shore. Being apprehensive of being driven on shore by the current and the chop, we stood off on drag anchor [*drek*]. In the morning the wind suddenly grew strong. We were unable to hoist the drag anchor and had to cut it off. Thus, while we escaped one danger, a greater one awaited us. The sky darkened, a thick fog hid from

our eyes not only the mountaintops, but even the shore itself. The strong wind continued to press us toward the
land. We had no prospect of safety. The fearless spirit of
our navigator, the Englishman Barber,[67] who had spent his
life since his earliest youth ceaselessly at sea, began to
flag. Throughout the entire day our *Sitkha* fought the
waves. Luckily, in a break in the thick fog we saw a small
bay [cove] and sailed for it, passing between steep cliffs
and sharp offshore rocks, at six sazhen depth. Everyone's
heart beat at this moment. The ground was not secure, the
depth drew less. The severe wind was turning into a
frightful storm. What was there to do? We dropped anchor, lowered the topmasts [*sten'gi*] and waited through
the entire night for death.

On the 6th, with sunrise, a ray of hope pierced our exhausted souls. The wind began to abate and by noon
dropped completely. On the 7th, we left the above mentioned cove and commenced our course for Petropavlovsk,
where we dropped anchor on the 12th, at 6 o'clock in the
afternoon.

On the 23rd of October I dispatched to the Governor of the
Kamchatka Region the following memorandum:

Copy

Your Excellency,
Benevolent Sir!

When I was leaving St. Petersburg with the circumnavigating expedition, His Eminence Metropolitan Amvrosii,
member of the Holy Synod, instructed me, among other
matters, to inspect the Kamchatka churches and clergy.
For this purpose, I intend to set out by land first for
Nizhne- Kamchatsk and then to other localities, as it will
be possible to do so. With all due respect owed your person, I am addressing to you my humble request to provide
me on this journey with all assistance within your authority.
    I leave it for the future to personally present myself to
Your Excellency,
                                With sincere respect,
                    I have the honor to remain etc.

In response, I received on the 12th of December from His
Excellency the following reply:

Copy

Most Holy Father Gideon!

In response to your memorandum addressed to me of 23rd
October last, which gladdened my heart and my soul, I
made all [necessary] dispositions to ensure your safe arrival here. I await with impatience the pleasure of re-
ceiving personally through you Holy Blessings.

With extreme feeling, I have the honor to be
Your Worthiness' diligent servant
Ivan Petrovskii
Nizhne-Kamchatsk, 17th November 1807

On the 30th January 1808 I departed from the Petropavlovsk on a trek around Kamchatka by a sled to which were
harnessed 12 dogs. I was accompanied to Nizhne-Kamchatsk by the Russian-American Company agent [kom-
missioner], the Irkutsk merchant Petr Il'ich Miasnikov.
Out of Nizhne-Kamchatsk I was accompanied by the commander of the local battalion, Lt. Colonel Semen Iakovle-
vich Sibiriakov and by protoierei [archpriest] Nikifor
Nikiforov. My inspection tour lasted about two months.

In the whole of the Kamchatka region there are eight
churches. Two of them are in the city of Nizhne-Kamchatsk.

1) The Church of the Dormition of the Holy Theotokos,
    founded in the year 1793, consecrated 12th November
    1796. It is 10 sazhen 2 arshin long, 9 arshin and 10
    vershok wide, and 7¼ arshin high. It is sturdy and
    warm, hence the Divine services are held there only
    in winter.
2) [Church] of the Church Teacher and Miracleworker
    Nikolai [St. Nicholas]. founded in 1759, consecrated
    22d May 1761 7 sazhen 2 verkh [vershok] long, 3 sa-
    zhen 12 verkh wide, and 4 arshin and 13 verkh high.
    It is dilapdated, but it is safe to conduct the Divine
    services there.
    Both churches are supplied with all that is neces-
    sary for well-appointed appearance and conduct of
    services [blagolepie]: 26 priestly vestments [rizy], 12
    cassocks [albs, podrizniki], 16 sticharions, 13 priestly
    stoles [epatrachileon], four thigh shields [nabedren-
    niki], five zones [priestly belts, poiasa], six deacon's
    stoles [orarion], 12 cuffs [maniples, poruchi], eight

chalice covers [veils, *vozdukhi*]. There are sufficient books, and the church treasury is 628 rubles 14 kopeks.

3) The third church, of the Dormition of the Holy Theotokos, is in Bol'sheretsk ostrog. It is of wood, founded in the year 1783, consecrated 2nd January 1784. It is 6½ arshin high, 10 arshin wide, 9 sazhen in length. It is dilapidated and it is very dangerous to hold services therein. A new one, to replace it, is under construction. Appurtenances [*blagolepie*] are sufficient. The vessels are of silver, with gold trim. There are 16 rich priestly vestments, four cassocks, seven sticharions, seven stoles, 12 pairs of chalice covers, 12 icon stand covers [*peleny*], 10 pairs of cuffs, three belts, five deacon's stoles, two curtains, a sufficient number of books. The church treasury is 966 rubles 38 kopeks

4) The fourth church, of the Lord's Ascension, is in the Verkhnekamchatskii ostrog, of wood, founded in the year 1747, consecrated in 1748. Since August 1805 no Divine services have been held there because of its dilapidated condition. Icons and books are also old. There are 12 priestly vestments, four cassocks, three stoles, four pairs of cuffs, 27 covers for icon stands, 13 chalice covers, seven pairs of table covers [*pokrovtsy*], and two curtains. Church treasury is 702 rubles.

5) The fifth church, of the Nativity of the Holy Theotokos, is in Petropavlovsk, built and consecrated Setpember 1, 1748 on Paratunskii Island. To replace it, a new one, in the Harbor itself, is being finished nowadays. Appurtenances are few: six priestly vestments, two cassocks, two belts, two stoles, four pairs of cuffs, six chalice covers. There are very few books. Church moneys are 714 rubles, by the record [*po raspiske*] 545 rubles 21 kopeks.

6) The sixth church, in the Tigil'skaia fort [*krepost'*], of the Nativity of Christ, was founded in 1764, consecrated on the 12th day of February 1766. It is safe to hold Divine services there. Appurtenances are sufficient: two silver vessels with gold trim, 20 priestly robes, eight cassocks, 15 stoles, four belts, 18 cuffs, five sticharions, 11 icon stand covers [*peleny*] Church moneys are 514 rubles 11 kopeiki.

7) The seventh, of the Life-creating Trinity, in the Kliuchevskoe settlement, was founded in 1783, consec-

rated 2nd October 1784. It is possible to conduct
Divine services there. There are 11 vestments, four
cassocks, six stoles, 12 cuffs, three belts, seven chalice covers, two pairs of table covers [*pokrova*] three
(one word unreadable] icon stand covers [*peleny*], 16
covers with Holy Icons thereon, a sufficiency of
books. Church moneys are 285 rubles 47 kopeiki.

8) The eighth church, in the Ichinskii ostrog [Ishiga or
Gizhiga?], of the Lord's Ascension, was founded in
1800, consecrated on 30th December 1801. It is 8 sazhen 7 arshin and 10 verkh long, 7 arshin and 10
verkh wide, and 5 arshin and 2½ verkh high, and
rather well beautified. There are expensive vessels,
11 priestly vestments, four cassocks, six stoles, three
belts, seven cuffs, four chalice covers, five icon stand
covers, four covers for the Holy Icons. Church moneys are 991 r[ubles] and 73 k[opeiki].

All celebrants and church servitors are skilled [*iskussni*] in
their knowledge of their duties. Their behavior is decent. Because of the high cost of living locally, their substance and
supplies are not much; they derive their subsistence from putting up fish and, to a very small extent, from cattlekeeping.

The Kamchadals are very well disposed toward the church,
but because of the immense distances between their settlement
and the churches, and because they are constantly employed in
their own pursuits [*promysly*], they seldom come to church.
The priests perform the services they request [*treby*] for the
most part in winter, as in summer transport by means of the
baty (wooden native boats) along the rivers is very difficult.

On the 28th of June I boarded the vessel *Mariia* which is
owned by the Russian-American Company. On the 30th [June
1808], at 2 o'clock in the afternoon we weighed anchor and
sailed out of Avacha Bay. Unfortunately, as we were leaving
the bay, a sailor fell overboard and drowned. Our voyage
lasted two weeks and was safe. On the 15th of July we weath-
ered a storm. On the 19th, our vessel was guided [piloted] into
the Ohkota River.

Because of the rainy season, I remained in Okhotsk until the
17th of August. On that date, I left Okhotsk. I travelled to Iakutsk on horseback, accompanied by two Iakut guides. The
trek was very bothersome and difficult because of many
mountains, thick forest, frequent swamps, and rivers.

I reached Iakutsk on the 20th of September and took up
quarters in the house of the Russian-American Company. I
frequently visited the Iakutsk monastery. All buildings there

are very dilapidated, the Superior [*nastoiatel'*] himself lives in
rooms that are not roofed. The Iakutsk seminary [*dukhovnaia
shkola*] lacks supervision, students are few, and therefore,
successes are also few, as can be seen from the appended report [not present in the available microfilm copy of Gideon's
papers from the Synod file]. In the years 1801, 1802, 1803, and
1804 the school was in better shape and was better organized.

I stayed in this city two months and nine days, awaiting a
fair winter trail along the river Lena. On the 26th of November
I left it, traveling by post horses. Without stopping anywhere
en route, on the 23rd of December I arrived at Irkutsk.

[Here], after Archimandrite Apollon became the Superior of
the Ascension Monastery in the year 1807, the following measures were introduced: Commensality [*obshchaia trapeza*],
while before...[illegible, meaning unclear; the illegible passage
is followed by an unnumbered folio and it is not clear if it is in
order, or one or more folios are missing]...remains, so then 300
rubles annually are realized from fishing; also from fishing,
500 rubles annually have been bespoken for the reorganization
of the monastery. Two churches have been painted with fres-
coes, and this did not cost the monastery a single kopek.

As a decent vestry was lacking, 24 priestly vestments were
made, by subscription, of the richest brocade, also 12 sticharions, and eight cassocks. Five *rizas* [icon covers] of silver,
gilded, were made for the local icons and ten gilded *kioty* [icon
cases]. A kitchen with an adjoining apartment, of stone, has
been built. It includes storerooms and cellars [*pogreby* root and
ice cellars].

It has been whitewashed, both inside and outside, and
equipped with decent furnishings. A bell tower clock with
music [minuet] "Who strongly hopes in God" [*Kto krepko na
Boga upovaet*] has been constructed.

A military watch has been requested for the monastery and
granted. Finally, during my visit to the Archimandrite on the
27th of December, he managed to persuade the merchant-be-
nefactor Chupalov to [agree to] construct new stone living
quarters for the monks.

I append the register of the vestry and books of the Kad'iak
church, the inventory of the Kamchatka churches, church register for the Kamchatka clergy and the church register for the
Iakutsk seminary [not present in the available microfilm copy
of Gideon's papers from the Synod file].

I have the happiness to render the report to your Most High
Eminence, with the greatest respect.

Appendix I

Initiation of the Voyage
Proposal
To the Holy Ruling Synod

The Cathederal Hieromonk of the Alexander Nevskii Lavra Gideon who participated in the circumnavigating sea voyage submitted to me, in accordance with instructions I issued to him at his departure, an historical account as well as an account of his activities and achievements while on Kad'iak and on the return journey.

I present the same in the original, together with other pertinent papers, to the Ruling Synod for study and request that the Synod pay its benevolent attention to his efforts [made] on behalf of the Church and of the Fatherland.

Amvrosii,
Metropolitan of Novgorod,
St. Petersburg, Estland and Finland
#86 8th day of May 1809

[The above document is translated from the microfilm copy of the original in the Synod file, Shur collection, Rasmuson Library. It is suggestive in the sense that Gideon's report as it appears in the SV may have undergone editing by Amvrosii. Below, the covering letter by Gideon and the copy of instructions which he received from Amvrosii prior to his departure for Alaska in 1803 are presented in translation from the microfilm copy of the documents in the Synod file, Shur collection, Rasmuson Library.]

To the Member of the Holy Ruling Synod His Eminence Amvrosii, Metropolitan of Novgorod, St. Petersburg, Estland, and Finland, Archimandrite of the Alexander Nevskii Lavra, and Cavalier of various Orders.

Report
by the Cathederal Hieromonk of the Alexander Nevskii Lavra
Gideon

On the wish of His Imperial Majesty, and with the blessing of Your Eminence, it was my flattering lot to be assigned on the 19th day of May 1803 to serve with the [expedition] on the voyage around the world.

On the 14th of June, at my departure from Kronstadt, I had
the honor to receive from Your Eminence's archpastoral hand
a certificate [of the award of a pectoral cross, see below] and
[your] instruction of the following content:

Copy

* * *

Certificate

Issued to the Cathedral Hieromonk of the Alexander Nevskii
Lavra Gideon to certify that His Imperial Majesty, in recognition of his willingness to serve with the departing circumnavigating expedition which sails for the Russian establishments
in America has awarded him a pectoral cross on a chain.
   This cross, inscribed by the Synod, was put upon his person
in this year 1803, on the 24th day of June.

Amvrosii, Metropolitan

* * *

Instruction

Issued to the Cathedral Hieromonk of the Alexander Nevskii
Lavra Gideon, who is departing with the circumnavigating expedition for the Russian American settlements.

1.   While aboard ship and in harbor, celebrate whenever pos-
     sible Divine services, and at all times conduct yourself
     with the dignity appropriate to a Christian pastor.

2.   Begin to keep a record book, in which you are to enter en
     route whatsoever may be worthy of notice, noting all per-
     taining to celebration of Divine services and participation
     therein. Specifically, while in Kamchatka you are to in-
     vestigate if the local clergy understand their duties,
     whether they conduct their lives in respect to morality and
     husbandry [economy], if they are diligent in teaching the
     Christians, and whether the Christians are favorably dis-
     posed toward performance of their Christian and civil
     obligations. What is the condition of the churches there
     and how are they frequented?

3.   Upon reaching the American settlements, you are to act
     as the Dean of Clergy [blagochinnyi] and, paying attention
     to the copy of descriptions which have been previously

submitted here [reference is in all probability to reports and descriptions submitted to the Synod by Ioasaf in 1795-1796 and by Makarii in 1796] you are to learn in detail from the local clergy or others about performance of the Divine services, also about the teaching of literacy and God's Law and other subjects, and then while on Kad'iak you are to investigate everything that pertains to Christianity, specifically: do they have enough books, Church books, educational and instructional [of moral content] ones? How were [the people] taught about the faith and the Law, and what is the level of their understanding?

Following this, offer support and supplement and correct whatever needs it, do so with the utmost care and caution, so that nothing is taught which may be superfluous and nothing is omitted which needs to be taught in respect to faith and civil virtues.

All that you find and all that you do there is to be described in the aforesaid record book.

4.   You are to remind the teachers that they are not only to teach the Law of God but live it, thus encouraging others to follow their example.

5.   Lastly, you are to compile a report about all that you will discover there which pertains to Spiritual matters and all that you correct. This report is to be handed over, if special circumstances demand it, to the Expedition's Commander who will deliver it to the Holy Synod; otherwise, you are to deliver such a report yourself upon your return to St. Petersburg.

6.   Do not under any circumstances interfere in worldly matters.

Amvrosii, Metropolitan of Novgorod.

* * *

Appendix II

Record of baptisms, chrizmations, marriages, and confessions heard by Gideon while at Unalaska July 1-6 (July 12-18), Alaska Church Collection, Box D-11, Manuscript Division, Library of Congress, Washington, D.C.

"Received 6 July 1807 under the no. 174"
To the Unalashka office of the Russian-American Company

Records of chrizmation of children and persons of other ages, on marriages performed, and how many were admitted to confession during my sojourn here are appended.

Cathedral Hieromonk of the Alexander Nevskii Lavra
Gideon
In the year 1807
6th day of July
Settlement of Soglasiia
[Good Accord, Illiuliuk, later Unalaska]
on the Island of Unalashka.

* * *

Register

of children born to the Russian promyshlennye and to the Americans in the settlement of the Russian-American Company of Accord [sic] and [to the Americans] from other settlements and islands who were chrizmated 5th July 1807.

No. Children born to Russian promyshlennye
in the Accord settlement

M	F		(age)
1		Aleksei Zyrianov	3
2		Ivan Sorokovin	3
3		Filip Iachenianin [?]	2
4		Vasilii Butorin	3
5		Iov Sukin	4
6		Fedor, son of Fedor Stepanov	10
	1	Fekla, wife of the above	30
	2	Elena, their daughter	6
	3	Mariia, wife of Egor Netsvetov	25
7		Iakov, their son	5
8		Osip (Iosif), their son also	1
9		Iakov Argunov	3
10		Pavel Kozhevnikov	5
11		Egor Burenin, foster son of Manager Burenin	9mo

by Americans in the Accord Settlement

M	F		(age)
	4	Irina, daughter of toion Ivan Kuznetsov	6
12		Ivan, son of the zakazchik Daniil Galanin	1
13		Mikhailo [Mikhail], same as above	6
14		Semeon, son of Stepan Sutagin	8
	5	Nastasiia, daughter of Mikhail Khramov	4
	6	Irina, same as above	1

Children of Iul'ian Shelikhov:

M	F		(age)
15		Prokopii, his son	2
	7	Onis'ia [sic, Anisiia], his daughter	7
	8	Evdokiia, his daughter	9
16		Ivan, son of Ivan Sapozhnikov	7
17		Matvei, son of Abram Bel'kov	8
18		Mikhailo, son of the late Aleksei Achkanik	4
	9	Anna, his daughter	1
19		Konstantin, son of widow Evdokiia [Shein? illegible]	2
10		Evdokiia, her daughter	5
20		Andrei, foster son of Ivan Achkanin	7

11	Akulina, daughter of Timofei Zelemchenov [?]	4
21	Elisei, son of the late Grigorii [D?]ol'gin	4
12	Feodora, daughter of Ivan Serebrianikov	3
13	Paraskov'ia, daughter of Ivan Prianishnikov	4
14	Elena, daughter of Egor Shaiashnikov	5

[The last entry is not numbered in original]

From the Settlement Pestriakovskoe [Eider Point] on the Island of Unalashka

| 22 | Stepan, son of Dementii Polutov | 1 |
| 23 | Nikifor, son of Mikhailo Kochutin | 2 |

From the settlement Natyka [var. Natyki, modern Natikin Bay]

24		Ivan, foster son of the toion Andrei Shudrov	7
	14[sic]	Evdokiia, his foster daughter	2
25		Mitrofan, son of Nikita Zakharov	7
	15[sic]	Agrafena, foster daughter of Egor Pankov	7
26		Timofei, son of Nikita Pankov	
		Anis'ia, daughter of same	1

[The above entry, female -16- is not numbered, subsequent numbering continues with this error]

| 27 | Boris, son of Koz'ma Kondrat'ev | 6 |

From the settlement Imagnia [Morris Cove in Summer Bay]

28		Iakov, foster son of the toion Abram Svin'in	6
29		Prokopii, son of Boris Pankov	2
	16[sic]	Marfa, his foster daughter	3
30		Eremii, son of Foma Dolmennikov [?]	3
31		Osif[sic], son of Vasilii Kamchadalov	4
	17[sic]	Evdokiia, his fosterling	2
32		Stepan, son of Daniil Makar'in	4
33		Nikolai, son of Ivan Lukanin	6
	18[sic]	Evdokiia, daughter of Egor Markov	5
34		Kirill, son of the widow Mariia Krivoshein	7
	19[sic]	Irina, her daughter	2

From the settlement Borkinskoe [Biorka]
on the Island of the same name

35		Ivan, son of Luka Pankov[sic]	5
	20[sic]	Palagiia[sic], foster daughter	
		of Andrei Mel'nikov	8

From the settlement Veselovskoe [Reese Bay]
on the Island of Unalashka

| 36 | Gavrilo, son of Iakov Vasil'ev | 1 |

From the settlement Makushinskoe [Volcano Bay]

37		Ivan, son of Lavrentii Kondrat'ev	6
	21	[error, ought to be male 38]	
		Mikhailo, son of Ivan Krivoshein	7
	22[sic]	Nadezhda, wife of Nikita Galanin	30

From the settlement Chernovskoe Children of Petr
Mukhoplev:

38[sic]		Petr, his son	1
39[sic]		Fedor, same	5
40[sic]		Ivan, son of the late Antipin	3
	23[sic]	Matrena, his daughter	1

From the settlement Tanamykhta [Konets Head]

| 41 | Petr, son of Aleksei Pankov | 4 |
| 42 | Ivan, son of Ivan Burchevskoi | 1 |

From the Akutan Island, settlement Basinskoe [?]
The children of Ivan Miasnikh:

| 43 | Mikhailo, his son | 7 |
| 44 | Konstantin, same | 6 |

From Veselovskoe settlement, Unalashka Island

| – | Pavel, son of Iakov Vasil'ev | 6 |

Akun Island, Artel'noe settlement [Chulkax]
Children of the late Lestenkov [?]

45	Foma, his son	4
24[sic]	Natal'ia[sic], his daughter	7
46	Lavrentii, son of the late Lavrent'ev	6

From the settlement Sukhovskoe [Akun Island]

47	Karp, son of Aleksei Stepanov	7
25[sic]	Evdokia, his daughter	8
26[sic]	Matrena, the same	1

From the settlement Uskhinatskoe [Usxinax?]
The children of Sila Makar'in:

48	Lev, his son	2
27[sic]	Evdokiia, his daughter	3

From the settlement Artel'noe [Chulkas, see above]

28[sic]	Pelagiia, daughter of Grigorii Sapozhnikov	7
29[sic]	Anna, the same	6
30[sic]	Matrena, daughter of the widow Elizaveta	5

From the Island of Umnak, settlement Tulik Children of Vasilii Merkul'ev:

49	[sic] Agei [?Agnii?], his son	3
31[sic]	Katerina, his daughter	5

From Tigalda Island, settlement of the same name

50	Andrei, son of the widow Nastas'ia	$\frac{1}{2}$

From the settlement Derbenskoe [on the same island]
Children of Koz'ma Dolmatov:

51	Ivan, his son	8
32[sic]	Mar'ia, his daughter	5

From the Island of Unimak, settlement Pogromnoe

33[sic]   Agrafena, daughter of Petr Toporov

From the settlement Shishalda [Shishaldin, Unimak Island] Children of Luka Burenin:

34	Faiana [Faina?], his daughter	1
35[sic]	Palageiia, the same	3
–	Iakov, son of Ivan Savel'ev	2

From the Island of Atkha, in the Andreianov Chain

36[sic]	Widow Marfa – [one letter illegible]	30
52[sic]	Vladimir Gromov	10
53[sic]	Egor Arkasheev	45

School students of minor age, in the Accord harbor

54	Mark Mordvin
55	Karp Lotoshnikov
56	Maksim Lanin
57	Fedor Lanin
58	Ivan Borodin
59	Ivan Oborin, the elder
60	Ivan Oborin, the younger
61	Osip Volkov
62	Grigorii Petukhov
63	Petr Sakhlatov [?]
64	Ivan Olenin
65	Egor Zharov
66	Stepan Burenin
67	Luka Vikulov
68	Roman Fomin
69	Ivan Iaranskoi
70	Vasilii Proshev
71	Dmitrii Kondrat'ev
72	Vasilii Sinitsyn
73	Stepan Govorushin
74	Koz'ma Bakhov
75	Andrei Bakhov
76	Elisei Bakhov
77	Elisei Dolmatov
78	Danilo Proshev

79		Koz'ma Ustiugov
80		Matvei Sorokin
81		Egor Kurmin
82		Maksim the Second [Vtoroi]
83		Zakhar Basinskoi
84		Semeon Gladyshev
85		Ivan Petukhov
	37	Aleksandra Krivdin
	38	Dar'ia Mordvin
	39	Dar'ia Mordvin (the two are sisters)
	40	Nastas'ia Petukhov
	41	Avdot'ia Ustiugov
	42	Varvara Zharov
	43	Palageia Verkhovinukov
	44	Mar'ia Proshev
	45	Anna Proshev
	46	Anna Bobova
	47	Paraskov'ia Kolesov
	48	Natal'ia Kudrin
	49	Katerina Borodin
	50	Irina Dolmatov
	51	Dar'ia Beloglazova

[Gideon's numeration is in error, as he himself realized: on the original, there is an attempt to correct the mistake. Actual number of those chrizmated was 88 males, 52 females, a total of 140 persons].

Register

Of marriage entered into by Russian promyshlennye and by Americans of the various settlements in the islands on the 5th [corrected to 4th] of July of the year 1807, at the settlement of Accord of the Russian-American Company, Unalashka office:

No		Russian promyshlennye:	Age Male/Female
1		Fedor Stepanov, peasant of Vladimir district [uprava]	5
	1	[His] wife Fekla, of Atkha Island in the Andreianov Chain	28
2		Egor Netsvetov, teamster of Tobol'sk	34

2		[His] wife Mar'ia of Atkha Island in the Andreianov Chain	20
3		Vasilii Lazarev, burgher of the City of Irkutsk	30
	3	[His] wife Nastasiia of the Shishalda settlement on Unimak Island	–
4		Ivan Arkhimandritov, teamster of the City of Tiumen'	25
	4	[His] wife Natal'ia, of Chernovskii settlement on the Island of Unalashka	18
5		Gerasim Kozulin, peasant of Irkutsk government district	26
	5	[His] wife of settlement [illegible], Akutan island	19

Americans

In the Accord settlement:

1		Dimitrii Shaeshnikov [Shaiashnikov]	30
	1	Wife, Evdokiia	25
2		Ivan Lukanin	30
	2	Wife, Agrafena of Chernovskoe settlement	35
3		Ivan Sapozhnikov	40
	3	Wife, Anna	35
4		Tikhon Bakulin [sic, Vakulin]	40
	4	Wife, Malan'ia	40
5		Mikhailo Bel'kov	25
	5	Wife, Katerina	20
6		Ivan Paranchin	35
	6	Wife, Matrena	18
7		Mikhailo Khramov	35
	7	Wife, Evdokiia of Koshiginskoe settlement	25
8		Vasilii Bel'kov	40
	8	Wife, Matrena of the Avatanakskoe settlement of Goloi Island	20

Of Imagnitskoe [Morris Cove] settlement, Unalashka Island:

9		Ivan Lukanin	30
	9	Wife, Melan'ia	30
10		Foma Dolmatov	30
	10	Wife, Matrena	25
11		Vasilii Svin'in	20

11	Wife, Mar'ia	25

Of Accord settlement, Unalashka:

12	Vasilii Shelikhov	40
12	Wife, Katerina	40

Of Kalekhtinskoe settlement [Kalextax]:

13	Nikita Iachmenev	30
13	Wife, Matrena Makar'in of Sukhovskoe settlement [Akin Island]	25

Of Bobrovskoe settlement [Beaver (Sea Otter) Bay]:

14	Marko Shelikhov	25
14	Wife, Tat'iana	30

Of Borka [sic] Island, settlement of the same name:

15	Andrei Borkinskoi [Andrew of Borka, Biorka Island]	25
15	Wife, Iul'iana of Avatanak settlement	20

Of Natykinskoe settlement, Unalashka Island:

16	Zakhar Shudrov	20
16	Wife, Feodosiia, of the same settlement	20
17	Nikita Pankov	25
17	Wife, Irina, of the same settlement	20
18	Ivan Polutov	26
18	Wife, Katerina of Basinskoe settlement, Akutan Island	20

Of Veselovskoe settlement, Unalashka Island:

19	Iakov Vasil'ev	25
19	Wife, Anna	20
20	Ippolit Kochutin	20
20	Wife, Faina [?]	18
21	Grigorii Izmailov	27
21	Wife, Matrena of Artel'noe settlement [Akun Island]	16

Of Makushinskoe settlement [Volcano Bay], Unalashka Island:

| 22 | | Nikita Makushinskii [Nikita of Makushin] | 50 |
| | 22 | Wife, Evdokiia of the same settlement | 30 |

Of Chernovskoe settlement:

| 23 | | Ivan Burchevskoi | 35 |
| | 23 | Wife, Anna of the same settlement | 40 |

Of Umnak Island, Tulikskoe settlement:

| 24 | | Vasilii Mershenin | 40 |
| | 24 | Wife, Anna of Borkinskoe settlement [Biorka] | 40 |

Of Tanamykhtinskoe settlement [Konets Head], Unalashka:

| 25 | | Osip Tanamykhtinskoi [Iosif of Tanamykhta] | 29 |
| | 25 | Wife, Katerina of the Accord settlement | 35 |

Of Veselovskoe settlement, Unalashka Island:

| 26 | | Danilo Izmailov | 40 |
| | 26 | Wife, Vera of Chernovskoe settlement | 25 |

Of Tanamykhta settlement:

| 27 | | Aleksei Isakov [Aleksei, son of Isak] | 35 |
| | 27 | Wife, Agaf'ia | 30 |

Of the Island of Avatanak, settlement of the same name:

| 28 | | Mikhailo Vlasov | 35 |
| | 28 | Wife, Matrena of Makushinskoe settlement | 25 |

Of Tigal'da Island, settlement of the same name:

| 29 | | Aleksei Makar'in, employed by the company | 29 |
| | 29 | Wife, Irina of Accord settlement | (?) |

Of the Island of Unimak, Pogromnoe settlement:

| 30 | | Petr Toropov | 30 |
| | 30 | Wife, Evdokiia of Accord settlement | 45 |

[Of the Island of Unimak], Shishalda settlement:

31		Luka Burenin	30
	31	Wife Elena of Nosovskoe settlement [Unimak Island]	25
32		Timofei Zelenchanov [?]	35
	32	Wife, Anna of Accord settlement, Unalashka Island	35

Of Akun Island, Artel'noe settlement:

33		Klementii Makar'in	25
	33	Wife, Tat'iana of the same settlement	35

Of the Mainland Aliaksa, Severnovskoe settlement:

34		Semeon Danilov	30
	34	Wife, Anis'ia of Akun Island, Artel'novskoe settlement	20

Of the Island of Unalashka, Accord settlement:

35		Luka Pankov	25
	35	Wife, Anis'ia of the same settlement	20

From Kad'iak Island:

36		Ivan Prianishnikov	35
	36	Wife, Nastas'ia Makar'in, of Akun Island, Seredkinskoe settlement	[?]

Register

How many Russian promyshlennye and Americans of both sexes were chrizmated in lieu of partaking in the Holy Mysteries [Communion] on the 4th of July 1807, Unalashka office of the Russian-American Company at the Accord settlement.

No.	Civil status, Christian and Surname	Age
1	Egor Netsvetov, teamster of Tobol'sk	34
2	[His] wife Mar'ia Alekseeva [daughter of Aleksei] of Atkha	20

3	Fedor Stepanov, peasant of Panteleev village, Vladimir gubernia, Ovchinnikovskoi [?] 'oprichi'	58
4	[His] wife Feona Kondrat'eva of Atkha Island	28
5	Aleksei Andreev Beianov [Buianov?], merchant of Velikii Ustiug in Vologda gubernia	30
6	Vasilii Danilov Lazarev, burgher of the city of Irkutsk	30
7	[His] wife Nastas'ia Vasil'eva, of the Island of Unimak from the settlement Shishaldinskoe	18
8	Dmitrii Afans'ev Nozikov, peasant of Sol'vychegodsk	40
9	Vasilii Dmitriev Kulikov, of Chernaia Rechka in Tomskaia gubernia, newly baptized Tartar	25
10	Dmitrii Isaev Zyrianov, Biliktinskoi [?] peasant, of Irkutsk gubernia	57
11	Dmitrii Prokop'ev Miasikhin, burgher of the city of Irkutsk	46
12	Timofei Ivan's son Dolgopolov, burgher of the city of Tiumen', of Tobol'sk gubernia	60
13	Gavrilo Ignat'ev Ponomarev, retired cossack of the city of Tobol'sk	65
14	Ivan Arkhimandritov, teamster of the city of Tiumen', Tobol'sk gubernia	25
15	[His] wife Natalia Danilov of Chernovskoe settlement, Unalashka Island	18
16	Ivan Platon's son Tatarinov, Anginskoi peasant of Irkutsk [*oprichi*]	57
17	Vasilii Fedorov Zakharov, peasant of Iarenskaia sloboda, of Vologda gubernia	45
18	Gerasim Kozukhin, peasant of Balaganskoe vedomstvo, City of Irkutsk	25
19	Semeon Samoilov Petelin, burgher of Irkutsk	25
20	Vasilii Ivanov Kilychev, newly baptized Iakut of the Iakutsk vedomstvo	30
21	Toion Ivan Stepanov Glotov, of Umnak Island, Recheshnoe settlement [modern Nikolski]	60

22   Widow Marfa Ivanina [Ivan's widow
             Marfa] of the Island of Atkha   30

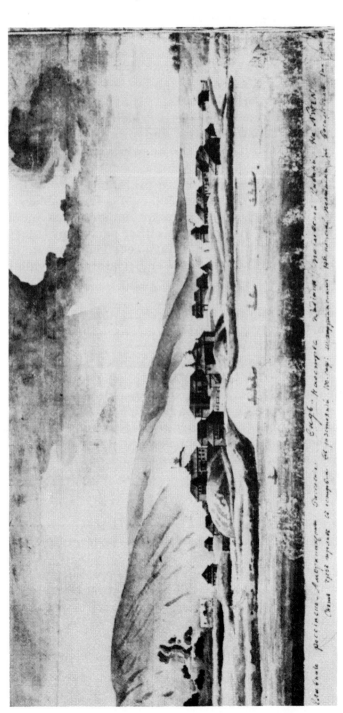

Pavlovsk Harbor, Kad'iak Island, 1808

Appendix III

Gideon's Sworn Testimony [from SV documents, Shur Collection]

This document is headed with a notation: "Father Gideon is to testify." Five questions are posed on the left side of each folio, with Gideon's answers on the right. The answers are in Gideon's own hand and each answer is "certified" that is, following each answer a part of rank and title is written and Gideon's name signed at the end of the answer to question five.

1. Did you receive at your departure for America from the [His Imperial Majesty's] Cabinet 500 rubles for expenses?

    This sum was awarded me as a special single payment for outfitting and did not comprise either part of my salary or maintenance costs. Indeed, I have received this sum in St. Petersburg from the Actual Chamberlain and Cavalier Rezanov.

2. Did you receive from the St. Petersburg [one word illegible] treasury an advance against your assigned salary of 500. – rubles per annum?

    I have received from the Actual Chamberlain Rezanov while in the Kronshtadt Roads, 257 piasters which sum was at the then current rate of exchange equivalent to 500. – rubles. [The monies] were an advance against my salary. I have received no [other] salary payments subsequently, either on the outbound voyage, or on my return journey.

    It is for this reason that I have requested payment of my salary, in accordance with the records of which the government is cognizant.

3. What kind of maintenance [subsistence] did you receive from the Russian-American Company, at sea, on Kad'iak, and during your return journey?

    My subsistence, until my return home, according to the assurances by the Actual Chamberlain and the company's Representative Rezanov, was to be provided by the Russian-American Company at the same level as for the officers [serving] with this expedition. His Eminence Amvrosii, Metropolitan of Novgorod and St. Petersburg, was not notified.

    At sea and on land, until return to Kronshtadt, each officer received besides the regular pay 800 rubles annually for [one word illegible]. I was on the same footing as the rest of the officers, in accordance with this general regulation, until our arrival on Kad'iak. On Kad'iak, I received subsistence from the local office upon a special recommendation issued by the Actual Chamberlain and company representative Rezanov to the Manager, Collegiate Counsellor Baranov. This is evidenced by the original memorandum #176 appended herewith in the original, and from a copy of the memorandum #99 addressed by the Kad'iak office to the Spiritual Mission.

On my return journey to St. Petersburg, my subsistence was provided by the Okhotsk and Irkutsk Company Offices against an account opened [for me] by the Manager Baranov [Baranov's private account, see correspondence above]. His memorandum [to the company offices] to that effect is appended herewith in original together with the records of expenditures charged against this account.

It is necessary to explain that while on Kad'iak, items were issued in my name but were expended for all the Monastics jointly, excepting Hierodeacon Nektarii, who lived separately. These items were: flour, tea, sugar, grain, molasses, vodka, tobacco, candles, leather and soles [for footwear], a variety of cloth [*kitaika* and *pestred'* or *debret* from Iaroslavl': cotton and coarse homespun linen]. Some of these were expended for the five students who serve in the Church and for other orphans.

The two buckets of vodka, shown for October 1805 were spent on promyshlennye performing seamen's duty during my [attempted] voyage to Baranov Island, Port of Novo-Arkhangel'sk, as their rations were not provided.

The *chrevii* [food delicacies?] mentioned in three [? plastina] and food supplies [*kharchi*] and furs mentioned on one, were given to Monk Ioasaf; 30 pud of grain were left for the Spiritual Mission.

On the return journey, I did not deduct [indicate] the sum expended for the maintenance en route and upon arrival here of the student Prokopii Lavrov who was sent in my company by the Manager to enable him to receive here, in St. Petersburg, a better [clerical] education, achieve the rank of a celebrant [priest] and return [to Alaska].

4. Did you receive, besides the 500 rubles paid you here, either from the Russian-American Company or from the

funds which were allocated to the Bishop's resident on Kad'iak, salary payments of 500 rubles per annum?
I never received anything.

5. How many Americans of the Kad'iak Island were converted by you to the Christian Faith? How many students are there in the school which had been established there to teach the Christian Law? Are there any students who have completed their training and remain now at the school? After your departure, who from among the original Spiritual Missionaries remains there and to whom are entrusted the school and the conversion of the Americans to the Christian faith? Append all documents pertaining [received and issued] at the transfer [of authority].

In regard to conversions, establishment of the school, arrangements which I made at my departure and so on, I am to submit, in accordance with my instructions, a separate report to His Eminence Amvrosii, Metropolitan of Novgorod and St. Petersburg.

Out of the former Mission's personnel, there remain on Kad'iak three: Hieromonk Afanasii, 53 years of age, and monks Herman, age 50, and Ioasaf, age 35. As the Headship has been given to Monk Herman, by common agreement with the local Manager, by reason of insufficient literacy [end of sentence and possibly one or more folios are missing, text resumes on separate page].

The school has been entrusted to him also. The teacher, Ivan Kad'iakskii, 21 years of age, has been accepted and confirmed [in office] by the Manager, also his associates, Khristofor Prianishnikov, 19 years of age, and the interpreter Paramon Chumovitskii, 22 years of age, all of them local fosterlings of the Spiritual Mission. They also perform the offices of sub-deacons in the Church.

Gideon.
The year 1809,
17th Day of April.

Appendix IV

Below is the surviving text of the Lord's Prayer in the Alutiiq language attributed to Gideon. It was published in 1816 by Dr. Johann Severin Vater, based on the papers of Johann Christoph Adelung, in a compendium entitled *Mithridates oder allgemeine Sprachenkunde mit dem Vater Unser als Sprachprobe in bey nahe fuenf hundert Sprachen und Mundarter* in Berlin, Vossische Buchhandlung. The prayer in question appears as no. 442, on p. 465 with provenance data on p. 464.

According to these, a copy of the prayer was transmitted to the editor/author of the compendium by Adelung who allegedly received it from Baranov. According to Adelung, it was collected at Yakutat, on the north shore and was ascribed to the Ugalentsy, in modern terminology Eyak. Both, Adelung and Severin Vater, however, recognized it as being Eskimoan. Modern linguists clearly identify it as Alutiiq. Modern Alutiiq transcription was provided by Mr. Jeff Leer of the Alaska Native Languages Center, University of Alaska, Fairbanks on April 30, 1986.

The text as written by Gideon is given here in the German transcription by Adelung, with German glosses (presumably by Adelung) from the Russian glosses (*presumably* by Gideon). Alutiiq transcription accompanied by English glosses by Leer follows.

442.

Jakutat,

mitgetheilt von Hrn. v. Baranoff.

| Vater | unser | welcher | ist | Himmel im |
| Adaut | fankuda, | imai | ituduen | kilagmi; |

| geehrt | werde | Nahme | | dein |
| Pejutschkikok | | atchuen | | ilpit |

| es | komme | Herrschaft | | dein |
| Taitschikok | | pitschhhichkjuutschin | | ilpit; |

| geehert | werde | Wille | dein | wie |
| Pejutschkikok | | pejuchtschetschin | | ilpit, kaju |

Himmel im Erde auf
kilagmi nunami

Nahrung	unsere	noethige	gib
Nukchut	fankuta	pejuchtschiknabuet taitsch-	
		kut fankuta taminni;	

vergib	uns	Schulden
Uniwikikut	fankuta	schulanwautschibit

unsere	wie	wir	vergeben
fankuda,	kaju	fankuda	unitibit

Schuldnerunsern

ajuk-schtbuet   fankuda;

fuehre nicht uns	Boesen,	von 'Autnickut
		fankuda ikmonwautschi-
mik.		

Es	sei.
Ta	waduen.

Mithrid. 3 Thl. 3 Abth. Gg

Modern transcription and glosses by Jeff Leer:

Ata'ut	ggwangkute,	ima'i	et'utan gilagmi;
Our Father	[of] us,	somewhere yonder you are in the
sky;			

	Piurciiquq	atrem	ellpet;
it will come into being	your name	[of] you;

	Taiciquq	picirkiu'ucin	ellpet;
it will come	your rule	[of] you;

	Piurciiquq	piqcicin	ellpet qayu
it will come into being your will	[of] you, how

	qilagmi	nunami;
	in the sky	on earth;

Neggwet	ggwanquta	piugcikengarpet	taiskut
ggwangkuta			
our food	[of] us	that we want bring usus

	tamiini;
	everywhere;

Uniggwikikut   ggwangkuta   sulanqua'ucipet
Leave to us   us   our   misappropriations

ggwangkuta qayu   ggwankuta   unitapet
           [of] us   how   we   we   leave
them
           ayugestepet   ggwangkuta:
           those who are like us – us

Agutenillkut   ggwangkuta   sulanqua'ucinun;
do not lead us   us   to misappropriations;

           Awauskut   ggwantuta   iqlunqua'ucimek;
take us aside   us   from falsehood;
                          Tawatan.
                          Thus.

Notes

1. *Posluzhnoi spisok Sviato-Troitskoi Lavry Sobornogo Iero-monakha Gedeona.* This record of Gideon's service up to 1803 was submitted by his ecclesiastical superiors on occasion of Gideon's appointment to the circumnavigating expedition and to America. It is available in the Shur Collection, Rasmuson Library, University of Alaska, Fairbanks, microfilm reel no. 12, document 86. Original is in TsGIA, USSR, Fond 796, opis' 84, delo 408.

2. The term *lavra* indicates a major monastery. Consequently, the Russian *Aleksandro-Nevskaia Lavra* is rendered initially as Monastery of St. Alexander Nevskii. In the body of the translation, the term *lavra* is retained. This monastery was dedicated to the Holy Trinity and is so designated in some documents. In still others, both designations are used. Alexander Nevskii, Prince of Novgorod, by skillful negotiation and agreement to pay tribute appeased the then invincible Mongols, so that he was able to defeat the Teutonic Knights. Shortly before his death he became a monk and later a Saint of the Russian Orthodox Church.

3. An excellent account of the publication history of Gideon's papers is given by Dr. Roza G. Liapunova, who traced it as follows: Valaam 1894, *Ocherk iz istorii Amerikanskoi Pravoslavnoi Missii (Kad'iakskaia Missiia 1794-1894)*, published in 1978 in English translation by Colin Bearne as *The Russian Orthodox Religious Mission in America 1794-1837*, Kingston, Ontario, The Limestone Press, Richard A. Pierce editor; Valaam 1900, *Valaamskie Missionery v Amerike*, and an abridged version of Valaam 1894 in the August issue of the journal *Pravoslavnyi Vestnik* ("Orthodox Messenger"), 2 (16):349-367. For additional articles concerning Gideon, published in *Pravoslavnyi Amerikanskii Vestnik* ("Russian Orthodox American Messenger"), the readers should consult *Alaska Names and Places in the Russian Orthodox American Messenger (1896-1973), an Index and Annotated Bibliography* by Barbara S. Smith and Anne C. Sudkamp, published 1985 by the Alaska State Historical Commission, Studies in History no. 36, Anchorage, Alaska.

4. The quotation is from Proverbs 30:18-19, cited here after the *New American Bible*: "Three things are too wonderful for me, yet four I cannot understand: the way of an eagle

in the air, the way of a serpent upon a rock, the way of a ship on the high seas, and the way of a man with a maiden." In VC and in Valaam 1894 the quote appears as given in this translation, in VV and SV it appears as in the quote from the Bible above.

5. Gideon's reference to a *korabl'* – ship – may refer to a ship-of-the line but the context does not make this clear. However, a *korabl'* was larger and had more fire power than a frigate.

6. Gideon consistently uses ewes and rams *(ovtsy i barany)*. The more common "sheep" is adopted in the translation.

7. In Valaam 1894 and VV and VC, Rezanov's letter appears after the conclusion of the text, which ends with Gideon's preparation to depart from Kodiak. In the SV, the letter follows, in chronological order, as Gideon gives the account of the expedition's sojourn in Brazil, as it appears in this translation. In SV and VV, the letter text appears to be copied, while the original appears to be in the Synod file as a separate document.

8. Gideon describes here, and in greater detail subsequently, the penis sheath, known anthropologically from Micronesia, New Guinea and South America.

9. Vasilii Berkh, midshipman, later lieutenant, of the Imperial Navy, afterwards historian of Russian explorations in the north and in America. Author of *A Chronological History of the Discovery of the Aleutian Islands*, English translation by Dmitri Krenov; Richard A. Pierce, editor; Kingston, Ontario, The Limestone Press. Originally published in Russian in 1823, St. Petersburg, Russia.

10. The Frenchman was Jean Josef Le Cabry, who eventually reached France via Kamchatka. The Englishman was Edward Robarts. His journals were published in 1974, G.M. Dening editor, in Canberra, Australia.

11. VC and SV has *posy* while VV has *moka*. The word *posa* (see glossary) in archaic Russian is equivalent to the anthropological term *bridewealth* or, in common usage, bride price. The word *moka* may be a native term.

152

12. *Skaznaia bolez'n*: the meaning is unclear, it may refer to leprosy or any disfiguring skin disease, from *iskazhat'*, "to disfigure."

13. This attitude toward tattooing may have been by 1803 due to European influence and thus of recent origin.

14. Gideon uses the term *pataty* or *sladkoi pataty* to designate sweet potatoes; for yams, he uses the term *in'iamy*; when dealing later on with agricultural experiments on Kodiak, he uses the term *kartofel'* for potatoes.

15. *Vyboika* as a rule refers to the coarsest grade of cotton print (see glossary for details).

16. Most of this information is also contained in the letter dispatched by Gideon to Amvrosii via Lt. Arbuzov and Lt. Povalishin (see below). The wording of the SV text given here differs somewhat from the wording in the letter as given in VV and VC.

17. The term *kazhim* derives from the name of the men's house, widespread in Alaska, where meetings, feasts, and rituals were held. Gideon occasionally uses this term for a communal dwelling.

18. See Gideon's description of the *pavlina* in an earlier section in which he talks about activities at the Three Saints Bay artel. See glossary.

19. These "rattles" are better described by the term "tambourine". A number are preserved in ethnographic collections, notably of the Museum of Anthropology and Ethnography in Leningrad, the National Museum of Finland and in the British Museum. An excellent illustration of this rattle appears in the portrait of the "Kad'iak" toion Nankok, christened "Nikita" painted by Mikhail Tikhanov, staff artist with Golovnin, in 1818. Nankok's chin is tattooed, which means, according to Gideon, that he was a shaman (see below). Nankok may have been the Kodiak chief, an experienced war leader, who headed the Kodiak islanders at the taking of the Tlingit fortification on Sitka in 1804 (Khlebnikov 1973:48).

20. This is a reference to the method of sea otter taking by the "drive" which Gideon describes in detail later on. The

drive method seems to have spread from Kodiak to the
Eastern Aleutians in the proto-historic or even possibly
early historic period, and throughout the Aleutian Chain
during the Russian period, eventually becoming the standard method which persisted everywhere into the American period. It was employed as late as 1911 when sea
otter hunting was prohibited by provisions of an international treaty.

21. In Russian usage, collaterals of the same generation, in
English nomenclature "cousins", are referred to by the
terms "brother" and "sister" depending on the person's
gender, with a qualifier indicating the degree of distance
preceding the basic term. In the original text, the term is
used twice, at the beginning and the end of the sentence.
Initially, Gideon specifies "first cousin of the female
gender" (*dvoiurodnaia sestra*) but omits the qualifier at
the conclusion of the sentence. Unfortunately, he does not
specify if Vasilisa and Afanasii were related agnatically
or matrilineally.

22. Gideon's glosses are remarkably accurate and sensitive to
the aboriginal meanings. Two inferences suggest themselves:

   a)   as a trained foreign language specialist, he acquired
        some knowledge of Alutiiq (he is known to have
        translated into Alutiiq language several prayers, of
        which only the Lord's Prayer is believed to survive
        (see Appendix IV) and that he had an excellent ear;

   b)   that his interpreter, presumably Paramon Chumovit-
        skii, or Prianishnikov, was excellent.

23. The reference here is to the custom to cover oneself with
black paint to indicate mourning.

24. Aminak is presumed to be a personal name. The Alutiiq
personal names, which appear in many Russian archival
sources, cannot be retrieved at present.

25. The word "Agnak" which may be a name, may also con-
ceivably mean *arnaq*, "woman" (Jeff Leer). The meaning
of the text then may be interpreted as suggesting that in
the past women, or more precisely "grandfather's women",

possessed sea otter skins and the gloss should read: "I am looking diligently for the woman (women) who possessed sea otters."

26. Though the Russian term *gnilushka* may be rendered in translation as "rotting or rotten wood", which may mean in certain context a rotting tree stump, here the meaning "fungi (which grows on a rotten tree stump)" is more likely.

27. Earlier, I mentioned the term *kislitsa*, assuming that it was a synonym for *kliukva*, cranberry (see *Arctic Anthropology* 14(2):106). Further research demonstrated that the term refers to *Rumex acetosa*, sorrel.

28. *Chistiak* refers to several wild plants, among them *Iris siberica*. *Kosichki* refers to *Iris germanica*. Since only the former occurs on Kodiak, I identify it as such.

29. The term *kutagarnik* continues to present problems. In Eastern Siberian and Alaskan Russian usage the distinction is made between sweet and bitter kutagarnik. The sweet kutagarnik, sometimes called *puchki kutagarnye*, is in all probability a Polygonum species, most likely *P. viviparium*, though on Kodiak I am informed by Jeff Leer of the Alaska Native Language Center, the Alutiiq term at present equated with kutagarnik, refers to an Angelica species. Bitter kutagarnik remains unidentified.

30. Neither the Alutiiq nor the Russian term can be identified at present. According to the "Dictionary of Russian Language Usage" (Dal', 1912), the term designates colloquially the Andromeda species and also the following: *Petasites vulgaris* and *officianalis*, *Tussilage farfara*, and Achillea species (yarrow). Based on ethnobotanical usages in Alaska, this plant is probably an *Achillea* species, but it may be coltsfoot. Both plants are used medicinally.

31. There are several discrepancies in transcription of this song between SV, VV and VC. Only the SV text has been analyzed linguistically by Jeff Leer.

32. Apparently among the people of Kodiak, as is the case among some groups in the Amur region of Eastern Siberia, a woman who stretched her leg in the direction of a male

was considered to be issuing an invitation to sexual dalliance.

33. Reference is to the fact that only ne'er-do-wells and slaves wore sealskin parkas, while men of any substance wore parkas of highly valued furs: marmot, ground squirrel, fox, caribou and bear. Sea otter skins were also used for garments, but it is not clear if men, women, or both wore them. Among the Chugach, who are linguistically and culturally close to the Kodiak people, men wore sea otter clothing.

34. The term probably means *ks'arlluk*, translated by informants in modern times as "evil priest", while the term *kas'aq* had come to signify "priest". The usage seems consistent with the demiurge figure of raven, present in Alutiiq cosmology (courtesy Jeff Leer).

35. Early sources indicated that all male transvestites, and not only shamans, had faces tattooed in feminine fashion and that a shaman was likely to be a transvestite.

36. According to the records of Kiril Khlebnikov, for many years manager of the Novo-Arkhangel'sk (Sitka) office of the Russian-American Company, who came to Alaska in 1818, O'Cain was the first foreigner with whom Baranov contracted to hunt sea otters on shores as far as the coast of southern California. O'Cain arrived at Kodiak in 1803, with the *Eclipse*. Leaving goods valued at 12,000 rubles as a bond, he took on 20 baidarkas (20 Kodiak islanders), under supervision of Shvetsov and Tarakanov. O'Cain set out for California 26 October 1803, returning in June 1804 (See Khlebnikov 1984:46).

37. The passage to Ugamok (Chirikov) Island is a very dangerous one.

38. Early in his tenure Baranov established two bases on the Alaska Peninsula, one called Katmai, at the portage to Bristol Bay, the other at Sutkhum, modern Sutwiik. See Khlebnikov 1979:46-47 for a description of these two outposts.

39. This information is of extreme importance, as it indicates that already in early Baranov tenure whale hunting was

becoming a company oriented enterprise. It is known that later on Kodiak whale hunters were settled on Unalaska and in 1828 on Atka in order to improve, and in the latter case to introduce, whaling in the Aleutian archipelago. This suggests that whaling spread to the Aleutians from Kodiak in relatively recent times. It should also be noted that whale products were shipped as trade goods by Russian-American Company to the north, when trading through St. Michael and at Buckland River with the Inupiat.

40. This is, so far, our only record of impressment of the Aleuts from Unalaska at this early date though there is a terse note by Khlebnikov that initially "16 baidarkas" were transported. Khlebnikov states that in the first major move in 1804 (with Rezanov), and in the second in 1807, 60 hunters were moved. He estimates the total number of resettled people, including the "16 baidarkas", to have been, with families, "150 souls" (See Khlebnikov 1979:108-109).

41. Compare Khlebnikov's casualty figures for Kodiak Islanders during the Baranov administration: 12 men killed in 1792 in Prince William Sound during the attack on Baranov's party by the Chugach; 20 drowned en route from L'tuya Bay (Lituya Bay) to Kodiak and 2 captured by the Tlingit; 8 died and 10 drowned returning from the "Aglegmiut shore"; 135 died from eating contaminated mussels (Gideon's figure is 140 and he says that 40 more died en route later). For 1800 Khlebnikov lists 33 men drowned sailing from the Semidi Islands (Gideon says 32 baidarkas or 64 men). Khlebnikov's figures, however, by far exceed those of Gideon for the year 1805. While Gideon says that 300 men were drowned on the return voyage from Sitka, Khlebnikov lists (in addition to 14 killed in 1804 while storming the Tlingit fortified camp and 165 lost to hostilities following the destruction of Old Sitka in the hunting party led by Urbanov) "up to 250 men drowned near Aglegmiut shores when Dem'ianenkov's party was returning from Sitka" and states that at Kodiak itself, during strong winds, 100 persons were drowned in 6 baidaras. Khlebnikov gives the total casualty figure as 751 men (Khlebnikov 1979:25).

42. Iasak collection was abolished in 1788 but it appears that this measure was not implemented until after 1791.

43. Reference is to seining which the Russians have introduced.

44. This incident of administration of the oath of allegiance to Kodiak men is a single major symptom of the general conflict between the Mission and Baranov's administration which focused on the company's policies of impressment.

45. The colloquial Russian term *pop* (singular; *popy* plural) has an express connotation of disrespect, not to say contempt, for the clerical office.

46. In order to understand the meaning of this and the following passages, it is necessary to realize that Easter celebration in Russia was customarily accompanied by bell ringing, beginning at midnight service in the night from Saturday to Easter Sunday. Obviously, the monks at the Mission failed to ring the bell, causing frustration and dissatisfaction to Baranov and his promyshlennye, who presumably were feeling homesick, on this particular day more so than usual. This is one incident when the reader has some sympathy with Baranov's crew, especially since Baranov went to a lot of trouble to cast the bells for the church in 1795 (the bell that was now cracked): "Sapozhnikov has founded bells for our church here, 5 puds, 3 pounds in weight" (*A History of the Russian-American Company*, vol. 2:72).

47. Baranov obviously likened his crew to the Tartars (Mongols) who invaded Russia in the 13th century. The brutality of that conquest was legendary. After re-conquest, of which the taking of the Tartar city of Kazan' on the Volga is symbolic, Tartar communities continued to exist in the Kama-Volga basin.

48. This is a reference to the fact that Baranov employed the natives of Kodiak, the eastern Aleutians, and Prince William Sound not only as his labor force but as his army in southeastern Alaska. In their dealings with the local people they followed their own notions about warfare and perpetrated various atrocities. According to Khlebnikov (1833, 5:80), the attack on the Redoubt of St. Michael on Sitka Island (Old Sitka) was believed to have been revenge, provoked by the killing by the Aleuts (Kodiak Islanders) of close to ten important kinsmen in a quarrel (Khlebnikov

himself, however, tends to ascribe the outbreak to agitation by American and British skippers who supplied the Tlingit with firearms). Another incident relatively well known was the massacre of the Indians on the island the Russians called Il'mena off the California coast which took place shortly before Baranov's removal in 1818. The promyshlennyi Iakov Babin who was in charge of the hunting party was shipped by Ianovskii to St. Petersburg to be called to an account (see *The Russian-American Company, Correspondence of the Governors, Communications Sent: 1818*, translated and Edited by R.A. Pierce, 1984, Kingston, Ontario, The Limestone Press, pp. 11, 138-139 and 172. See also the children's story *The Island of the Blue Dolphin*). Anthropologist Frederica de Laguna in her 3-volume book *Under Mount Saint Elias: The History and Culture of the Yakutat Tlingit (1972*, Washington, Smithsonian Institution Press) reports extensive Tlingit traditions about "Wars with the Aleuts" (vol. 1, pp. 254-255 and related stories p. 175). Though the incidents she recorded, says de Laguna, cannot be dated with any degree of certainty, a number of them undoubtedly refer to the early Russian period. Harrington in 1939 recorded the Aleuts: "These buggers are too mean...they sneak up on you and kill you when you are asleep. They are sure going to get you when you are asleep" (George Johnson; 1939 or 1940, quoted after de Laguna 1972:1:256). And further: "The Aleuts just killed – no limit. They did not declare war, they just come down and fight when they do not expect it. They used to catch the Yakutat people when they come to Cordova to trade" (de Laguna 1972:1:257)

49. Aboard ship, Rezanov and the expedition's commander, Kruzenshtern, clashed head on over authority. The dispute became aggravated by personal dislike. The navy officers, to a man, sided with their commander while the company employees, such as the supercargo Shemelin, sided with Rezanov. In the Marquesas, matters came to a head, and after a series of confrontations Rezanov remained in his cabin until his arrival in Kamchatka aboard the *Nadezhda*. There Rezanov pressed charges against Kruzenshtern, who was forced to apologize. Shemelin's description of Rezanov's behavior following the Marquesas incidents suggests some degree of mental instability. Certainly, his demonstrated excessive fear suggests a touch of paranoia. Rezanov continued to denounce the navy officers even while in Alaska, blaming them for dis-

turbing the peace in the colonies "at its very roots" (see letter to Board of Directors, February 15, 1806, in *A History of the Russian-American Company* 1979 v. 2:190-197). In the quarrel between Kruzenshtern and Lisianskii on one hand and Rezanov on the other, Gideon, obviously, was caught in the middle. In Alaska, Rezanov managed to become at odds with almost all officers manning the company ships, including Lt. Khvostov, with Langsdorff, who accompanied him to Alaska as his personal physician, and finally apparently even with patient and long suffering Gideon (see documents in Shur collection and correspondence below).

50. The reference pro ably is to the son of Demid Il'ich Kulikalov, who in 1805 was in charge of the RAC department on Atkha Island. In a letter dated April 29, 1805, written by Baranov to Kulikalov, the former states: "I am trying to take your son away from the clergy. If this comes to pass he will sail to Petersburg with the expedition ship *Neva*, with four other schoolboys. On the way they will be taught the English language and navigation and upon arrival will go to a boarding school at company expense. The request for that will be forwarded to the main office. They will be outfitted here with everything necessary for this journey" (*A History of the Russian-American Company*) vol. 2, translated by Dmitri Krenov, R.A. Pierce and A.S. Donnelly, eds., Kingston, Ontario, The Limestone Press, 1979:36).

51. Gideon refers to Rezanov's letter written on St. Catherine Island, see above.

52. This letter, to judge by the date, must have been written by Rezanov while in Brazil. It is not clear what channels he used to mail it to Baranov: a company vessel from Kamchatka or with Lisianskii? The former seems more likely, especially in view of the fact that Banner was notifying the Spiritual Mission about Gideon's authority about seven months after the clergyman's arrival on Kodiak aboard the *Neva*.

53. Banner's letter (which Gideon later submitted to the Synod) is evidence of Rezanov's bad faith: it seems that in writing to Baranov he intimated that Gideon was on Kodiak on Rezanov's (and hence the company's) request and

employed by the company, so to speak, while in reality Gideon was responsible to Metropolitan Amvrosii and the Synod.

54. In this letter we find one of the foundations for the subsequent myths about the death of Father Iuvenalii (Juvenal in English language literature), culminating in the writing by Ivan Petrov of the fictitious "Daily Journal of the Reverend Father Juvenal". We cannot know at this point what motivated Rezanov to repeat this story about the clergyman, which as far as we know originates with Lieutenant Davydov, on Kodiak in 1802 (then about 17 years old). As Rezanov in 1805 was intimately associated with Davydov, who for a time even shared his quarters, it is likely that he was the source. Nor do we understand why he felt it necessary to lie about the bloody conflicts in the Iliamna lake region where the outposts of the rival Lebedev-Lastochkin Company were exterminated by Alaskans – according to information provided at the time by Archimandrite Ioasaf on behest of Baranov. Rezanov's version is at odds with Baranov's own accounts contained in several letters to his co-workers (published in the same volume as Rezanov's letter).

55. This letter, written such a short time after most cordial letters to Gideon and other Fathers, clearly indicated Rezanov's double-dealing with the Church.

56. Rezanov refers to his plan (one is tempted to say obsession) to revenge himself on the Japanese, something he seemed to brood upon and plan since his poor reception in Japan the previous year. In a letter addressed to Alexander I from Unalaska, dated 18 July 1805, (en route to Kodiak) he wrote: "I do not believe that Your Imperial Majesty will consider it an offense if I, with the able assistance of Messrs. Khvostov and Davydov, build ships and sail next year to the Japanese coasts to destroy their settlements on Matmai Island, push them from Sakhalin, and ravage their coasts. By cutting their supply of fish and depriving about 200,000 people of food, we will force them to open trade with us" (*A History of the Russian-American Company*, vol 2, p. 150). Later on, the two young Lieutenants, Khvostov and Davydov, did, on Rezanov's instruction, raid the Japanese and almost wrote paid to their careers, as the Imperial Russian government was displeased.

57. According to Langsdorff (see his account of the voyage, published in 1812, *Bemerkungen ueber eine Reise um die Welt in den Jahren 1803 bis 1807*, Rezanov dispatched Khvostov in the newly acquired *Juno* to the settlement of Three Saints Bay (far enough from the company office at St. Paul Harbor so that any protest would be too late) to raid it for food supplies and women. It appears likely that Baranov neither consented nor knew about this. Lack of women seems to have been another obsession with Rezanov, as several of his letters published in the second volume of *A History of the Russian-American Company* amply demonstrate.

58. *Okoisk* appears to be a literary allusion of the time, possibly to some work of theological or moral content. I was not able to find the reference, but the context seems to indicate the meaning "edge of despair".

59. This reference to violence done to Hierodeacon Nektarii by person or persons unknown remains enigmatic. The episode may have had something to do with Nektarii's unexpected return to metropolitan Russia.

60. The records of the Alaska Orthodox Church indicate that three of these young Tlingits in later years were associated with the Russian-American Company (one of them up to 1867) as interpreters, and that all had the surname "Gedeonov".

61. Rezanov died 1 March 1807 in Krasnoiarsk, on his return journey to St. Petersburg overland. Obviously, the news of his death was still unknown in Alaska at the time when Gideon was preparing to leave Kodiak.

62. This procedure was followed even in the absence of the priests and was considered to constitute legal marriage as late as 1816, as a document about the marriage of Ivan Petrovich Prokhorov to a Tlingit spinster from Sitka named (of the clan or moiety?) Kut, baptized Glafira, goddaughter of the burgher of Tobol'sk Dmitrii Eremin clearly demonstrates. The document is dated April (day omitted) 1816, and is signed by Baranov, witnesses and those who are standing bond (A.A. Dolgopolov file).

63. Of the remaining Mission members, only Afanasii (of unsound mind) was a celebrant, that is was able to perform the Liturgy and the sacraments: marriage, chrizmation (baptism could be administered by lay persons and lesser clergy, the servitors, the Monks Herman and Ioasaf), and last rites.

64. This reference to the late Archimandrite's travel to Yakutat is puzzling, as in 1796 not he, but Iuvenalii sailed with the first group of settlers. Iuvenalii, however, did not get to Yakutat, but stayed with Polomoshnyi on Hinchenbrook Island and from there travelled via Kenai Peninsula to the Iliamna area and from there to the Kuskokwim; he was killed on the way back, travelling apparently toward Bristol Bay, at Quinhagaq. It remains unclear if Ioasaf visited Yakutat the following year (1797). Ioasaf sailed for Siberia in 1798.

65. By custom married couples were characterized in terms of the ethnicity of the male partner.

66. The chief Ivan Glotov was, as all evidence indicates, Ivan Stepanovich Glotov, formerly the boy Mushkal' about 12 years old, who was baptized by Stepan Glotov in 1758 on the shore of modern Nikolski Bay, taken to Siberia where he learned the Russian language, and later returned with Glotov to the Aleutians. In 1762 he accompanied Stepan Glotov as his interpreter to Kodiak. The icons in the Church of St. Nicholas in modern Nikolski deserve study by an expert in Orthodox iconography. Two date by inscription to the 1770's.

67. This seems to be Henry Barber who, in command of the *Unicorn*, arrived at Sitka on June 28, 1802 (Gregorian calendar), just after the destruction of Old Sitka, the Russian redoubt of Archangel St. Michael, by the Tlingit. His account of the incident was published in *Sydney Gazette* in 1803 (reprinted in *Alaska Journal* 9(1): 58-61, Winter 1979, in an article by W.W. Schumacher. Gideon's information suggests that Barber (an Englishman and not a German as some would have it) survived the near-wreck of the *Sitka* in Kamchatka, and sailed the vessel to Okhotsk where she was wrecked again. The date of his death has not been established but Filip Kashevarov in his answers to Khlebnikov's questions about the 1790's – early 1800's in

Alaska mentions that Barber died in Kamchatka (Shur collection).

A.A. Baranov   *N.P. Rezanov*

Glossary

ALEUT: Originally, the name for inhabitants of the Near Islands, derived from their autonym. Eventually the term became extended to the inhabitants of the entire Aleutian archipelago and then to those of Kodiak with the qualifier "Kad'iak Aleut". Today, the term has become the autonym for the Aleutian and Commander Islanders when identifying themselves to outsiders, as well as for the Kodiak Islanders, for some of the Yup'ik speakers of Alaska Peninsula and Bristol Bay area, and is also used occasionally in the Prince William Sound and Cook Inlet regions. When Gideon uses the term, he refers primarily to Kodiak Islanders and those resettled from the Eastern Aleutians.

AMANAT: A hostage.

AMERICAN: A native of America (Alaska).

AMERICAN CYPRESS: (*dushnoe derevo* or fragrant wood): Cedar.

ARKHIMANDRITE: A senior priest-monk, usually head of a monastery or mission, a ranking member of a monastic community.

ARSHIN: A measure of length, 0.7112 m, 28 inches.

ARTEL': (In English spelling *artel*): A permanent work crew. In this context, a small, permanent, subsidiary settlement of the Russian-American Company, established for performance of specific tasks and composed of hunters-laborers, a manager, and supporting personnel.

BAIDARA: A large skin boat. In Russian America of two types: native type, resembling the umiaq of the Northern Eskimo and Russian type, which was adapted to carry a sail and had a rudder. The native baidara was capable of carrying more men and cargo than the Russian one.

BAIDARKA: a) A kayak. b) Mussels, primarily black mussels, considered a delicacy.

BAIDARSHCHIK: Chief of a work crew (artel) who was also responsible for the management of the territory where his artel was located. Head of a hunting party.

BALAGAN: A storage shed, a cache, usually for fish, constructed on piles, with a plank floor, planks spaced to permit air passage.

BARABARA: (In English, spelled variously: barabora, bor-abora etc. and pronounced with a shift in stress). In Russian usage, semi-subterranean storage structure, also used to designate a small summer dwelling or camp. In the American period the term began to be applied to the late 19th century-early 20th century native semi-subterranean small-size houses (see yurta).

BIZAN': Mizzenmast. On three-masted vessels, the aft mast (on two-masted vessels the aft mast is the main mast and called *grot machta*, see below).

BLADDER: (Russian, *puzyr'*) Containers made of stomachs of large sea mammals, primarily sea lion.

BRAM: Prefix used in Russian sailing terminology (generally derived from the Dutch) to indicate the third tier of sails and their appurtenances, also to indicate a certain strength of wind (see below).

BRAMREI OR BRAMREIA: Top-gallant yard.

BRAMSEL': Top-sail, top-gallant-sail, square sail on bramsten'ga.

BRAMSEL' WIND: A light steady wind, under which the masts and yards can carry the topgallant sails without danger.

BRAMSTEN'GA: Topgallant mast, topmast.

BRANDVAKHTA: Sentry vessel, in a harbor.

BRUSNITSA: (var. *brusnika*): *Vaccinum citus idea*, cran-berry. Identified variously in literature as mountain cranberry, red bilberry, red huckle-berry. Oxford English Dictionary lists four varieties of *Vaccinium* under this term.

BURDUK: A mixture of crushed edible roots (most often *sarana*) prepared with water so as to be of paste-like consistency.

CELEBRANT: Member of the cleros, that is those who parti-cipate in services or care of the temple in official capacity, and are consecrated priests of all ranks. The lowest rank is deacon, who holds the third degree of priesthood, priests, bishops and metropolitans. Although the word means a "ministrant", who assists in all functions, a deacon may not perform the sacraments.

CHERNITSA: (var. *chernika*): Commonly identified as "blueberry", "whortle-berry" or "hucklebbery". Botanically, chernitsa is identified as a *Mirtillum*, *Vaccinium myrtillius* and *Vaccinium uliginosum L.*, sub-species *microphyllum Lange*.

CHERNOGOLOVNIK: *Sanguisorba officianalis* (burnet?)

CHRIZMATION: The sacrament of confirmation, by the grace of the Holy Spirit, in the Christian faith. Administered at baptism by a priest, also annointment with the Holy Myrrh (*miropomazanie*).

COUNTER HALSE: Sailing on the wind.

DAGLIKS: Forward port anchor.

DEAN OF CLERGY *(blagochinnyi)*: in a given region, in charge of administrative and disciplinary matters and protocol. Immediate ecclesiastical superior of parish priests.

DESIATNIK: Foreman, from "foreman of a crew of ten."

DREK: Grapnel, drag anchor, from the Dutch *dreg*.

EVRASHKA: Ground squirrel, *Spermophilus undulatus ablusus (Osgood)*.

FOKA: Fore, foresail.

FOKMACHTA: Foremast.

FOKA-REI: Fore-sail-yard.

FRENCH MILE: 4.17 Russian versts or ca. 2.76 miles. A French geographic mile is 1.15078 statute miles.

GALS: *Naut.*, tack halse (sailing by the wind either on right halse – starboard – or left halse – port; see also *kontra-gals*, counter halse, opposite tack – sailing on the wind).

GANSHPUG: *Naut.*, a lever, or handspike, of several kinds.

GERMAN MILE: A distance equivalent to a range from $3\frac{1}{4}$ to 6 English miles, the short German mile being equal to 6,272 m.

GITOV: *Naut.*, clue-garnets, clue-line; Brail; *vziat'na gitovy*: to brail (sailing terminology).

GNILUSHKA: Rotten wood, also fungus of genus Agaricus (A. sulphurotus, A. alcalinus).

GOLETS (PL. GOL'TSY): A term variously applied to a number of fish species occurring in Eastern Siberia and in Alaska. Here, it is applied to Dolly Varden trout (*Salvenius malma Walbaum*), the steelhead or rainbow trout (*Salmo gairdnerii Richardson*) and to Arctic char (*Salvenius apalpinus Linnaeus*). On Kodiak, the term refers, most likely, to steelheads.

GOLUBITSA: *Vaccinium ulginosum*, bog bilberry, or low-bush blueberry varieties.

GORBUSHA: Pink salmon, *Oncorhynchus gorbusha*.

GROT: *Naut.*, mainsail, square; also a triangular storm sail used on the mainmast.

GROT MACHTA: Mainmast.

GROT MARSHEL': *Naut.*, main topsail; a sail on the first extension of the main mast (on *grot sten'ga*).

HIERODEACON: A deacon who is also a monk (see "celebrant").

HIEROMONK: A priest who is also a monk.

IAL, IALIK: *Naut.*, from "yawl", a small ships's boat rowed with four or more oars. Not to be confused with the modern usage which refers to a type of sailing yacht.

IALO: *Naut.*, "the head," latrine.

IAMANINA: Goat's meat and/or skin, depending on context.

IN'IAM: Yam (vegetable).

INTRIUM (TRIUM): *Naut.*, hold; bilge.

ISHKAT: A large grass basket of native manufacture.

ITALIAN MILE: developed from the ancient Roman mile, variable, ranges from   to 1¼ English miles.

IUKOLA: See Yukola.

IURTA: See Yurta.

IUT: *Naut.*, poop, quarterdeck, aft (cf. *shkantsy*)

KABEL'TOV: *Naut.*, cable

KACHEMAZ: A form of yukola (dried or air cured fish strips) with the backbone left in.

KAIUR (Male), KAIURA or KAIURKA (female), KAIURY (plural): indentured laborer of the Russian-American Company. Sometimes, persons who were slaves of various native groups, were liberated by the Russians but were not able to return to their homes. Originally, the word meant "dog team driver".

KAIUT KAMPANIIA: wardroom.

KALABAS: A gourd ; *Naut.*, container, calabash.

KALGA (plural *kalgi*): in Alaska, enslaved war captives.

KALINA: Viburnum species which bears edible berries.

KALIUKAKH: Basket of slats, twigs, roots.

KALUGA, KALUZHKA: Wooden containers of various sizes.

KAMLEIA, KAMLEIKA: Waterproof hooded outer garment made of sea mammal (inc. whale), sometimes bear, intestines.

KAMZOL: A long vest, from the French *camisole*.

KARONADA (KORONADA): A short barrelled artillery piece
                     (gun).
KARTECH':   Case shot or canister shot, in certain contexts
               grape shot.
KATER: *Naut.*, a naval term of the 18th c., applied to a
               single-masted vessel, a tender. Also, an oar-
               propelled craft, slightly smaller than a long-
               boat (*barkas*), of eight to 24 oars.
KAZHIM: A special structure or part of a large com-
               munal dwelling which served as the men's
               house, meeting place, and ritual chamber.
               Ceremonial house or room. In early Russian
               sources occasionally applied to a communal
               dwelling, particularly if a ceremonial space
               was present.
KEKUR (sing., plural KEKURY): Off-shore rocks, an isolated
               rocky islet, or rock, often in the shape called
               pillar.
KHAIKO (haiko): Dog or chum salmon, *Oncorhynchus keta
               Wallbaum*.
KISLITSA: Wild sorrel, *Rumen acetosa*.
KIZHUCH: Silver or Coho salmon. *Oncorhynchus kisutch
               Wallbaum*.
KNIAZHENIKA: Salmonberry, *Rubus stellatus*.
KONTR-GALS: Counter-tack, sailing on the wind.
KOPEIKA: One hundredth of a rubl', smallest Russian
               monetary unit.
KRASNAIA RYBA: Red salmon, *Oncorhynchus nerka*.
KRIUISEL':   *Naut.*, mizzentop, mizzentopsail; square sail
               on the aft (third) mast of a three-masted vessel,
               from the Dutch *kruizeil*.
KUBYSHKA, KUBYSHEK, pl. KUBYSHKI: square   wooden,
               sometimes metal, container.
KUNSTKAMERA: Museum.
KUTAGARNIK: Sweet kutagarnik is a *Polygonum* species.
               Bitter kutagarnik is unidentified.
KUIKAK: Of Alutiiq origin, labret of sea shell.
KVAS: A fermented drink prepared from various
               bases (bread, honey, grasses, roots, ferns etc.).
               The alcoholic content of *kvas* is extremely
               variable, depending what base is used and the
               method of preparation. May be very mild,
               practically non-alcoholic and thirst quenching,
               or extremely potent.
LABAZ: Platform for drying, curing fish; a storage
               platform.

LAVRA: A major monastery, of ecclesiastical and/or historical importance.

LAVTAK: Dehaired processed sea mammal skin used for a variety of purposes. Primary technological material for kayak covers.

LUKOSHKO: Russian twig, root or slat basket.

LYKO: Bast.

MARSEL': Topsail.

METROPOLITAN: Bishop in charge of a large and populous province. In the Orthodox hierarchy, rank above archbishop and below the patriarch.

MOCHALO: Processed wood fiber, bast.

MOLEBEN: A service of thanksgiving or petition, usually rendered by the Latin "Te Deum".

MOROSHKA: Cloudberry, *Rubus chamaemorus L.*

OSTROG: Stockade, palisade; in Siberia, a fortified post, fortified town.

OVERSHTAG, TO TURN OVERSHTAG: to jibe, to turn a vessel on another tack.

PANIKHIDA: Derived from the Greek, a service for the dead, sung prior to and following funeral, memorial service.

PARTOVSHCHIK: Leader of the large hunting parties which Baranov dispatched from Kodiak to southeastern Alaska and beyond, along the northwest coast of America.

PAVLINA: Cured whale meat made of choice belly part of fresh whale, processed with sorrel and fish roe.

PECTORAL CROSS: A cross, on a chain, worn by priests and bishops of all ranks outside their robes. Ornamental crosses are given in acknowledgement of outstanding service and achievements.

PESTRED': Jute cloth.

PIPA: Portuguese measure of volume, 500 litres, but the old pipa equaled 429 litres.

PLEKHT: *Naut.*, starboard forward anchor, or best bower anchor.

PODBEL: A plant which cannot be identified with certainty, probably a yarrow (Achillea) species.

PODLEKAR': Surgeon's assistant.

PODSHTURMAN: Navigator's assistant, second mate.

POLOVINSHCHIK: A half-partner or sharer; the term Russians applied to a partner in a polyandrous marriage or household.

POSA: (Archaic, from *posag*), dowry, wedding gifts, bridewealth.

POVARNIA: A communal kitchen in a settlement or artel; also a blubbering and food processing station.

PRIKAZCHIK: An agent of the Russian-American Company, of middle management position; a supercargo; a store manager.

PROMYSHLENNYI (Sing.): also PROMYSHLENNIK, sometimes spelled PROMYSHLENNOI (from *promysel*, industry): An entrepreneur, hunter, provider. A rank and file employee of the Russian-American Company.

PROVESNA: Cured whale meat, less choice than *pavlina*, prepared from fins of a fresh whale and belly part of a whale that has drifted for some time.

PUD: A measure of weight, equals 36.11 pounds.

REAUMUR: Designating temperature in accordance with a scale introduced by Reaumur, in which water's freezing point is 0° and boiling point is 80°.

REI (REIA):   *Naut.*, yard.

RUBL':   A monetary unit of 100 kopeikas.

RUMB: Rhumb, point of the compass, compass heading.

SAMOVAR: An apparatus for boiling water wherein fuel burns in a central chamber while water is heated in the surrounding one. Widespread in Asia, Russia and E. Europe, from China to the Mediterranean.

SARANA: Applied to a variety of edible roots of the *Lilium* and *Fritillaria* species. Most frequently, *Fritillaria kamtschatkenensis*.

SAZHEN':   In English spelled *sazhen*. A measure of length equalling 7 feet (3 arshin). However, in Russia there were at least four variations: *sazhen' pechatnaia* 2.13 m; *kazennaia* (official) one equal to 7 English feet or 6 French feet, measuring 3 arshin and 12 chetveriki; *sazhen' makhovaia* measuring both arms outstretched equal to 2½ arshin; *sazhen' kosaia*, from the heel of a foot to the tips of fingers of the opposite arm, raised and stretched: larger than the *pechatnaia* or *kazennaia* sazhen.

SHIKSHA: Crowberry, *Empetrum nigrum*, also Voronitsa.

SHKANTSY: Quarterdeck, middle section.

SHKOT: *Naut.*, block.

SHPIL':   Naut., capstan.
SHTURVAL: Steering-wheel.
STEN'GA: Naut., Topmast.
TAKELAZH: Running-rigging; *takelazh stoiachii*: standing-rigging.
TENDER: A single-masted seagoing sailing vessel.
TOLKUSHA: Native Alaskan dish made of fat and berries or roots whipped together.
TORBASY: Native footwear, usually made of sea lion esophagus, seal skin, and seal flippers for soles.
TREBA: A religious service, performed upon individual demand: a prayer service of petition or thanksgiving, burial and memorial services, baptisms, chrizmations, marriages etc.
TUNTAI (sing.): A Kamchatka term for a large birch bark container of 2½ pud of butter.
TYK: Peach.
URUN: Sleeping benches or sleeping compartments in a communal dwelling.
VANTY: Naut., shrouds.
VERKH (plural VERKHI): See *Vershok*
VERP: Sea anchor, a small anchor with four blades, as a rule.
VERSHOK (plural VERSHKI): measure of length, 44.45 mm or 4.4 cm., ca. 1.25 inches (see VERKH).
verst and *versts*):
VERSTA (plural VERSTY, in English usage 1.067 km., 0.6629 miles. Equals 500 sazhen or 1500 arshin.
VOLYNKA: A Russian peasant musical instrument resembling a bagpipe. It is constructed from the skin of a goat or calf, taken off whole like a bag, sewn together tightly and equipped with a pipe on top into which the musician blows, and several playing pipes at the bottom. The bag is held under the left arm and pressure is exerted on it, while with the right hand the musician manipulates the bottom pipes.
VYBOIKA: Coarse printed cotton (rarely, linen), printed on one side only in single color.
YUKOLA: In Library of Congress transliteration, *iukola*. Dried fish strips.
YURTA (IURTA): A native style dwelling, usually a large semi-subterranean one.
ZAKAZCHIK: A native who was a middleman in Russian-Aboriginal trade.

ZHELEZKO (plural ZHELEZKI): small iron items or tools
    which could be inserted into a haft and used in
    various ways, as a spear blade, drill etc. Also
    small pieces of iron cut up for trade for the
    above use.

Father German (Herman), now Saint Herman, as recalled by
I.A. Ianovskii

Bibliography

A. Published Sources

Barratt, Glynn   Russia in Pacific Waters, 1715-1825. *A*
1981   *Survey of the origins of Russia's Naval*
                 Presence in the North and South Pacific.
                 Vancouver and London, University of
                 British Columbia Press.

Berkh, Vasilii N.   *A Chronological History of the Discovery*
1974   *of the Aleutian Islands.* Translated by D.
                     Krenov, R.A. Pierce, editor, Kingston,
                     Ontario, The Limestone Press. Originally
                     published in Russian in 1823.

Dening, G.M., ed.   *The Marquesan Journals of Edward*
1974   *Robarts, 1797-1824.* Canberra, Australia.

De Laguna, Frederica   *Under Mount Saint Elias: The*
1972   *History and Culture of the Yakutat Tlingit.*
                       Smithsonian Contributions to Anthropology,
                       vol. 7 in three parts. Washington, D.C.,
                       Smithsonian Institution Press.

Documents on the History of the Russian-American Company.
1976   Translated by Marina Ramsay, R.A. Pierce
                     editor, Kingston, Ontario, The Limestone
                     Press. Originally published as *K istorii*
                     Rossiisko - Amerikanskoi Kompanii (Sbornik
                     dokumental'nykh materialov), Krasnoiarsk,
                     1957.

Fedorova, S.G.   See Khlebnikov.
1985

Khlebnikov, Kiril   "Pervonachal'noe poselenie Russkikh
1833   v Amerike." *Raduga,* Special Supplement,
                     2:1-13; 3:15-24; 5:69-83.

1973   *Baranov, Chief Manager of the Russian*
                     Colonies in America. Translated by Colin
                     Bearne, R.A. Pierce editor. Kingston,
                     Ontario, The Limestone Press. Originally
                     published in Russian in 1835.

1979   *Russkaia America v neopublikovannykh za-
              piskakh K.T. Khlebnikova.* R.G. Liapunova
              and S.G. Fedorova editors. Leningrad,
              Nauka.

1985   *Russkaia Amerika v neopublikovannykh za-
              piskakh Kirila Khlebnikova:* Novo-
              Arkhangel'sk. S.G. Fedorova editor. Moscow
              Nauka.

Korobitsyn, Nikolai Ivanovich - prikazchik (supercargo)
              aboard the *Neva*, Archive of the All-Union
              Geographic Society (Vsesoiuznoe Geografi-
              cheskoe Obshchestvo), raz. 99, opis' 1, no.
              141. "Journal..." Published in *Russkie
              otkrytiia v Tikhom Okeane i Severnoi Amerike
              v XVIII-XIX vekakh*, A.I. Andreev ed.,
              Moscow-Leningrad, Academy of Sciences of
              the USSR, pp. 118-214, with appended RAC
              instruction to Korobitsyn (pp. 214-220).
              Translated in: *Russian Discoveries in the
              Pacific and North America in the Eighteenth
              and Nineteenth Centuries*, Ann Arbor, 1952,
              pp. 118-208.

Kruzenshtern, Ivan Fedorovich *Puteshestvie vokrug sveta v*
1809-1812   *1803, 4, 5 i 1806 godakh po poveleniiu Ego
              Imperatorskogo Velichestva Aleksandra
              Pervago, no korabliakh Nadezhde i Neve pod
              nachal'stvom Flota Kapitan-Leitenanta, nyne
              Kapitana pervogo ranga, Kruzenshterna...* in 3
              volumes, vol. 1 in 1809, vol. 2 in 1810, vol. 3
              in 1812. Accompanying atlas was published
              in 1813.

              Kruzenshtern's account was translated into
              German and published as: *Reise um die Welt
              in den Jahren 1803, 1804, 1805 and 1806...,*
              also in three volumes, vol. 1 in 1819, vol. 2
              in 1811, and vol. 3 in 1812, and into English
              as *Voyage Round the World...* London, 1813, 2
              vols.

Langsdorff, Georg Heinrich *Bemerkungen auf einer Reise um die*
1812   *Welt in den Jahren 1803 bis 1807.* In two
              volumes. Frankfurt-am-Main, Friedrich
              Wilmans. Originals of the illustrations,

Wilmans. Originals of the illustrations, drawn by Ivan Kuziakin, are in the Honeyman collection, Bancroft Library, University of California, Berkeley. For a translation (abridged): *Voyages and travels in various parts of the world, during the years 1803...and 1807*, London, 1813, 2 vols.

Liapunova, Roza G.   *"Zapiski ieromonakha Gedeona kak istochnik*
1979   *po etnografii eskimosov o. Kad'iaka."* Istoriia i *etnografiia Ameriki.* Moscow, Nauka.

Liapunova, Roza G., and Fedorova, S.G., eds.   See Khlebnikov.
1979

Lisianskii, Iurii Fedorovich   *Puteshestvie vokrug sveta v 1803,*
1812   *4, 5 i 1806 godakh...* Two parts in one volume. Atlas, entitled *Sobranie kart i risunkov prinadlezhashchikh k puteshestviiu Flota Kapitana 1-go ranga i Kavalera Iuriia Lisianskogo, na korable Neve* was published by the Naval Printing office the same year (1812). An English language edition followed in 1814, but the text differs from the Russian edition.

Pierce, Richard A.   *The Russian-American Company. Corre-*
1984   *spondence of the Governors. Communications Sent: 1818.* Translated, with an introduction, Kingston, Ontario, The Limestone Press.

Pierce, Richard A. and Donnelly, A.S.   See Tikhmenev.
1978

1979   See Tikhmenev.

Ratmanov, M.I.   *"Vyderzhki iz dnevnika krugosvetnogo puteshestviia*
1876   *na korable Neva"* [sic; Makar Ratmanov was the first officer of the *Nadezhda*]; in the journal *Iakhta*, no. 32 (cited after Glynn Barratt 1981).

Rezanov, N.P.   "Anekdoty is puteshestviia Rezanova." *Otechest-*
1820   *vennye zapiski*, 1829, pp. 226-228.

1822-25   *"Pervoe puteshestvie Rossiian vokrug sveta..."* *Otechestvennye zapiski*, 10:194-219; 11:90-144;

15:248-274; 20:131-163 and 204-223; 23: 173-188 and 366-396; 24:73-96 and 242-253.

1866   *"Pis'mo Rezanova k I.I. Dmitrievu."* Publishec in the journal *Russkii Arkhiv*, pp. 1331-1335.

Roberts, Edward   See Dening.
1974

Schumacher, W. Wilfried, ed.   "Aftermath of the Sitka Massacre c
1979   1802." *Alaska Journal* 9(1):58-61.

Shemelin, Fedor   *Zhurnal pervago puteshestviia Rossiian vokrug*
1816   *zemnogo shara...* St. Petersburg, Meditsinskai tipografiia.

1823   *"Istoricheskoe izvestie o pervom puteshestvii Rossian vokrug sveta."* *Russkii invalid*, 146, no. 23-28, 31-36, 49 (cited after Glynn Barratt 1981).

Smith, Barbara S. and Anne C. Sudkamp   *Alaska Names and Place*
1985   *in the "Russian Orthodox American Messenger 1896-1973). An Index and Annotated Bibliography.* Anchorage, Alaska, Alaska State Historical Commission.

Tikhmenev, P.A.   *A History of the Russian-American Company*,
1978   Vol. 1, Translated and edited by Richard A. Pierce and Alton S. Donnelly. Seattle and London, University of Washington Press. Originally published in Russian in 1861.

1979   *A History of the Russian-American Company*, Vol. 2. Translated by Dmitri Krenov. Edited by Richard A. Pierce and Alton S. Donnelly. Kingston, Ontario, The Limeston Press.

U.S. Department of State, et al.   *United States and Russia, The*
1980   *Beginning of Relations 1765-1815,* Joint Soviet-American Editorial Board, Washington, D.C.: documents no. 188, N.P. Rumiantsev to Alexander I; no. 191, Rumiantsev's instruction to Rezanov; no. 230, Rezanov's letter to Rumiantsev June 17/29 1806 from Sitka (see also Tikhmenev 1979:199-227,

Sitka (see also Tikhmenev 1979:199-227,
version with deletions); no. 233, Rezanov to
Baranov July 20/August 1, 1806.

B. Archival Sources

The archival materials in the USSR which pertain to the first
Russian circumnavigating expedition are enormous and I am
listing only the few references known to me from published
sources:

TsGAVMF (Navy archives), Leningrad
    fond 14 (Kruzenshtern)
    fond 25 (I. de Traverse)

TsGADA (Central Archive of State Documents), Moscow
    fond 89, delo 89
    fond 796, delo 290 (Rezanov)
    fond 21 of the Gosarkhiv

TsGIA (Central Historical Archive), Leningrad
    fond 853 (Buldakov)

TsGIA Narodnogo Prosveshcheniia (Education), Leningrad
    fond 15

TsGIA, of Estonian SSR, Tartu
    fond 1414, Kruzenshtern family papers.

Saltykov-Shchedrin Public Library, Manuscript Division, Leningrad
    Shemelin ms.
    Ratmanov ms.
    Romber, letter (Titov coll).

Microfilm copies of selected documents from the Soviet archives,
Shur collection, Rasmuson Library, University of Alaska
Fairbanks are:

Correspondence on organization of the expedition, outfitting,
crew, objectives, etc.: from TsGIA, fond 15, op. 1, d. 1, Microfilm
roll 10, no. 78 (1803-1806).

Levenshtern, Ermolai - Travel diary kept aboard the *Nadezhda*,
    from TsGIA of the Estonian SSR, Kruzenshtern archive,

no. 116 and from BIM of the Estonian SSR, F. 225, op. 1,
delo 20 microfilm roll 26, no. 174.

Ratmanov, Makar - Journal kept aboard the *Nadezhda* (gragment)
GPB fond 1000, delo 1939-68, microfilm roll 26, no. 72 and
Letters to Karamzin, BN Slav. 104, microfilm roll 27, no.
177.

Romberg, Fedor - Letter to friends, GFB, Titov collection, delo
791, microfilm roll 26, no. 172.

Tilesius von Tilenau, Wilhelm Gottlieb - staff artist with the
expedition, drawings and sketches (from GBL archive,
fond 178, delo M. 10693 a and b), microfilm roll 21, no.
142 and drawings and sketches from LOAAN, R.IV, op. 1,
delo 800a, microfilm roll 23, no. 155.

Kruzenshtern, I. - Fragment of a Journal kept aboard the
Nadezhda. From TsGIA of the Estonian SSR, fond 1414,
op. 3, delo 5, microfilm roll 18, no. 117.

Index

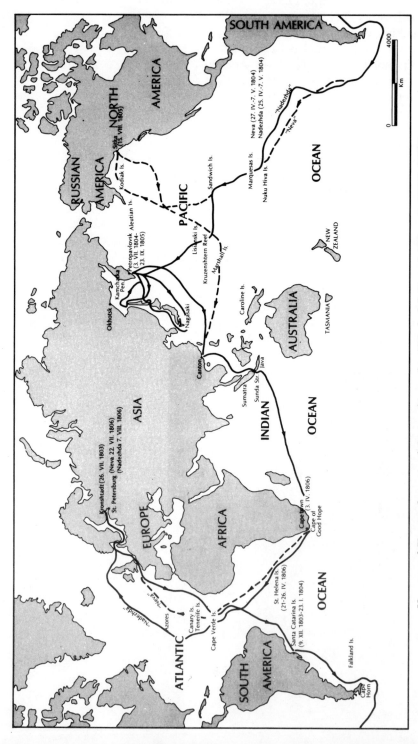

Voyage of Kruzenshtern and Lisianski on the "Nadezhda" and "Neva" (1803-1806)

THE LIMESTONE PRESS

ALASKA HISTORY SERIES

19.　G.I. Shelikhov. VOYAGE TO AMERICA, 1783-1785. 1981. 162 pp., illus., maps, index, supplementary materials. Transl. from the Russ. edition of 1812. Includes Shelikhov's book, publ. in 1791, with additional materials erroneously attributed to him since early 19th century. Data on Shelikhov's origins, family, and achievements, dispelling some of the mythology about the "Russian Columbus," but adding to his stature as an organizer and entrepreneur.

20.　KODIAK AND AFOGNAK LIFE, 1868-1870. The journals of Lts. E.L. Huggins and John Campbell, and of merchant Frederick Sargent, with other materials relating to the first years of the American regime in Alaska, including portraits, and early map of Kodiak. Details on ship movements, personnel, trade and life style. 1981. 163 pp.

21.　M.D. Teben'kov. ATLAS OF THE NORTHWEST COASTS OF AMERICA FROM BERING STRAIT TO CAPE CORRIENTES' AND THE ALEUTIAN ISLANDS' WITH SEVERAL SHEETS ON THE NORTH—EAST COAST OF ASIA. Compiled by Teben'kov while governor of Russian America, and published in 1852. 39 sheets, boxed, with softbound vol. with rare HYDROGRAPHIC NOTES (109 pp.) and supplementary information. 1981.

22.　George R. Adams. LIFE ON THE YUKON, 1865-1867. 1982. 219 pp. Illus. Diary of a participant in the Western Union Telegraph Expedition, and his autobiographical account, written later, both publ. for the first time. Describes life in the then little known Alaska Interior, supplementing Whymper, Dall, and others.

23.　Dorothy Jean Ray. ETHNOHISTORY IN THE ARCTIC: THE BERING STRAIT ESKIMO. Articles, assembled in one volume for the first time, on early trade, the legendary 17th century Russian settlement, the history of St. Michael, Eskimo picture writing, land tenure and polity, settlement and subsistence patterns, and place names. Transl. of Russ. accounts of the Vasil'ev-Shishmarev expedition (1819-1822). 280 pp., illus., maps.

24.　Lydia T. Black. ATKA. AN ETHNOHISTORY OF THE WESTERN ALEUTIANS. 1984. 219 pp. Illus. Problems of prehistory, ethnography, and 18th century foreign contacts, with a list of Russian voyages, the account of navigator Vasil'ev (1811-1812), Fr. Ioana Veniaminov, and biographical materials.

25.　THE RUSSIAN-AMERICAN COMPANY. CORRESPONDENCE OF THE GOVERNORS. COMMUNICATIONS SENT: 1818. 1984. xiv. 194 pp, illus., index, notes. Transl. of seldom-used manuscript material in U.S. National Archives.

26.　THE JOURNALS OF IAKOV NETSVETOV: THE YUKON YEARS, 1845-1863. 1984. 505 pp., illus., maps. Tr. by Lydia Black from the unpubl ms. in Library of Congress, with notes and appendices on the history and ethnography of the Yukon and Kuskokwim regions of Alaska.

27.　Ioann Veniaminov. (St. Innokentii). NOTES ON THE ISLANDS OF THE UNALASHKA DISTRICT. 1985. 511 pp., illus. Tr. of Russ., ed., St.P., 1840. Classic, encyclopedic account.

28.　R.A. Pierce, BUILDERS OF ALASKA: THE RUSSIAN GOVERNORS. 1818-1867. 1986. 53 pp., illus. Biographies of Alaska's thirteen forgotten governors, from Hagemeister to Maksutov. 1986.

29.　F. Litke (Lütke) A VOYAGE AROUND THE WORLD: 1826-1929. Vol. I TO RUSSIAN AMERICA AND SIBERIA. Tr. from the French ed., Paris, 1835. 1987. 232 p.

30.　A.I. Alekseev. THE ODYSSEY OF A RUSSIAN SCIENTIST: I.G. VOZNESENSKII IN ALASKA, CALIFORNIA AND SIBERIA 1839-1849. Tr. from Russ. ed., Moscow, 1979. 1987. 140 p.

31.　A. Fienup-Riordan, ed. THE YUPIK ESKIMOS AS DESCRIBED IN THE TRAVEL JOURNALS AND ETHNOGRAPHIC ACCOUNTS OF JOHN AND EDITH KILBUCK. 1885-1900, 1988.

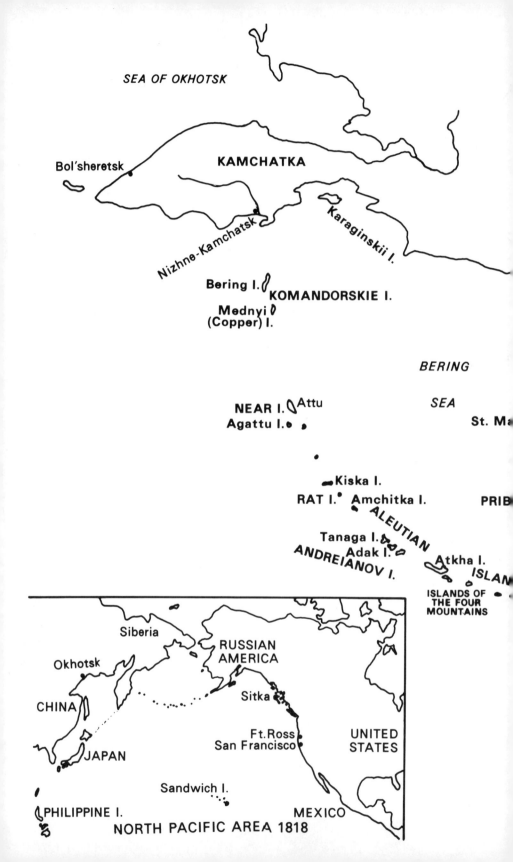

SEA OF OKHOTSK

Bol'sheretsk

KAMCHATKA

Nizhne-Kamchatsk

Karaginskii I.

Bering I.
KOMANDORSKIE I.
Mednyi
(Copper) I.

BERING

NEAR I. Attu
Agattu I.

SEA

St. Ma

Kiska I.
RAT I. Amchitka I.

PRIB

Tanaga I.
Adak I.
ANDREIANOV I.

ALEUTIAN

Atkha I.

ISLAN

ISLANDS OF
THE FOUR
MOUNTAINS

Siberia

RUSSIAN
AMERICA

Okhotsk

Sitka

CHINA

Ft.Ross
San Francisco

UNITED
STATES

JAPAN

Sandwich I.

PHILIPPINE I.

MEXICO

NORTH PACIFIC AREA 1818